The Key to the Qigong Meditation State

by the same author

Chinese Medical Qigong
Editor in Chief: Tianjun Liu, O.M.D.
Associate Editor in Chief: Kevin W Chen, Ph.D.
ISBN 978 1 84819 023 8 (hardback)
ISBN 978 1 84819 096 2 (paperback)
eISBN 978 0 85701 149 7

of related interest

Chinese Shamanic Cosmic Orbit Qigong
Esoteric Talismans, Mantras, and Mudras in
Healing and Inner Cultivation
Master Zhongxian Wu
ISBN 978 1 84819 056 6
eISBN 978 0 85701 059 9

Tranquil Sitting
A Taoist Journal on Meditation and Chinese Medical Qigong
Yin Shi Zi
Forewords by Master Zhongxian Wu and Glenn H. Mullin
Translated by Shi Fu Hwang and Cheney Crow
ISBN 978 1 84819 112 9
eISBN 978 0 85701 090 2

Daoist Meditation
The Purification of the Heart Method of Meditation and Discourse
on Sitting and Forgetting (Zuò Wàng Lùn) by Si Ma Cheng Zhen
Translated and with a commentary by Wu Jyh Cherng
Foreword by Eva Wong
ISBN 978 1 84819 211 9
eISBN 978 0 85701 161 9

The Key to the Qigong Meditation State

Rujing and Still Qigong

Tianjun Liu

Foreword by Master Zhongxian Wu

SINGING
DRAGON

LONDON AND PHILADELPHIA

English language edition first published in 2017
by Singing Dragon
an imprint of Jessica Kingsley Publishers
73 Collier Street
London N1 9BE, UK
and
400 Market Street, Suite 400
Philadelphia, PA 19106, USA

www.singingdragon.com

Copyright © Tianjun Liu 2017
Foreword copyright © Master Zhongxian Wu 2017

Library of Congress Cataloging in Publication Data
A CIP catalog record for this book is available from the Library of Congress

British Library Cataloguing in Publication Data
A CIP catalogue record for this book is available from the British Library

ISBN 978 1 84819 232 4
eISBN 978 0 85701 177 0

Printed and bound in the United States

Contents

Foreword

In Chinese wisdom traditions, when we study an art, whether it be music, painting, calligraphy, martial arts, medicine, internal alchemy, meditation, or Fengshui, we know that the very foundation of our art lies within SanBao, or the Three Treasures—Jing, Qi, and Shen. Jing, Qi, and Shen are also commonly known as SanCai, the three materials we use to achieve our greatest aspirations. In our Qigong practice, Jing, Qi, and Shen hold the keys to the most incredible methods for healing and spiritual transformation. So, you may now be wondering, what exactly are Jing, Qi, and Shen?

In the context of internal cultivation, Jing means essence—it is the essential fluids of the physical body and is the source of all life. Through our Qigong practice, we learn to strengthen Jing through TiaoShen, our physical adjustment. (Tiao means adjustment, tune, transfer, move, change, switch, melody, or harmonious; Shen means body or posture.)

Qi is our vital energy, the subtle, invisible (for most people) steam-like vitality that spreads throughout the body and is the momentum of all life processes. Qigong allows us to strengthen Qi through TiaoXi, our breathing adjustment. (Xi means breath, breathing, rest, gain, or increase.)

Shen represents our spirit, our emotion, our thoughts, and our consciousness. It is Shen which brings clarity and joy to our lives. We learn to awaken Shen through TiaoXin, our mental or psychological adjustment. (Xin means heart, mind, or psyche.)

Although there are countless Qigong forms, the unifying principle of all traditional Qigong practice is Rujing, or entering into the tranquil state. We reach Rujing by working with the three aforementioned techniques—TiaoShen, TiaoXi, and TiaoXin. One of the primary tenets of Chinese cultivation practices is "JingNengShengHui," which literally translates as "tranquility generates wisdom." In other words, the tranquil state is the path to enlightenment. To truly master our Qigong cultivation, we must be able to achieve Rujing.

In *The Key to the Qigong Meditation State: Rujing and Still Qigong*, Tianjun Liu explains the fundamentals of Qigong practice and ancient Rujing methods through physiological and psychological principles, making it a valuable resource for modern people interested in pursuing the methodologies of ancient Chinese wisdom. The original version has been a part of my personal library since it was published in China in 1990. Indeed, it is one of the best-selling Qigong books in China, bringing great benefit to many Chinese Qigong practitioners for over 25 years. I am honored to help introduce this book to the English-speaking world and I hope it will enrich your personal practice and support you on your path towards enlightenment.

Master Zhongxian Wu
Lifelong Daoist practitioner and teacher
Phoenix Nest, Sweden
www.masterwu.net

Preface to the First Edition

When the People's Sports Press first published Mr. Liu Tianjun's book *The Key to the Qigong Meditation State*, both the publisher and the author expressed their wish for me to write a preface for the book. I accepted the request with great pleasure since Mr. Liu is one of our graduates and is now teaching at our college as a young lecturer. Besides, I myself have a great interest in Qigong.[1]

Alongside the ever-rising Qigong boom in China, modern research on Qigong has been following its development. The study of Qigong from physical, chemical, biological, and medical perspectives has brought up some fruitful and significant results. On the other hand, the study of Qigong from the perspective of psychology and cognitive science is still inadequate. The academic aspect of this book demonstrates a remarkable breakthrough in this difficult and little studied area of research. In the book, Mr. Liu Tianjun proposes a set of new concepts by combining classic Qigong theory with the theories of modern psychology, parapsychology, cognitive science, etc. He provides us with a detailed exploration of the psychological fundamentals of Rujing (a type of Qigong meditation state characterized by attaining a mental stillness in which the consciousness has ceased working and has itself become just pure, ultimate existence). In general this meditative state is achieved by practicing a certain thought process, the thinking process in Rujing. Based on his new theory he describes a type of Qigong exercise that takes Rujing as its main goal. Mr. Liu is confident of his viewpoint as a thoughtful researcher. Yet it will come as no surprise if it gives rise to controversy. Science develops through debate. Without dissenting voices, it would be too quiet in the world of science, wouldn't it? I have also learned that Mr. Liu is willing to listen to different voices and will further his study through more experiments.

This book is not only of academic value, but also a good introduction for Qigong beginners. The state of Rujing is the key issue as one enters the state of Qigong. Most types of Qigong require the practice of Rujing. The mastery of Rujing is a fundamental skill in the practice; therefore, how to develop this skill by a scientific approach will be a main concern for many Qigong practitioners. The author explains the complex theory of Qigong in detail and in simple language, so that it is easy to read and understand. All these features make this academic book exceptional.

Qigong is a treasure of our nation. Its impact extends far beyond national boundaries. It is spreading steadily overseas. China should be the leading nation in the study of Qigong in modern times when high technology is changing the world at dramatic speed, and we are certainly capable of achieving this goal. We should have a group of ambitious scientists dedicated to this promising quest and working for it throughout their lives. From this book it is clear that Mr. Liu is one of those offering themselves to the cause, and is working diligently for it. I sincerely hope that he, as a promising young researcher, will contribute further to this great cause. Finally, I would like to present Mr. Liu with a quotation from the great Chinese writer Mr. Lu Xun[2] in concluding my preface: "Work persistently on it and never give up."

Gao He Ting, President of the Beijing Chinese Medicine College,
Director of the Research Institute of Chinese Medical Qigong
10 April 1990

Introduction

Future Qigong masters will show a great interest in the last decades of the twentieth century when they look back on the development of Qigong. During this dynamic and vigorous period, Qigong, an ancient skill, entered the halls of modern science. This marks a new century in the history of Qigong, a new era of the scientific, extensive, modern study of Qigong.

No one knows for sure about the origin of Qigong. Some say it originated about 1000 years ago, some say tens of thousands of years ago, still others say hundreds of thousands of years ago. It is believed that back in prehistoric times diligent and intelligent Chinese primitive man learnt to make stone needles that he could use to sew animal skins or to practice acupuncture. Acupuncture is closely associated with Qigong. Many doctors, past and present, believe that meridian[3] and acupuncture points, the foundation of acupuncture and moxibustion treatment, were discovered during the practice of Qigong. Li Shizhen, the outstanding Ming dynasty physician and the author of the *Compendium of Materia Medica*,[4] once commented, "The inner landscape of one's body can only be observed by those who can see within."

Without seeking to find the exact time when Qigong originated, we can say that Qigong can be traced back to about 4000 years ago to the period called Tanyao, based on recorded history. In the subsequent dynasties, from the time of slavery to the period of feudalism, many people, from the monarch and his subjects to ordinary citizens, were engaged in Qigong. They used it as an esoteric therapy to keep themselves in good health. A lot of them even developed extraordinary power. A great number of Qigong masters were also found among warriors and entertainers in cities and towns, or monks and nuns in the villages and countryside.

After the founding of the People's Republic of China, Qigong as a means of medical treatment and physical fitness gained support from the government. Although Qigong was also abused during the time when the extreme leftists prevailed in China, it has survived, and has never become extinct. Qigong, the precious gem of oriental culture, has always been adored by the Chinese people, from ancient times to the present.

As with everything, Qigong has been through ups and downs during its history, just like the flow of a stream. In the 1950s and 1960s, the flow almost stopped during the ten-year turmoil of the Cultural Revolution, but from the late 1970s, Qigong quickly re-emerged in China like bamboo sprouts erupting after a spring shower. The surge of enthusiasm did not abate and this soon became known as the "Qigong boom." Various social, economic, political, and national factors led to this enthusiasm and had an effect on the promotion of Qigong. Everyone was working diligently and fighting intensely towards the goal of social and economic reform and internationalization. When they gained respite from intense labor, people looked back and suddenly rediscovered Qigong as an economical, easy way to help them to relax and recover from fatigue, cure their diseases, and strengthen their physical constitutions, as well as develop their latent potential. They grasped it as if they had captured a valuable treasure.

History has advanced, and now Modern man, educated and forged by modern science, requires a scientific explanation of Qigong. Even an ordinary student of Qigong is no longer satisfied with the ancient, ambiguous theories of Qigong. He wants something different, and so do the scientists whose task it is to explore the mysteries of nature. Scientists of natural and social science have investigated Qigong, using modern research techniques. As a result, understanding of Qigong has advanced. There is a saying in China that one hand cannot clap. The marriage between Qigong and modern science is the result of a mutual attraction. While Qigong is approaching modern science, the latter is also approaching the former. Modern science that is based on the study of nature in terms of different subjects and branches has tended to move from the analytic approach to an integrative approach. In the study of the macro and micro world, modern science has discovered the common language of oriental science and philosophy, which has always studied the world using a holistic approach. In modern science's description of the duality of wave and particle in quantum physics, the invention of the binary system, and the deciphering of DNA, we can see the enlightenment that modern science has received from the ancient Chinese theory of Yin and Yang.[5] Qi (vital energy) is a fundamental concept of ancient philosophy and science in China. Qigong is a fruit of the marriage of ancient philosophy and science. The study of Qigong might eventually lead to a revolution in modern science, and so it has to be addressed by modern science. Nowadays, the study of Qigong has come to be regarded as the "high tech in high tech" and has attracted a great deal of attention. My book has been completed just as Qigong is beginning to thrive in China.

If we think that Qigong is a wonder, Rujing is the wonder within a wonder, the central secret of that esoteric knowledge. It is an essential, vital element of Qigong. Discussing Qigong without mentioning Rujing misses the soul of the skill. Rujing is an excellent starting point for research into Qigong. Furthermore, in practicing Qigong, the ability to reach the state of Rujing is one of the challenges that beginners will encounter, and it is certainly helpful for Qigong practitioners to be given an explicit description of the theory and method of Rujing.

For these reasons Rujing is the subject of this book. My research not only translates the classic theory into modern scientific terminology, but aims to integrate the classic theories and the modern scientific approach. I have tried to develop a new theory of Rujing that is richer, more explicit and profound than in the past. My account aims to be easy to understand yet academically based, so that it can satisfy both ordinary readers and researchers and specialists.

Achieving this is indeed a challenge. I have done my best to achieve it, but at times I still feel my ability is not up to achieving my best intentions. Errors are inevitable in this book. I sincerely hope my readers will be warm-hearted critics, helping me to correct the errors and weaknesses. Thus my heart and soul and yours will join, and together we will be able to lay the foundation for the future course of Qigong.

Chapter 1

Rujing and Qigong

"Ming zheng ze yan shuen" ("One is able to advocate one's opinion confidently only when one is in perfect control"). This Chinese proverb tells us that we should have a good reason before we act. I'd like to borrow this proverb but alter its meaning slightly. My interpretation is: Before we start to explain a matter we should get to know the concepts clearly so that we'll be able to express our opinion without much difficulty. As we are studying the theory and method of Rujing⁶ (Qigong meditation), we should first clarify the two concepts "Qigong" and "Rujing."

Two Concepts

One of the key issues in setting forth a new theory or establishing a new discipline in science is to propose new concepts. Complete and adequate concepts can be seen as the mark of a complete and adequate theory or discipline, but the acceptance and clarification of the basic concepts are not complete once it is has been proposed. This is done in a process of development. The extent to which the concept is clearly explained is somewhat limited by the level of development of the entire subject area, and its current degree of adequacy at the time. This is true of any subject, and Qigong is no exception.

The practice of Qigong has a long history in China. Yet the term "Qigong" itself is not a very old term. Although the notion of Qigong was reported in much of the ancient Chinese medical literature, it was never labeled by the precise term "Qigong." It was actually called by various other names such as "Daoyin" (lead and guide), "AnQiao" (massage), "TuNa" (exhaling and inhaling), "ZhiGuan" (stop thinking and observing yourself from outside), "CunXiang" (maintain thinking), "YangQi" (nurturing vital energy), "TingXi" (listen to the breath), etc. (the meanings of these names differ to some extent but they still belong to the same family of Qigong). According to textual research, the term "Qigong" first appeared as a religious quotation in *Jing Ming Zong Jiao Lu* by the Taoist Xuxun, written during the Jin dynasty (1115 AD to 1234 AD). Another instance of the term is the chapter "Supplementary of Qigong" in the book *Yuan He Pian* (a classic on Qigong written in the late Qin dynasty). The term Qigong is indeed rare among ancient Chinese references.

The official use of the term "Qigong" began in the 1950s when China established its first institution of Qigong, the Tangshan Qigong Sanitarium, for the purpose of studying Qigong and its medical function, in the small town of Tangshan in Hebei province. From then on the term became popular and eventually replaced other terms. Now the name is fixed. But what about its definition? So far there is no commonly agreed explanation. For instance, in the book *Exploring Qigong*,[7] the definition reads, "Based on the classic holistic view of life, Qigong is a skill that forges and enhances the genuine Qi (vital energy) in man's body; it is the knowledge of balancing one's body and mind; a science of exploring the mystery of life." In the book *Void and Bright Qigong*,[8] the study of Qigong is defined as "a science studying the theory and the methods for adjusting man's body, mind, and breathing under the guidance of consciousness in a unique state to achieve the ultimate emptiness; to manipulate the Circulation of Qi and to benefit the good temper of the body so as to cure disease, maintain good health, adjust energy, and live a longer life." In answering the question "What is Qigong?" the book *Magic Qigong in China*[9] states that "Qigong is an ideal skill to strengthen both one's body and mind; it is a skill to maintain good health, to cure diseases, to prolong your life, defend yourself, save your energy, and cultivate your intelligence." Judging by the modern study of Qigong, it should be more than just the skill mentioned above. It is also a science and a multidisciplinary branch of knowledge related to both social and natural science in modern times. Some influential Chinese scientists have commented that "it is a high technology within high-tech, or it is the most sophisticated technique."

The uncertainty in defining Qigong is associated with and manifest in the development of the entire study of Qigong. The current study of Qigong can be described as the proclamations of hundreds of different schools. Hypotheses proposed by scientists in various fields emerge, one after another. Their views of Qigong vary depending on the different approaches and starting points of their study, so it is no surprise to see many different definitions. These will narrow to a single adequate definition only when the study of Qigong has discovered its own approach and unique angle of observation.

Based on my own focus, I define Qigong as "a skill that aims at cultivating man's potentials by means of the unified three adjustments of mind, breath, and body." My definition regards Qigong as a skill and so differs from other definitions that take Qigong as a theoretical concept or an approach. My notion emphasizes the practical and technical aspects of Qigong, in particular its operative aspect. Understanding this is essential for the learning and study of Qigong. The *three adjustments* relate to the adjustment of mind, breathing, and body. In other words, the adjustment of consciousness, inhalation and exhalation, and posture and movement. I'll give a detailed explanation later. The term "unified" refers, crucially, to the idea of combining the three adjustments all in one. Whether or not the three adjustments are unified is the key to distinguishing Qigong and general physical exercise. The latter is a self-controlled movement. The brain gives orders to the body, accompanied by the rhythm of breath. So it may also be regarded as a kind of integrative exercise of mind and body when one applies the three adjustments. But in physical exercise, each of the three adjustments is independent and coordinated with the other two, and operates constructively or simultaneously during the process, whereas the three adjustments in Qigong work quite differently. They are unified into one modality. Each adjustment now contains the other two and loses its independence. It only exists while operating with the other two. This feature distinguishes Qigong from physical exercise.

In my definition the term "potential" is used in a broader sense. It not only refers to the so-called extraordinary power that has not been generally cultivated, but also to the ordinary power that can only be cultivated through the practice of Qigong. For instance, the ability to self-heal: The practitioner has his illness cured by practicing Qigong. This ability to recover from illness is an ordinary power that is cultivated through the practice of Qigong.

Now I will explain the notion of Rujing. Many other concepts similar to the concept of Rujing have been adopted by experts in health care throughout history. The notion of "Wu Ru" (five entries) is an example. The five entries are Ruxu, Rujing, Ruding, Rushen and Ruji. The ancient scholars regarded them as five different concepts.

Ruxu means quiet and inactive; *Rujing* means fresh and alert and in a state of extreme calmness; *Ruding* means to clear out worries and concentrate on the understanding of Zen (a notion in Buddhism referring to the meditation), and wisdom and peace combine; *Rushen* means being free of mental burdens and being able to apply the wisdom of the supreme being; and *Ruji* means everything becomes quiet and disappears—there is no pain and no rejoicing. These five entries can be understood as the five different stages of one realm. Apart from the term "Rujing," all the rest are rarely used, and the notion Rujing is not just one of the stages, but includes all five concepts, and stands for all of them. Rujing is also called Zen Qigong (Buddhist meditation or Zen) and is used by Buddhists.

Like the concept of Qigong, Rujing also has a variety of definitions. Each researcher holds his own opinion. In the chapter "Understanding Rujing" in *The Study of Chinese Qigong*,[10] the author states that "Rujing is a relaxed and comfortable state achieved by the practitioner having a clear mind based on the practice of concentration of consciousness during the process of Qigong. It is also a state of calm and peace and being cut off from the outside world." *Xu Ming Gong* adopts the notion of Ruxu. It defines Rujing as "a developing physiological stabilization initially achieved through the adjustments of body, breathing, and mind. It is a special state characterized by profound calmness and peacefulness in mind, and a demonstrated function of reinforcing constitutional health, recovery from illness, expanding the life span, and balancing the consumption of energy." In *An Introduction to Chinese Qigong*,[11] the author states that "so-called Rujing actually refers to the mono-thinking process, with the reduction of unrelated thoughts and weakened response to stimuli."

Despite these variations in definition, the process of defining Rujing remains the same—that is, to describe its state if possible and then point out the essence of the state. My definition of Rujing focuses on its process. I think that Rujing is a process during which thoughts gradually die away and the form of thinking changes. The term Rujing is both a noun and a verb. As a noun it indicates a special state. As a verb it emphasizes the complete process of entering that particular state. This particular aspect of Rujing as a verb corresponds with my express purpose of revealing the essence of the dynamic changes in one's mind and body in the process of Rujing. My definition shows that the essence of this process is the alteration of thinking in strength and mode. I will discuss the essence of Rujing from a multidisciplinary angle. My focus will remain the study of Rujing from the perspective of cognitive science. I will discuss these topics in detail in the later chapters.

The definition of Rujing that I have presented in this chapter is to illustrate the way the concept is used, and this also applies to the definition of Qigong.

Rujing and the Three Adjustments

As stated before, the three adjustments are the adjustment of mind, adjustment of breath, and adjustment of body. The practice of Qigong is actually the practice of the three adjustments. The adjustment of *mind* is also called adjustment of spirit or adjustment of consciousness. This adjustment includes the balance of thinking, senses, emotion, etc. The adjustment of *breath* is sometimes called adjustment of exhaling and inhaling; it is to adjust the mode of breathing (abdominal breathing, regular breathing, and other modes of breathing), frequency, rhythm, strength, etc. The adjustment of *body* is to adjust the posture and movement of the body. Inactive Qigong, the still type, is to set posture. Active Qigong, the moving type, is to control the body movements. Both types of Qigong are developed by selecting the necessary contents of the three adjustments and combining them for a particular goal. The priority of each adjustment depends on the type of Qigong. For most types of Qigong, adjustment of mind is primary. It leads the other two adjustments. However, the superiority of one adjustment over the others does not mean it can replace the others. They cannot be subtracted either. In any type of Qigong, each of them makes its own respective contribution, and at the same time they act as one unit. Therefore, the practice of any type of Qigong involves the unification of mind and body.

Rujing, as a process or state in the practice of Qigong, is, of course, a changing process of mind and body. In other words, it is not merely an isolated psychological or physiological state or change, but the unification of these states or changes. I lay great emphasis on thes because many people often consciously or unconsciously regard Rujing only as a psychological state or process of adjusting one's mind. This view is biased, though not wrong; the state of quiet, comfortable, and ultimate emptiness indeed starts from Tiaoxin. Gradually, the psychological alteration affects one's physiological state. Rujing is connected with all three adjustments but is primarily connected with the adjustment of mind.

The content of Tiaoxin is abundant. Rujing is a vital part of it, but not the entirety. A lot of mental activities one does during the practice of Qigong do not aim at Rujing (for example, the consciousness used in martial arts, or in diagnosing and treating diseases). A 70-year-old lady once reported her experience when she was practicing standing Qigong with ten other practitioners. She closed her eyes for a little while and then she felt that her body was floating and slowly rising up. The trees and people around her remained where they were. She was flying higher and higher. It was just wonderful. When she looked down, she found the people and objects around were only an inch in size, as if in a mini-landscape. When she opened her eyes at the end of the practice, she found herself still on the ground and was just swaying slightly. This is termed "soul wandering" or "the consciousness departing." It usually occurs when one has been in the deep *state* of Rujing and is quite different from the active consciousness during the *process* of Rujing.

The adjustment of mind aiming at Rujing consists of two parts: the adjustment of consciousness and the adjustment of emotion. Adjustment of consciousness can be further classified into two subtypes: concentrating on consciousness, including concentrating inwards or outwards; and not concentrating on consciousness. Concentrating inwards refers to concentration on a particular part of your body, normally the Dantian[12] or Baihui,[13] Yongquan,[14] or other acupuncture point. If you practice Qigong for the purpose of curing disease, you can also concentrate on the organ affected, such as the liver for liver disease, or the stomach for stomach troubles. In doing so you can collect the vital energy to attack the illness. Concentrating outwards refers to focusing on an object or a space outside your body. For instance, you can concentrate on a mountain peak in the distance, a tree, or a flower nearby. You can also concentrate on a point in three-dimensional space, such as a point three inches away from the Shanzhong[15] point in your chest. Given so many types of concentration, plus other kinds of activities of consciousness and the adjustment of sense and emotion, it is easy to see the complexity of Rujing.

The adjustment of breathing, while not the most important part of Rujing, is a significant part. We can hardly say that someone who is panting is in the state of Rujing. On the contrary, once you really reach the state of Rujing, your breathing should be very slow and soft. It is also possible that for a certain period of time your breathing may even stop. An Indian yogi is reported as sitting in a wooden box that was then buried for several days. During the time he was buried, the instruments connected to his body did not register any breathing, blood pressure, or pulse. His body restored normal functioning only several hours after he was back from underground. There was no sign of any harm to his body. So we may suppose that he was in the deep state of Rujing while he was in the box. His breathing must have completely stopped. (Here I'm referring to Lung breathing. Cell breathing was still going on.) In our general practice of Rujing, we may not reach that level. Our breathing will not stop, but should be very soft and slow. The diminished breathing correlates with the different states of Rujing.

The adjustment of body has the least influence on Rujing, yet it should not be neglected. The different postures one may assume in practicing Rujing have a different impact on Rujing. The standing posture, for example, usually leads to a lower level of Rujing than the sitting posture. This is because of the difficulty in maintaining stability and balance while standing, it requires coordination of the leg and waist muscles, and these muscles are always in a state of tension so that the nerves that control them must be intensely stimulated. Moreover, the cerebral cortex is also on the alert for potential falls; therefore, one could hardly be in a state of complete physical and mental relaxation. This will definitely affect the state of Rujing. So when you choose the standing posture for practicing Rujing, all you need is to banish distracting thoughts and minimize your thinking. You still have to maintain a sense of your body. Things will be quite different when you assume a sitting posture. You can be much more relaxed compared to the standing mode. The state of Rujing will be deeper than in the latter. As far as the standing posture is concerned, there are also differences in posture, such as Sanyuan Shi (three rings type), Fu An Shi (hold and press type), etc. Each has a slightly different impact on the state of Rujing. This is also true of the sitting mode. Besides these two modes there is another: the lying mode. All have a subtle impact on the state of Rujing.

Rujing and the Types of Qigong

We have learnt that the type of Qigong chosen is specified by the combination of certain elements of the three adjustments to achieve its purpose. No one knows the exact number of Qigong variants. Some say that there are about 3600 sorts of Qigong developed by Taoism, and 84,000 by Buddhism. These numbers are, of course, not literally true. They just show the abundance of the variants. There are about 3000 different types of Qigong that have traceable titles and records. In the years of the Qigong boom, over 3000 variants became popular, among which the most popular are Crane Flying Qigong, Wild Goose Qigong, New Qigong Therapy, Standing Qigong, and Zen Meditation Qigong, amongst many others.

To understand better the varieties of Qigong, we need to put them into different categories. Criteria for classifying Qigong have been proposed according to the different goals of study, and have resulted in various categories. We can classify them according to the origin and schools of Qigong, which can be classified as Buddhism, Taoism, Medicine, Confucianism, and Martial Art. Based on the emphasis placed on different aspects of the three adjustments, Qigong can also be classified into three different schools aiming at adjustments of body, breath, and mind. There are also other synthetic classifications that divide Qigong into relaxed type, gymnastic type, massage type, and autokinesis type; or into five schools: Inhaling and Exhaling, Buddhism Concentration, Thought Preserving, Circulation of Qi, and Leading and Guiding Qi.

For the purpose of research, it is most appropriate to classify Qigong into two types: active and inactive. Rujing is mostly associated with the inactive type. This does not mean that the active type of Qigong does not require Rujing. Many require an element of "stillness in motion." The state of Rujing in active Qigong differs from that in inactive Qigong only in scale and level. On the other hand, the concepts of active and inactive are just relative. There are not only the active types that involve inactivity, and vice versa, but also intermediate types that involve both activity and inactivity. Standing Qigong with certain postures is regarded as either inactive or active by different people. This shows that it is actually an intermediate type. All the classifications of Qigong are relative, and all have intermediate or transitional forms.

Although Rujing is mainly concerned with still Qigong, it is not the goal of all inactive Qigong, and even among the many types of still Qigong that take Rujing as their main goal, the requirement of Rujing is not all the same. Differences are reflected in the depth of the level of Rujing, and also in its operational variants. It is important to know those differences. It directly affects our choice of Qigong and how to do it.

The type of Qigong that requires the highest level of Rujing is Zen. During the period of the North and South dynasty (420 AD to 589 AD), Bodhidharma, who brought Buddhism to China, sailed across the Indian Ocean and landed in Guangzhou. Then he went to Jinling (the city of Nanjing), the capital of the Liang dynasty (502 AD to 557 AD), and met Xiaoyan, the emperor of Liang, who was said to have a great interest in Buddhism. After a few minutes talking with the emperor, he found the emperor did not have the "wisdom root" and could not understand his witty words. He was quite disappointed and hid himself in Shaolin Temple at Songshan mountain in Henan province. He prayed and meditated for nine years, facing the wall. He never moved an inch in those nine years, and did not even notice the birds that had built a nest on his shoulder. The validity of this legend cannot be attested, but even if half of the story is true, we can still see that the state of Rujing this monk achieved was quite magnificent.

As for the sorts of Qigong which ask for a shallower state of Rujing, such as the recently developed Health Preservation Qigong, this only requires the practitioner to achieve a state where one feels comfortable and feels the body levitating in the air. Obviously this is still far from the state of ultimate emptiness. Of course, some practitioners who have better mastery of the skills may reach the deeper state of Rujing, even close to the ultimate emptiness, but this is not regarded as a general requirement of Health Preservation Qigong.

Zen Qigong and Health Preservation Qigong are also different in process. In other words, the contents of the three adjustments are different in these two types of Qigong. The difference in the adjustment of body is obvious, as one is done in a sitting posture while the other is done in a standing posture. As for the other two adjustments, one may not be able to tell the difference at first sight. If you observe and study them carefully, you will find surprising differences underneath. Zen Qigong requires a conscious adjustment of breathing, followed by the way of counting the number of breaths or following the breath. This not only stabilizes one's emotion and makes it easier to enter the state of Rujing, but it is also good for adjusting the breathing to soften the inhaling/exhaling until it becomes a sustained soft, almost ceased breath. Health Preservation Qigong does not require a conscious adjustment of breathing. It takes soft, abdominal breathing or even body breathing as something developed naturally: one does not need to be trained to achieve it. It only requires a smooth, steady, natural inhaling/exhaling. This natural way of breathing adjustment is also effective. Good practitioners can also enter the state of the soft, extended inhaling/exhaling through Zen Qigong.

There is also a significant difference between these two types of Qigong in the process of concentrating thoughts. The adjustment of mind in Zen Qigong emphasizes the harmony of the adjustment of mind and breath. As I mentioned above, it often follows the idea of counting and following. One counts the numbers of inhales and exhales from one to 100, then counts it again in the same order or in a reverse order. By doing so, one can also concentrate consciousness on breathing, so as to banish other thoughts. Following the Breath is the method one applies after becoming good at Counting the Breaths. Now one's mind is peaceful and concentrating. There is no need to continue counting the breath—one just lets consciousness follow the breathing rhythm in inhaling/exhaling until one reaches the state where mind and breathing are in great harmony. Counting the Breaths and Following the Breath can be regarded as two different stages of Rujing achieved through concentration on breathing.

Health Preservation Qigong does not pay attention to breathing at all—its basic activity of consciousness is to "hold the ball." Hold your hands in front of your chest in a circle, as if you are holding a very thin, light paper ball full of air. Since it is very thin, you cannot hold it tightly, otherwise it will deflate. Because it is very light in weight you need to hold it with the least effort, otherwise it may fly away from you. Your consciousness is concentrated on how to keep this ball from deflating and flying away; thus you banish all other thoughts and get into the state of Rujing gradually. This activity of consciousness also has some other functions in Health Preservation Qigong, which we will not explore here.

Many other types of inactive Qigong, such as Circulation of Qi, and Vital Energy Moving, aim to manipulate inner Qi. They also require the state of Rujing at various levels as preparation for the manipulation of inner Qi, but is not the final goal of the practice. Let's use Circulation of Qi as an example to explain this.

Circulation of Qi aims at making the inner Qi circulate around the two routes in your body. The Ren meridian, starting from the Huiyin[16] point, runs along the mid-line at the front of your body and then ends at the Chengjiang[17] point. The Du meridian, starting from the Changqiang[18] point, runs along the mid-line at the back of your body. It goes up along the spine, crosses over the Baihui point at the center of your head, and ends down at the Yinjiao acupoints. The practitioner should start by concentrating on the Dantian point. When you feel it being filled with inner Qi, you guide the Qi down to the Huiyin point and move it up along the Du meridian to Baihui to join the Ren meridian back to the Dantian. Once you become skilled you can circulate inner Qi along the two meridians in rhythm with your breath. You will feel fresh and alert, and your body light and full of energy. This is of great benefit to your health. These types of Qigong characterized by the movement of inner Qi are mostly found in schools of Taoism. Circulation of Qi also means Qi moving along the meridians of Du and Ren, which is regarded as a technique for developing Dan.[19]

Some forms of still Qigong take the control of breathing as a main component. Neiyanggong (a kind of Qigong for preserving the health of your organs), the earliest Qigong implemented after 1949, is one example of this kind. It lays importance on reciting words, stopping the breath, the tongue rising and falling with the rhythm of the breath, storing the Qi in the Dantian, and other features. Its breathing skill is quite sophisticated. It provides three fundamental breathing rhythms for you to choose from, according to your illness and physical constitution. The three rhythms are: "inhaling–pause–exhaling"; "inhaling–exhaling–pause"; and "inhaling–pause–inhaling–exhaling." It does not require the manipulation of inner Qi. Its emphasis is entirely on breathing. To summarize, there are various kinds of still Qigong and only some of them take Rujing as the primary content and ultimate goal.

Now let's explain the relationship between Rujing and the sections of one particular Qigong. Some types of Qigong have only one section; we are not concerned with those. Complex forms of Qigong always consist of sections, each of which may be comprised of several units. For instance, "New Qigong Therapy" includes sections called "a natural process in breathing with medium strength," "special fast skills," and "relax and calm in rising, falling, opening, and closing." "Relaxing Qigong" includes sections called "relax at three lines," "relax in sequence," "relax as a whole," "relax a particular part," and "relax inversely." These units sometimes have sequential relationships and sometimes have parallel relationships. Some relationships are fundamental and sophisticated. Some more complex Qigong forms consist of sections of both active and inactive types to achieve a better result in curing illness and maintaining good health. One example, entitled "Returning," has some its units focusing on Rujing. It is divided into active and inactive sections. The active section consists of eight units. The inactive section consists of four basic units.

"Keep-Fit Qigong," another type of inactive Qigong, is characterized by self-massage and movement of the limbs. It consists of 18 units, including clicking the teeth, washing the mouth with saliva, turning the tongue, and massaging the ears. Out of these 18 exercises, 17 are active and only one is inactive (that is the first unit, silent sitting). Such an arrangement helps the practitioner to calm down and breathe smoothly and quietly, and relax his body to prepare for the subsequent steps.

Our understanding of the relations between Rujing and Qigong and their different units will make it easier for us to select an appropriate Qigong without getting confused or lost when confronted by the thousands of Qigong varieties. In this chapter I have discussed the relations between Rujing and the three adjustments. We all know that Rujing has the closest connection with adjustment of mind. We have also discussed the posture of Rujing in Qigong in a holistic approach. This has prepared us for further discussion of the essence of Rujing.

It is worth mentioning that although my book studies mainly Rujing as the finest and core part of Qigong, I do not reject or devalue other elements of Qigong. Many well-known Qigong masters, past and present, have emphasized the practice of both active and inactive elements in Qigong. They are all correct, and so we need to consider the combination of both active and inactive Qigong when selecting the right type of Qigong to practice. When practicing active Qigong we should try to feel peacefulness in motion, and when practicing inactive Qigong we should try to feel movement in stillness. Once we can feel and undertake both, we will be able to extend our lifespan.

Chapter 2

The Realm of Rujing

If you have watched the incredible performances of Qigong masters, or their therapeutic magic on patients with various diseases, you may be bewildered by the magic of Qigong and eager to know how it is done. You may ask the Qigong masters directly, read a pile of classic medical works full of ancient terminology, or get to know some of the mysterious, unpredictable classic theories of Qigong and come to realize that behind the magic there are infinite secrets.

Why is Qigong so mysterious? Apart from the fact that it was purposely made hard to understand, and is usually taught on a one-to-one basis, another vital reason is that the state of Qigong can hardly be explained in words. And the most difficult thing to explain is Rujing. So Rujing is naturally regarded as a mystery within a mystery.

The Problem of Definition

Why is the concept of Qigong so difficult to describe? It is because of the limits of language itself. Language is basically a system of abstract symbols, and is a tool or medium of man's conceptual thinking that can precisely express concepts, judgments, and the process of deduction during man's conceptual thinking process. This is where language works best. When it comes to describing imagery, language is not quite so successful; it can only provide you with a vague account, but not a genuine interpretation of the image. We may be able to describe a man's appearance, but it won't be more accurate than a photo, no matter how hard we try. To teach the action of

Qigong, except for some very simple gestures that can be explained clearly in language, most of the complex actions cannot be learned or taught without the aid of illustration or demonstration. Few people can learn the 64-gesture Wild Goose Qigong by reading books, even with the help of illustrations. Language seems so limited in describing the action of Qigong, let alone the state of Rujing, which is motionless and involves no gestures at all. It is almost impossible to describe in words.

There are two obstacles that cannot be overcome when we try to explain the state of Rujing in words. One is the shortage of vocabulary. During the process of Rujing our mind's main activity is sensory thinking. This thinking needs to control all kinds of detailed senses. Our feeling is more difficult to describe than images. The vocabulary we have in any human language for describing feelings is inadequate and imprecise, relative to what we actually feel and sense in reality. The concept of pain may cover many similar or even different types of pain. Is the pain you get when pricking your finger with a needle similar to the pain you get when you have stomach ache? Is the pain in your waist after hard work the same as the headache you get when you have a fever? We may feel the differences, but it is difficult to describe them with appropriate words. This is also true of the sense of soreness, numbness, swelling, or itching. We have only a finite vocabulary to explain the infinite experiences of all kinds of feelings. This is the conundrum. This problem exists whenever language is needed as the medium of description. During Rujing, the sensory changes in one's body are far more complex than changes in one's everyday feelings, thus making the already impossible situation even more complicated.

The emotional changes during the state of Rujing are also worth mentioning. Nor do we have many words available to describe those changes. Commonly we might say "like ants on a hot pot" to describe a feeling of agitation. This might be a good choice of words in literature—but readers will feel bewildered if you use the same expression in defining a scientific theory.

The reason why we lack vocabulary for describing emotions is probably the same as it is in relation to describing feelings. If we look into the matter and try to discover why this vocabulary is so limited from a more profound point of view, we may observe that for thousands of years, and the last century in particular, man has been busy exploring, cultivating, and exploiting nature. He has done little in the field of understanding and cultivating his own inner world.

The second barrier is more difficult to break through, and is more critical. Rujing is a process during which consciousness is gradually weakened. Once one enters the advanced level of Rujing, the entire activity of consciousness, including thoughts and emotions, almost ceases (if it has not already stopped) in our subjective mind. In the lower level of Rujing, sensory thinking is still active, despite being impossible to describe. Since consciousness is still active, we can still talk in words. When we reach the advanced level of Rujing, during which thinking and the entire consciousness do not exist in our subjective mind, we have nothing to talk about. Though we can still feel the ultimate realm, we are not able to pinpoint where it is. It is not made concrete in the form of consciousness or thinking; therefore, it cannot be controlled or mastered by our consciousness and thinking—because once we start to think, it is no longer the same ultimate realm that we want to describe. Language is the vehicle or medium for thinking. No thinking, no words. That is why we can say that words are not capable of expressing everything.

The high level of Rujing is really indescribable. This is determined by the nature of Rujing, not by human factors. More precisely, it is not really indescribable—we just do not have the vocabulary available, and nothing to interpret. This is one of the main reasons why my definition of Qigong emphasizes its practical, operational aspect.

However, it does need to be passed on in one way or another, otherwise Qigong would not even exist. People have tried many ways to communicate the unspeakable state of Rujing and Qigong.

Words are still our first choice. After all, they are the most widely used means of communication. If we cannot find the right words for a direct, straightforward description, we tend to do it indirectly. To describe the Qi in the body one can say metaphorically that it is just like ants moving on the body, or a breath of cool breeze through the feet and hands. In *Four Hundred Words on Golden Don,*[20] the author described the production of Dan in practicing Circulation of Qi as:

> Starting from NiWan[21] you feel the wind blows, JiangGong[22] was as bright as the shining moon, the Dantian was heated by fire, and GuHai[23] like the clear lake. Jaji[24] is like the wheel rolling, and the four limbs are like rock and mountain. The pores open as if you had just had a bath. The bones of your body were in sound sleep, and the spirit brings you the joy of making love with your partner, and the soul, like a baby, wants to be with the mother all the time. This is the real circumstance but not the metaphor.

It says it is not a metaphor, but actually it is a metaphor. The entire account is metaphorical. Some use poetry to describe the state of Rujing. One Song dynasty poem, "Enlightenment in a Temple," edited by the monk Jue Fan, reads:

> The rising desires bring you back to the secular world,
> Realizing it makes you a saint.
> This is said to be the wakening, and genuine this wakening is
> Once to understand that everything is just of emptiness,
> Saint and Secular are nothing but a mirage,
> Sitting and remaining silent with a heart as clear as an ancient well.

The puzzling Zen texts may be regarded, to some extent, as the expression of a state of emptiness in linguistic form. This situation is quite similar to that of Qigong. One of the characteristics of the puzzle is the sharp conflicts in the dialogues. The questions and answers in the dialogue seem unconnected, not following the formal logic at all. For instance, in one puzzle a monk asks his master CongNian: "What is the purpose of Master Dam's coming from the west?" His teacher answers: "Hair grows on the teeth." It seems that the teacher tried to stop his disciple from thinking by giving an illogical reply. It brings the thinking to a stop and into a state of vacuum. The disciple was unable to continue his thinking and did not know what to think about his answer, and he was expected to obtain sudden insight from the vacuum of his mind. Sometimes teachers will use gesture instead of language to answer questions. A monk named LongYa once asked Master Cuiwei the same question. His master asked him to cross a panel they used for praying and hit him with it, without speaking a single word. The blow had the same meaning as the words used by CongNian. From words to action, this showed how language had reached its limits.

Are there other forms of nonverbal communication? There certainly are. We have to come back to Zen again. Some readers may ask why the study of Qigong is always associated with religion. Qigong does have a broad association, or even a bond, with religion. While not going further into this, I want to point out here that Qigong may have provided a practical foundation for religious doctrine, while religion to some extent promoted the development of Qigong. Actually the very fact that Qigong can improve health and life expectancy, cure illness, and cultivate extraordinary power provided a foundation for the Buddhist ideas that one could go to heaven and become divine. Equally, man's desire to be immortal and go to heaven, and his activity to that end, helped and enriched the content of Qigong. Understanding this enables us to distinguish the difference between superstition and modern science. Now let's go back to Zen. Zen was regarded as Sakyamuni's tutoring course; that is to say, Sakyamuni taught his disciples in secret and in private. It is a knowledge transferred through telepathy. No other media are required. The knowledge was transferred directly to one's mind, and the one who received the message became the Buddha. It is the mutual understanding and cooperation between teacher and student. One follows the other in great harmony.

The teacher's mind is the mind of Buddha; thus the student's mind became the mind of Buddha as well. Such a way of transferring the knowledge is said to have started when the Buddha picked a flower and showed it to his disciples at a gathering on LinSham mountain. All the disciples remained numb, not understanding its meaning, except for Mokejayi, who gave a smile to show his understanding. Then Buddha acknowledged that the mind of Buddha was transferred to Mokejayi. This is said to be the origin of Zen. Mokejayi became the founder of Zen, as he understood the Buddha in his heart, without language. In common sense terms, this sounds like nonsense. Yet if we re-examine it in terms of Qigong or extraordinary power, it was quite possible.

Everyone knows that Buddha would sit for hours in meditation as a kind of religious service. According to legend, he acquired the ultimate wisdom in his sudden understanding of the laws of nature while sitting under a banyan tree. It is obvious that he was quite good at Qigong. From the way he showed his disciples the flower, we may assume that he had certain extraordinary powers and was able to transfer his thoughts to others through thinking. Mokejayi was one of the truthful disciples. His mastery of Qigong was higher than others'. He was the only one whose power had been strong enough to communicate with Buddha through psychic communication. It is quite likely that Buddha sent out a message through the flower. The message could only be received by Mokejayi. So he smiled, and the others could only remain numb. This is the explanation of "heart-to-heart transferring" from Qigong's point of view.

Whether or not this explanation matches the original meaning in Zen, the phenomenon of psychic communication has been recorded in China and overseas, from ancient times up to the present.

It should not be a problem to admit its existence. There are numerous examples in modern scientific experiments, not to mention the past. In 1966 Yuri Kamensky, a well-known Soviet biologist, conducted an experiment in the city of Novosibirsk, 3000km from Moscow. The subject in Novosibirsk was an actor of the state theater with the power of psychic communication—Karl Nikolaev. He directly received graphic information sent by telepathy from Moscow. It is also reported that the American navy, working together with Stanford Research Institute, did experiments on telepathy with people who had extraordinary power. They were quite successful in an experiment with extrasensory communication in submarines.

In China, someone did some experiments and concluded that telepathy does not exist only among those who have extraordinary power. We all have this ability—it is just that the degree of energy we send out is quite weak compared to those who have extraordinary power. The experiment was as follows.

Two persons with extraordinary power were invited to try psychic communication. Once it was proved that both of them had the power, one of them was replaced by an ordinary person. This person was asked to send out a thought message, to see if the person who had the extraordinary power would be able to receive it. The experiment showed that his message could not be received by the man with the extraordinary power. Then another ordinary person was added, and the two ordinary persons were asked to send out the same message, to see if it could be received by the man with the extraordinary power. It was concluded that the message would be received by the man with the extraordinary power when five or six ordinary people joined together to send it. This experiment not only showed that the ordinary person also has psychic power, it also told us that the amount of energy emanated was in a ratio of 5 or 6 to 1. The experiments described above show that humans do have the capacity for ESP (extrasensory perception). It is the best, natural way of conveying to others the ineffable message of Qigong and Rujing. It strikes to the heart of the matter.

Actually, this kind of communication is not mysterious and inaccessible. Many beginners can also feel the existence of the Qi field when practicing Qigong in a large group. The feeling is a kind of nonverbal communication. It is not yet the transfer of consciousness. It has the character of "heart-to-heart information transfer" (psychic communication). To give another example, the sensations reported by a patient during treatment by a Qigong master could also be interpreted as the result of receiving nonverbal information from the master.

What indeed the Qi field or external Qi is remains a subject that the scientific world is studying assiduously. Former Soviet scientists reported their discovery of micro-particles around the human body. Chinese scientists have also reported the existence of the Qi field by measuring the dosage of radiation around the human subject. All these discoveries are very illuminating. It seems not impossible that we shall find the material basis for what we call telepathy.

We have discussed nonverbal communication at some length. We have a positive view on its feasibility and superiority in transferring messages during Qigong and Rujing. Unfortunately, we cannot use it to communicate at the same time as using language as a form of communication, which is the only way we can choose to talk about it. The difficulty is obvious, as I don't have the vocabulary to present to you a precise account and description. Therefore, it is far from adequate to learn Qigong merely from books.

The Levels of Rujing

Since ancient times the state of Rujing has always been divided into several levels. The divisions are used to indicate the various depths of Rujing one may achieve. The deeper one can reach in Rujing, the better their skill, and vice versa.

The most complex division of Rujing by the ancient Chinese was Zen in Buddhism. There are many types of Zen. In terms of "On Earth Zen" and "Beyond Earth Zen," On Earth Zen consists of Four Zen, Four Infinite Mind, Four Empty Stillness, etc. Beyond Earth Zen consists of Nine States of Thought, Eight Exclusions, Nine Grades of Stillness, and others. There is also a variety of other Zens. The content of Zen includes many different levels of Rujing as well as the visualization of thinking on the basis of the various levels of Rujing.

Liu Miao Fa Men[25] (Six Magic Skills) describes the different levels of Zen that result from the application of the six magic skills: Count, Follow, Stop, Observe, Return, and Purify.

To count is the first magic skill; the practitioner will reach the state of Four Zen, Four Infinite Mind, and Four Empty Stillness by counting his breath.

The second magic skill is *to follow*. By following the breathing, one will obtain the 16 special skills:

1. Knowing the breathing in

2. Knowing the breathing out

3. Knowing the length of breathing

4. Knowing the breathing through the whole body

5. Following the movement of the body

6. Receiving pleasure

7. Receiving happiness

8. Receiving all the feelings

9. Becoming pleasant

10. Becoming frightened

11. Becoming released

12. Observing the dynamic

13. Observing the floating out

14. Observing departing

15. Observing the disappearing

16. Observing abandonment of consciousness.

The third magic skill is *to stop*. As the practitioner stops at his heart, it results in five cycles of Zen.

1. First is the cycle of ground.

2. Second is the cycle of water.

3. Third is the cycle of emptiness.

4. Fourth is the cycle of gold sand.

5. Fifth is the cycle of diamond.

The fourth magic skill is *to observe*.
　　The fifth magic skill is *to return*.

The sixth magic skill is *to purify*.

There are sub-levels of the last three skills. Altogether the six magic skills contain almost 100 different Zen.

Dividing Rujing into so many different levels reveals the richness of the concept of Rujing. It shows positively that Rujing is not a state of inert tranquillity, but rather a dynamic world. The negative aspect of this division is that it scares beginners who come to think of Rujing as something too hard to learn, unable to see the entire picture of Rujing and control the process. As far as the practice is concerned, those divisions are too complex; even monks may not follow the whole process. If someone has to think about the levels they have to pass in the practice of Rujing, how can they become peaceful and calm?

Research papers on categorizing the levels of Rujing have been published occasionally in recent years. Most of them divide Rujing into three different levels: primary, intermediate, and advanced, based on the practice of Rujing and the practitioner's experience; others may not use the same terminology but apply more or less the same ideas.

For instance, in *Xu Ming Gong* the three levels are named as: a period of getting into the state of Rujing when one's consciousness is still working, a period of getting into the state of Rujing when one's consciousness is partially working, and a period of getting into the state of Rujing when one's consciousness stops working. A representative and concise account of the three-level idea might be the following excerpt from the article "Consciousness, Relaxation, and Calmness in Qigong."

1. *Primary stage:* The posture is natural and comfortable, the breathing gentle, the mind is better cleared. Distracting thoughts are cleared out quickly. One may experience one or two short periods when one feels the mind is clear and tranquil and comfortable. This is the primary state of Rujing.

2. *Intermediate stage:* On the foundation of the primary stage, you ignore interruptions from the outside world, feel your

body light and relaxed; your breath is slow and gentle. The feeling of light, heavy, warm, itching, and comfortable recurs now and then.

3. *Advanced stage:* On the foundation of the intermediate stage, outside interruptions will have no effect on you; the breath becomes even slower and softer. You allow it to come and go. You have freedom to control and manipulate it. It is such a deep feeling that the whole body seems floating and shapeless. Once you move, you might feel like you have just taken a shower. You feel very comfortable and energetic.

The advantage of this three-level division is that it is practical, concise, and accessible for beginners. The division also matches the natural process of Rujing, which tends to shift from the initial, shallow level to the advanced, deep level. Thus it can provide practitioners with effective guidance. A defect of this approach is that the uniqueness of each stage is not given enough attention. It is also difficult to demonstrate the specific features of each level when they are all described in terms of the same aspects of breathing, feeling, etc.

I therefore prefer to divide Rujing into four stages, according to the main differences one experiences at the different stages of Rujing. Each stage is named after its specific quality and it will not be labeled by gradients. Based on the general process of Rujing, I categorize the four stages as:

1. the stage of Relaxation

2. the stage of Moving and Touching

3. the stage of Pleasant Sensation

4. the stage of Ultimate Emptiness.

The first period, Relaxation, is the initial, shallow stage of Rujing. The main experience of this period is physically and mentally relaxing and calming down. It sounds easy, yet it is not easy to be perfectly relaxed. One may easily relax the limbs, but it is not easy to achieve the same effect on the inner organs, which turns out to be far more important than relaxation of the limbs. This is particularly true for those whose reasons for practicing Rujing is to heal afflicted organs, because it is the prerequisite for the treatment.

It is also easy to neglect certain parts of your body during relaxation (such as relaxing your eyes and brows). In practicing Rujing most people think that those parts are already relaxed. If you observe those practitioners carefully, you might find that they could still be frowning a bit, which reveals that not only have they not completely relaxed their bodies, but also they have not relaxed their minds. The indication of mental relaxation is to stop thinking consciously. You may not be able to clear your mind at this moment, and may still have many thoughts, which come and go frequently. So long as you do not initially start to think about something, you can be regarded as mentally relaxed. Real relaxation is the relaxation of both body and mind, inside and outside. Only by achieving this can you lay a good foundation for the next stage of Rujing.

Relaxation and tranquillity are very much connected to each other. They not only facilitate each other but also blend into one state of being that is both dispensable and indispensable. Only when muscles are relaxed can the rate of blood circulation slow down. Being relaxed is itself the beginning of being tranquil, and this is how they become blended into one state of being. To relax mentally means not to think about anything, and to stop thinking is the beginning of being tranquil, isn't it?

The deep state of tranquillity emerges from relaxation. In this period relaxation already retreats into the background, it seems to be forgotten, and tranquillity comes to the fore. As far as one's body is concerned, the limbs are motionless, the heartbeat slows down, and the breath becomes slow and soft. All of this can be experienced consciously or unconsciously. As far as one's mind is concerned, the thoughts are excluded through different methods in accordance with the various processes. One may use one thought to replace all other thoughts, stop thinking when it occurs so that it cannot develop, apply inner observation skills to have the thoughts vanish by themselves, etc. In the later part of this stage your limbs are still, your breath is smooth, and there aren't many thoughts in your mind. Your body and mind are in great harmony and proceed into the realm of tranquillity and comfort.

The Moving and Touching stage consist of two states. State one occurs on the foundation of the Relaxation stage. State two occurs after the achievement of the deep state of Rujing. The two might appear in the same or a similar way, but they are essentially quite different. Simply stated, the characteristics of the shallow level of the Moving and Touching stage could be classified into "16 feelings," an ancient notion that includes moving, itching, cool, warm, light, heavy, acerbity, slippery, falling, leaning, cold, hot, floating, sinking, hard, and soft. Once you are in the deep level of Rujing, the content of those 16 feelings may still exist, but will be more complicated. For example, you may have an illusion. We can also observe that the characteristics of the 16 feelings are mostly sensations from your body, what your muscles, skin, or organs can sense. Some may be changes in the way the whole body feels. They are still basically within the range of normal sensations that one experiences every day, though some of the sensations are actually illusions (for instance, one's body may feel as light as a feather, but one's weight has not actually changed at all). But the old lady's case is quite different. What she felt does not exist in reality. She did not float up from the ground.

The differences between these two feelings in terms of form and content reflect the different states of consciousness at the shallow and deep levels of Rujing. At the shallow level, some relatively active consciousness is still working. In other words, the consciousness is still active. At the deep level of Rujing, what is relatively active is the subconscious. The difference between consciousness and the subconscious determines how one acts. So feelings can be divided into two types: sense-based feelings and illusion-based feelings. The change between relatively active consciousness and the subconscious is not absolute, but rather they overlap each other. So do feelings and illusions.

Now when people talk about the Moving and Touching stage, they usually refer to the reactions at the shallow level of Rujing, or they may include some of the reactions at the deep level of Rujing. To our ancestors the so-called "moving and touching" mostly referred to all types of sensations, including some illusions. I clarify the boundary between feelings and illusions from the viewpoint of consciousness. Since they all belong to the process of consciousness, we can still place them in the category of the Moving and Touching stage. In my four-stage theory, the Moving and Touching stage is still the primary level of Rujing, as represented by the feelings and illusions whose manifestations are based on the 16 feelings.

The third stage—the period of Pleasant Sensation—is short and quite significant. Its occurrence indicates the progress of your practice in Rujing. It occurs after the Moving and Touching stage. The moving and touching during the primary level of Rujing is mostly what you feel when your inner Qi is not circulating smoothly and the three adjustments have not yet been integrated. These feelings are related to mastery of Rujing, to the balance between Yin and Yang in your body. For those who practice Qigong to cure illness, the incidence of moving and touching has a close relation with recovery from illness. Their vanishing indicates full recovery from the illness. The genuine integration of the three adjustments also depends on the state of one's health. Achieving the integration of the three adjustments is very difficult for someone whose illness has not yet been cured and whose circulation of blood and vital energy is still not smooth. When someone reaches the third stage, their health condition has reached a new level and has obtained the freedom of practicing Rujing. The occurrence of the Pleasant Sensation stage also indicates the advance of one's skill in Rujing.

It's hard to describe the pleasant sensation one experiences at this stage. It is quite different from any other pleasant sensation one may experience in life. Yet it seems to contain all the other pleasant sensations in life and be the realization of all in one. It's known in the theory of systemology that the whole does not equal the sum of the discrete parts. It actually exceeds the sum of the parts, because the whole has entered a new stage as a unified one. The mechanism of the matter at the advanced level may combine all of the lower-level functions. This does not mean a simple aggregation of the lower-level functions. All the same, the pleasant sensation one experiences in Rujing consists of all the other sensations, but it exceeds all those sensations put together and reaches a point that is new and inaccessible in everyday life.

Common pleasant sensations consist of two classes: the comfortable senses and the pleasant sensations. During the Pleasant Sensation stage of Rujing, the two merged into one. It's hard to separate them. The sensation is both mental and physical. To make it easier to understand, it is similar to sexual orgasm, if we are looking for an equivalent in everyday life. The orgasm is a pleasant sensation that involves both your body and mind. In general, it is much stronger than other sensations. It is quite similar to the pleasant feeling one experiences in Rujing. The ancient Chinese scholars frequently talked about it. Orgasm is usually strong, intense, brief, and hard to control. The peak of it is ejaculation. The pleasant sensation one experiences in Rujing is calm and mild, and from it you always sense the infinite, everlasting comfort and pleasure.

After the period of Pleasant Sensation you come to the Ultimate Emptiness stage. The turning point occurs naturally. It is not a leap across, but a transfer by osmosis. In this stage the pleasant sensation is not noticeable any more. You are not seeking the self-satisfaction of body and emotion. You actually forget yourself and are absorbed in an ultimate state of nature and the universe. If, in the Pleasant Sensation stage, you are still seeking physical and mental self-fulfillment, the search will become insignificant and vanish, along with the fading of your self-awareness.

Once self-awareness disappears, you will feel a sudden enlightenment, like rivers finally joining the sea. It goes from finite to infinite; from temporal to permanent. It is the moment when nature and man become one. At this moment your consciousness perceives not yourself, but the entire universe. Yet it is also yourself, since you and the cosmos are all one. Besides, consciousness itself changes too. It is no longer the consciousness of a particular individual, but the integration of consciousness of the individual and the universe.

Moreover, the consciousness and what the mind perceives have become one. The consciousness is simultaneously both itself and the object it uses to perceive. The object becomes simultaneously itself as well as the consciousness. It enters the state of chaos in which all differences disappear. Nature and man becoming one is the state of chaos. The final word we can use to describe the state of Rujing is perhaps "chaos."

Nature and man becoming one is not the same as the state of Ultimate Emptiness, since it can still be described by the word "chaos."

The state of Ultimate Emptiness can only be described by the word "nothingness." Yet just as the "nought" in math has significant implications, the word "nothingness" is a term of lexical enrichment. The key to the notion of ultimate emptiness is to "forget," which means to cease thinking. We may explain it this way: The function of thinking still exists, but it is not utilized. Therefore, the consciousness holds no content, and that is nothingness. No content leaves no need to express. Please be aware that to stop thinking does not mean that thinking is terminated. It nurses its vigor, waiting to be woken up. If thinking is terminated, it means the vigor dies and life cannot return. This is the key point that distinguishes Rujing from dead calm—just as in Buddhism, meditation is different from the monk passing away in sitting. When one enters the advanced level of Rujing, it tends to approach termination, yet it is not the same as termination. If the boundary is broken, it suggests you are entering heaven. Perhaps the monks who die in sitting fly to heaven this way.

Since Rujing nurses full vitality, when one enters the advanced level of Rujing, this vigor will manifest in a form that is outside the control of consciousness. It is formed in the Moving and Touching stage. Extrasensory power is perhaps the sublimation of Moving and Touching. But this is beyond the scope of my discussion of Rujing.

In my above discussion of the levels of Rujing, I need to emphasize two points. First, division between the different levels is relative. This relativity appears not only in the sequence of the different levels, but also in the content. From the natural progression of Rujing it generally develops in a sequence of four stages: Relaxation, Moving and Touching, Pleasant Sensation, and Ultimate Emptiness. This does not exclude the fact that they are interchangeable and overlapping. For example, in the stage of Pleasant Sensation, the occurrence of a certain thought could disrupt the stability of that stage and bring you back to the stage of Moving and Touching—sometimes even back to the Relaxation stage, so that you have to start all over again. This is not rare among beginners. The stability of the Ultimate Emptiness stage requires more power and skills. At the initial stage, one may just be able to achieve it for only a few minutes and then regress to other states. As far as the content of Rujing is concerned, the four stages are not distinguished in black-and-white terms. Each stage can more or less be thought to contain the content of the other three. The fundamental aspects of one's experience in different stages of Rujing are actually one entity. It simply weighs differently at the different levels of Rujing. So they should not be taken as absolute and isolated events. This principle of relativity regarding the different levels of Rujing accommodates the analysis of each individual's practice, and the evaluation of his skills and power, over a period of time.

Second, the level one enters varies from individual to individual. Those gifted from birth may leap ahead to the advanced level when they have only just started to practice Rujing. Ordinary practitioners who have reached quite a high level after hard practice may also begin from the higher stage, and not necessarily from the Relaxation stage every time. By contrast, those who are physically weak or not practicing in a correct way may still not be able to reach the stages of Pleasant Sensation and Ultimate Emptiness after long periods of practice. Therefore they may lose confidence in carrying on with the exercise. Knowing this variation will help the practitioner to control his practice procedure and help him to give full credit to his strong points and avoid his weaknesses.

As no way of classifying the levels of Rujing is perfect, my way of classifying it into four stages is also not without shortcomings. It is based on subjective experience, on the characteristics of different stages of the process of Rujing. The benefits of this division are mixed.

Each stage is clear-cut. They are easy to learn. However, these features are at the same time the shortcomings of my approach. Contrast and clarity are the result of emphasizing certain characteristics of the event, and because these characteristics do not represent the entirety of the event, emphasizing them can lead people to ignore the relatively non-characteristic elements. They may misunderstand relative aspects of the matter in the extreme, and assume that the part represents the whole. Therefore, in applying my approach, one should pay plenty of attention to the relativity principle that I have highlighted with reference to the stages of Rujing, and use my categories as points of reference for the content of the next section, so as to draw advantage from them and avoid unhelpful consequences.

The Experience of Rujing

In the last section we divided Rujing into four stages based on the characteristics of each stage, and provided a framework for understanding Rujing. In this section we'll study the issue synchronically. We'll follow not the temporal order but the type of subjective experience, to portray the concept of Rujing. At the same time we'll try to make our perception thorough and complete, without dwelling on the specific aspects.

The subjective experience of Rujing varies and is changeable. For convenience, we'll divide it into two types of experience: sensory experience and mood/emotion experience. Internal and external motion during the process of Rujing should also be regarded as part of subjective experience. As the causes of these are different from the two types of experience mentioned above, we'll discuss them in a different section.

Sensory Experiencing

The richness and refinement of sensory experience in the concept of Rujing are incomparable. This is partly because, although we experience all kinds of events every day, we only pay attention to the object we perceive. We do not notice the actual process of sensing and feeling. This happens subconsciously, and our attention will not be directed to it unless something happens. This will change when you enter the state of Rujing. Your attention will be, to a great extent, guided to the sense and the process of feeling itself. The object does not matter. Thus the feeling that you have never experienced, or which just flashed by in everyday life, now appears, is magnified, lasts longer, and even becomes the dominant feeling at the time. Such an experience is indescribable. What I have described here is still just an analogy from everyday life.

VISION

The most frequently occurring visual experience is the sense of light. I have mentioned earlier that Rujing is not the same as dead calm, nor is it the fall of darkness. Some practices require you to have your eyes slightly open or to focus on the top of your nose. In these circumstances you will not have a sense of darkness. When you practice with your eyes closed, external light can still pass through your eye lids and produce a sense of light (except in darkness). The sense of light we are talking about does not concern light caused by an outside light source, but the sense of light automatically generated during the practice of Qigong.

This sense of light may also have color. Any color of the palette may occur. It may be a cluster or a ray of colored light. It may just be in front of your eyes, or cover your whole body. It may be still or flashing. This is nothing to do with light stimuli from outside. During practice in the evening, it will be more clearly seen. The color of the light may relate to the physical constitution or illness of the practitioner. According to the theory of traditional Chinese medicine, the colors red, blue, yellow, white, and black are associated with the five organs of the body: heart, liver, spleen, lungs, and kidney. If one of the organs has a problem, you may observe changes in the associated color. For example, a patient with spleen or stomach disease may see black and yellow Qi while practicing Rujing. A different color of light may also be linked with the cultivation of one's extrasensory power. One Qigong master declared that white light may enable you to obtain the skill of clairvoyance; gray light enables you to see the heavenly body; red light gives you X-ray vision of the human body; black light is for detecting coal or oil reserves; blue light helps you to find underground water sources and deep-sea locations, and to X-ray plants; and yellow light enables you to detect copper, gold, and other ores with a red or yellow color. Nevertheless, this sense of light associated with extrasensory power usually occurs late in the Moving and Touching stage, while the sense of light associated with illness and health conditions mostly occurs during the early Moving and Touching stage.

People can observe their organs and skeleton during Rujing. One sort of Qigong stimulates and trains you to develop specialized clairvoyant skills. Some people acquire these abilities automatically when they enter the state of Rujing, without any special training. The most gifted may be able to observe their own organs, skeleton, muscles, and even their circulation and heartbeat if they wish. They can even zoom in for a closer look at part of the image. The image could be either black and white or in color. When, in the Ming dynasty, Dr. Li Shi Zhen described the origin of meridians, he said that man's inner parts could only be observed by those who were able to see inside. His statement was probably based on the clairvoyant skills of Qigong masters. We have no reason to question the reliability of his statement, as he was very rigorous in his academic study. He would not have spoken carelessly or been casual in drawing his conclusions.

Illusions are another common occurrence during Rujing. These appear at the higher level of Rujing. Usually they are the recurrence of feelings or thoughts for everyday life, particularly things you are in favor of, or something you are expecting or are scared of. For instance, a female patient who is physically very weak and frequently sick reported seeing a dancing python and a roaring tiger in the course of Rujing. When we tried to trace the possible reasons, we found out that it was related to a frightening experience at the zoo during her childhood, when she saw a giant python and a fierce tiger. Thirty years later, she came to experience the fearsome illusion over a series of days while practicing Rujing. Consequently, she had to stop practicing Rujing.

The ancient Chinese already knew quite a lot about certain illusions that one might experience during Rujing. Their accounts can be read in certain sections of Buddhist texts. Since illusion and hallucination disturb the stability of peace and calmness, it was regarded as something "obsessive or overwhelming" by the ancient Chinese. Obsession was divided into several types. It is said in the book *Elementary Self-Observation and Thought Adjustment*[26] that in positive illusions you might see everything going on smoothly; you might see your parents, brothers, and sisters, or the solemnly sitting Buddha, or a lovely man and woman, and be really attracted to them. In negative illusions you might see things go badly; you might see beasts such as a lion or tiger, ghosts, or other frightening kinds of things. If your illusions are none of these, they may just be ordinary, common things. In any case, your calm would be disturbed and you might lose your peace in meditation. Thus it is regarded as "obsession." According to this notion, the occurrence of illusion is also the occurrence of enchantment. Yet the occurrence of enchantment does not mean that you are already enchanted. You can still keep away from it. If you don't take it in or ignore it, you will not be enchanted. The book *Tian Xin Zhai Ke Wen* ("Inquiry from the Tenant of TinXin Building," a classic reference) provides us with an excellent footnote. It says that no illusion is real—it is an image created by your own mind. If you remain calm and ignore it, what you see will fade away naturally and there will be no illusions to enchant you. As for being enchanted by or infatuated with illusions, we'll discuss this in more detail in Chapter 7, "Malfunctions in Qigong."

During Rujing the phenomenon of clairvoyance may also occur. One practitioner from Henan province recalled that, at five o'clock in the morning, he was half awoken. A fog rose in his mind and then turned into the silhouette of two persons. One was short and the other was tall. They were about to leave the room. He could clearly see their actions but could not hear what they were saying. The figures gradually vanished. He came back to a normal state and his memory was still fresh, and everything in his memory was as real as if they were right in front of him. It looked like a dream and he was not sure if it really had happened. Yet when he returned home from his work at midday, he was surprised to see two strangers, one tall and one short, sitting in his living room. They were exactly the two men he had seen in the morning "mist." They were actually guests of his wife, two students of Qigong. Please note that this kind of remote viewing is not an illusion. It is cultivated extrasensory power. One should not be bothered about or believe in illusions. Although clairvoyance is reliable, you should not seek it, or there may be unwanted consequences.

Visual experiences during Rujing are various. Don't worry about whether it happens or not; just let it be. The basic rule is that you should anticipate its occurrence but not ask for it. This principle applies not only to the realm of visual perception, but also to all the other senses, as discussed in the following subsections.

HEARING

One tends to choose a relatively quiet place to practice Rujing. It is difficult to find a quiet place (even if there is one, it may not be ideal). You can always hear some slight noise of one sort or another. In the countryside you might hear the whisper of the wind and the singing of birds. In a city park, you may hear people talking and laughing. Even if you stay at home with your door closed, you may still hear the ticking of your clock; when beginning Rujing you can hear every sound. Try to ignore them. As you enter the deeper level of Rujing you may find they disappear or you only hear them occasionally, just as you intermittently hear car horns when you are absorbed in a book.

One method of practicing Rujing is called "listening to your own breath"—in other words, entering the state of Rujing by listening to the rhythm of your own breathing. This is applying the auditory sense to guide you into the state of Rujing. I think this is a wonderful method. Why is it wonderful? Because it asks you to listen to "soundless" breathing—it does not ask you to listen to the "sound" of breathing. During Rujing the breath should not be heard. We'll discuss this process later. If your breathing can be heard, it is the so-called "windy breath," which should be avoided in Rujing. So the idea of listening to your own breathing is actually listening to no sound, and by listening to soundless events, avoiding all sounds. By doing so, you adjust your breathing as well as leading yourself into the state of Rujing. This is akin to killing two birds with one stone. It is indeed the case that "the world of soundlessness is better than the world of sounds." This method was adapted from the book *Zhuang Zi*,[27] and the original script reads:

> YanHui asked Confucius: "Would you please tell me what the room of heart is?"
>
> Confucius answered: "If you are concentrating, don't listen to sounds coming into your ears but listen to your heartbeats. Then stop listening to your heartbeats but listen to your breath. Sound is connected with the ears; heartbeats are associated with the heart; air is something invisible and soundless, you must concentrate to feel it. This is the room of heart."

These words recorded the complete process and method of listening to your breathing for Rujing. Thus it is known as the "Zhuang Zi Mode."

It is possible that you will hear the beating of your heart in the early stages of Rujing. Sometimes, along with the circulation of your inner Qi, you may even hear sounds from your muscles and bones. In some cases, when one's Du meridian is about to open for the Qi and the Qi passes through the acupoints DaZhui and Baihui, one can even hear thunder-like noises. Don't worry about them, just forget them.

The occurrence of auditory illusion is relatively less common than visual illusions. Sometimes it occurs alone, and sometimes accompanied by visual illusions. One practitioner, while practicing Qigong one afternoon, once heard his master, who lived in another city, inviting him to come round. He heard the master telling him that he would like to help him change his job. So he got permission for leave and bought a railway ticket and arrived at his master's home the next day. He was told that the experience was not true. His master was asleep at the time when he thought he had heard his master's voice. This is an example of an auditory illusion occurring on its own. A different example is the one mentioned earlier, in which a female practitioner saw a tiger and heard it roaring. That is an example of auditory and visual illusions occurring together. These sensory experiences that occur during Rujing, no matter whether they are auditory, visual, or olfactory, are all "enchantment." They all occur when someone forces himself to enter the state of Rujing before he has cleared his mind and settled his mood. This was regarded by the ancient Chinese as "not having purified yourself during practice."

Clairaudience is likely to occur at the advanced level of Rujing. Like clairvoyance, it is an extraordinary power, the realization of a latent talent. I have heard of a middle-aged man with no prior medical training who could diagnose patients like a doctor, using his extraordinary power of remote hearing. When he was in the state of applying his psychic power he could hear a voice from out of nowhere telling him the diagnosis for his patient and the prescription. He just wrote down what he heard. His work was so simple that he was actually just the messenger of the mysterious voice. But it worked. The medicines he prescribed were somewhat strange, incredible in common sense terms, and the dosage was unusual, but it did cure the illness. When asked where the voice came from, he could not give a definite answer. He thought that possibly the soul of a famous doctor who had died years before attached itself to his body and guided him to accomplish the job. This account could never be tested. Whether to believe it or not is up to you.

SENSE OF SMELL
At the initial stage of Rujing, one is sensitive to the smells of nature. Of all the human senses, the most important are sight, hearing, and smell, in that order. During the process of Rujing this order may change. At the initial stage of Rujing the consciousness is still very

active, and one may, to some extent, still be aware of external stimuli. The visual sense has already been cut off, as the eyes are closed.

Since one usually practices Rujing in a quiet, subdued environment, auditory stimuli are also minimal. Therefore one's olfactory organs become more sensitive than usual. Some faint, unpleasant smell that was not noticeable before will be detected and become a problem. One feels particularly comfortable when breathing fresh, clean air. In ancient times, people would burn incense when practicing Qigong meditation. They must have believed that opening the olfactory channel had a relatively strong impact on their practice. Burning incense not only improves the environment but also keeps your mind alert, purifies the consciousness, puts you in a pleasant mood, and prevents you from falling asleep. It is quite beneficial for Qigong meditation.

The illusion of smell can accompany visual illusions in Rujing. One practitioner had been to the coast in summer and had a good memory of the beach. Once during the practice of Rujing, the beach appeared in his mind, and at the same time he could smell the salty, cool, fishy sea breeze. Smelling invisible flowers has also been reported by many practitioners. Please note that it is not easy to differentiate between the illusion of smell and the smell of a remote object. We use the term "illusory" to refer to all the hallucinations discussed here which we do not experience in real life. We use the term "remote smell" to mean the smell emanating from objects that actually exist, only far away from us. So it is not difficult to define and distinguish between an illusory smell and a remote smell. However, it *is* difficult to tell the illusory smell of flowers from the smell of genuine flowers that are far away. Other illusory sensations may be confused with other remote senses, but none is as hard to distinguish as the sense of smell.

There are several reports of Qigong masters who are able to emanate a fragrant odor. Some are able to emanate odor from the body in a natural way, while others will emanate the odor along with inner Qi. It was reported that a monk could send off the odor of sandalwood. A pioneer in Wild Goose Qigong once held Qi in both hands and sprinkled the Qi over her audience along with the sandalwood odor. She was said to be able to give off five types of fragrant odor, including jasmine. The founder of Zen Qigong once emanated fragrance into the air while practicing Qigong at midnight, and even his students miles away could smell it while practicing Qigong with the focus on receiving their master's message. One of the students of a master of Wild Goose Qigong said it took him quite a long time to develop the ability to emanate fragrance. There are also people who are able to emanate fragrance after only a few months of practice. A high-school teacher was able to emanate a sandalwood odor from his palms after just a couple of months' practice. Another practitioner who had just a few months' experience of practicing Qigong smelled fried green onion and eggs in his palms, as well as burning rubber and enameled copper wire. He also found that the smell emanating from his palms was associated with his mood. There are few studies on the mechanism of this phenomenon. It may be an illusory smell. It may also be a genuine odor. Whatever it is, the fact is that one will certainly experience olfactory changes when practicing Qigong.

TASTE

Taste does not refer to the taste of various foods but rather to the natural taste in our mouth without any food. For a healthy person the taste in his mouth is usually neutral and slightly wet. Those who have the problem of indigestion may have a sour or foul taste in their mouths. Those who have stomach heat may have a bitter taste in their mouths. The taste in your mouth will change in line with the process of Rujing. Many practitioners may find their saliva sweet and tasty. The quantity of saliva will increase. This was regarded as "jade fluid" by the ancient Chinese, who believed that it was the product of Qi when it passed the pool of jade (mouth). You should swallow it and send it back to the Dantian. You should also accumulate a quantity of the saliva in your mouth and slightly gargle it several times in your mouth before swallowing a bit at a time. As you do this, you should imagine the saliva moving along the Ren meridian down to the Dantian. Other good or bad tastes produced during Rujing are also mentioned in the ancient books. Generally speaking, the change in the sense of taste is less than it is for the other senses.

BODY AWARENESS

This refers to your awareness of your skin, muscles, organs, or the whole body. This is basically the 16 "feelings" or "touches" mentioned earlier. The term "touch" means an internal feeling of your body. The 16 touches are developed from the original eight touches: the feelings of pain, itching, coolness, warmth, light, heaviness, acerbity, and slipperiness. The 16 touches are quite similar to the eight touches in content, but the 16 touches are more detailed and delicate subdivisions of those senses. The eight touches could be described by the following phrases: they are as painful as a needle's pricking, as itchy as a bite from a bug, as cool as taking a cold shower, as warm as sitting by the fire, as heavy as carrying a bulky stone, as light as a floating feather, as acerbic as the taste of salt, and as slippery as lubrication with oil. All these feelings can be illusory, as well as genuine, concrete feelings. For example, when you feel heavy, this could be simply the feeling of yourself being pulled down by your body weight during Rujing, but your weight has not actually increased at all. Your body weight may indeed increase when your power of Qigong is strong and actually enhances your magnetic field; you will become too heavy to be carried by several men. The feelings and experiences arising in Rujing, from illusory to real, from the random occurrence to self-controlled skill, are often indicative of the process of acquiring extraordinary power. However, this process should come naturally and follow a natural development. It cannot and should not be actively pursued.

For most people, the most easily experienced of the 16 touches is the feeling of warmth. The feeling of warmth is adjusted either way; that is, it tends to reach the same degree of warmth regardless of the temperature in the outside world and protects you from both heat and cold. The power of maintaining your body at the right temperature is your body's response to nature through automatic adjustment during Rujing.

After special training, the ability to regulate one's temperature can be quite phenomenal. In 1984, 40 lamas entered two rooms for self-cultivation, secretly coached by masters at Baban Temple, the holy site of the White Lama[28] (a lama school in Tibet). The content of their self-cultivation was based on the White master Nanorba's Six Maxims. Their training began by developing the inner yoga fire to the point of realization of Qianshi (transfer of understanding)—that is to say, practicing Qigong to heat their bodies, entering the state of tranquillity, being released, and finally reaching the state of soul reincarnation. They stayed in the rooms for three years, three months, and three days. They walked out of the rooms barefooted, on 14 January of the Tibetan calendar, when it was bitter winter on the plateau. After walking around the temple they sat on the snow-covered ground and protected themselves from the cold by applying their power of Qigong. They were wearing only thin shirts, and icy water was poured over their heads to test their power.

The result was that those who had a strong power of Qigong remained as if nothing had happened. Their clothes were quickly dried by the warmth of their bodies. Please note, I said they looked as if nothing had happened to them. Apparently the way they felt had nothing to do with the external stimulus: they were still in a warm and comfortable state, feeling neither cold nor hot, no matter whether they were sitting in snow or drenched with icy water. In fact, the body had to emit enough heat to melt the ice, protect the body from the cold, and maintain body temperature. All this had happened subconsciously. And so they seemed unchanged. Of course, in the general practice of Rujing, one cannot regulate body temperature to such a degree. One can only increase one's ability to balance one's own temperature to a certain extent. One may not fear the cold in winter, or heat in summer. One's body is always as warm as it is in spring weather.

It is not necessary to give a detailed account of each of the 16 touches. Even if I discussed all of them, I might still not be able to cover all of the possible sensations from your skin and organs. The number 16 is used here only as an approximate number to suggest many possible sensations. The description of the 16 touches varies in different books. They are actually the most frequently occurring and most typical feelings. In fact, any feeling may occur during the process of Rujing. Its forms are infinite.

Some other feelings not included among the 16 touches are also quite common in Rujing—for instance, the feeling of big and small, soreness, numbness, swelling, etc. Many people have experienced the feeling that their bodies have became larger, or shrunk. They may feel that they have become taller and stronger. They may even have the feeling of becoming a giant with a head reaching heaven and feet on the ground; or they may feel their bodies have shrunk to the size of a child. All these feelings are just illusions. Their bodies have never really become larger, or shrunk. There are reports of certain Qigong practices that will actually help you to squeeze your body and make it smaller than before. One newspaper article reported how a 60-year-old Qigong master from Jiang Su province gave a performance of "body shrinking" in the city of Nanjing in October 1987. In the performance he managed to fit himself into the coat of a three-year-old child. It was proved that when he was in the state of Qigong he could shrink his body by 43 percent. After the performance someone asked him if shrinking his body was painful. He denied this and said frankly, "It is hard and miserable when you start to train yourself in this skill. There is no more suffering or discomfort once you have acquired the skill."

"Diao" and "Yi," two of the 16 touches, refer to the feelings of stirring and revolving. Like the feelings of big and small, and light and heavy, these feelings are no longer the sensation from any particular organ, but rather feelings from a whole body/mind perspective.

SEXUAL FEELINGS

Qigong, regardless of the schools of Taoism or Buddhism, certainly accounts for many of the sexual feelings one may experience during Rujing. *Xin Ming Gui Zhi* (Precious Instructions on Cultivating Mind and Body)[29] describes the feeling during the process of producing "yao" (vigor) as: "Suddenly you feel itchy. Your hair alive and your body as soft as cotton. You feel yourself in trance, your penis erect. This occurs when the Dantian is in harmony with your body and you feel joyful and relaxed. The pleasure is then transferred from the fingers to the whole body. You feel immobile and itchy. Your breathing is irregular and you are in an illusory state. It seems that you are about to ejaculate, but actually you have not." In the book entitled *Suo Yan Xu* (Some Words Continued) this moment is described as: "When your power reaches the ultimate tranquillity, you will suddenly feel something rising in your body. This is the initial making of vigor and then you will feel the drive of erection. This is the sense of activated vigor. It penetrates throughout your inner body and reaches the sex organ. The body is full of vigor." When the vigor is felt, this is the moment when "yao" is produced. *Chan MiGong* (Zen and Mystic Qigong)[30] believed that when you reach a certain state of Rujing you might experience sexual arousal. It is in fact the feeling of a mild sexual orgasm, particularly when Huiyin is hit by Qi. (*Chan MiGong* aims at developing Baopin ("sacred vase") Qi. It focuses not on the Dantian, but on Huiyin or Baihui.) Sexual intercourse itself is used by Zhangmi Qigong (Qigong of Tibetan origin) as one form of regular practice. It is also called the "male and female double practice." Some books on this practice in Tibet are actually sex manuals in modern terms. This illustrates the matter of sexual experience in practicing Tibetan Qigong.

The sexual pleasure one experiences in Rujing is weak, but of longer duration. It is somewhat different from normal orgasm, but the pleasure it brings is no less than orgasm, and may even be stronger. This is closely related to the state of Rujing. You may have had the experience that when someone bumps into you, or jokingly punches you in a noisy environment, you do not really feel it, so long as you have not been seriously hit in some critical part of your anatomy. When you are at peace in a quiet, tranquil environment, a tiny itching feeling like an ant crawling on the tip of your finger will immediately make itself felt and arouse a strong reaction from you. The state of Rujing is far deeper than that quiet environment. Any minute sense will be magnified, and you may even sense stimuli that would not be detected at other times. It is this function of magnifying the sensation that makes the tiny sexual pleasure that arises in the process of Rujing so magnificent. As the stimulus itself is actually tiny, you will not be sexually aroused. Some books mention that practicing Qigong can produce so-called Qigong orgasm, and regard it as the ultimate human orgasm experience. As far as content is concerned, the books are apparently referring to the tiny and lasting sexual pleasure we have just discussed.

Sexual pleasure is quite addictive. It should be avoided during the practice. If one pursues it in the process of Rujing, and even more so is fascinated by it, and it results in ejaculation, it is very harmful to health. Ancient teachings held that this was to turn the quintessence into impure sperm and then discharge it carelessly. All previous effort would be in vain as a result of this ejaculation.

SENSE OF OBLIVION

This sense occurs only at the higher level of Rujing. All the senses we have discussed so far are those mediated by your sensory organs and your body. Their existence relies on your body and sensory organs. Unlike these senses, the sense of self-forgetting is based on a feeling that your body and sensory organs have all disappeared and your body and consciousness no longer exist. It is therefore quite different from all the other senses we have discussed so far.

The lower level of self-forgetting is forgetting the existence of your body. It consists of two types of feeling: the feeling of weightlessness and the feeling of incorporeality. The two feelings are interrelated, and yet not without their own characteristics. Weightlessness is the loss of weight, and incorporeality is the loss of boundary. Together they result in a feeling of the dissolution of your whole existence. Initially you may not feel the complete loss of your weight and form. It may happen to part of your body. For example, if you assume the ball-holding posture while practicing standing Qigong, you lose the sense of your arms and hands after long practice. While you are practicing Qigong in a sitting posture, you can easily lose the sense of your legs. This also shows that the loss of part of your body is associated with the posture you assume in your practice of Qigong. On the other hand, it is also related to your state of health. For patients with certain illnesses, it is very difficult to experience the loss of their afflicted parts. If it happens, it indicates that the part has undergone a positive change, or even fully recovered.

The occurrence of such an experience often indicates a good mastery of Rujing and an improvement in your state of health. It is a vital step towards the advanced level of Rujing. If you assume a standing posture in practice, the feeling of your heels disappearing is the most difficult to experience. Yet only when you experience this will it be possible for you to experience the vanishing of your entire body. When you begin to feel the disappearance of your feet, your initial feeling will be that of standing on soft cotton, water, or a cloud. You have a feeling of floating in the air, not standing on solid ground, and gradually you find your feet disappear. In the sitting mode, to feel the disappearance of your buttocks is mostly difficult to achieve. Generally speaking, the supporting part of your body, or the afflicted part of your body, are the most difficult to experience disappearing. Yet only when you feel they have disappeared can you feel your entire body vanish. Sometimes, when you have reached this point, the Dantian is the only place that opens and closes along with the rhythm of breathing. It then seems that the whole body has gone except for the Dantian. If you take one step forward, your breathing gradually ceases and Dantian breathing then gives way to body breathing, and you will no longer feel even the existence of the Dantian.

The disappearing of self-awareness indicates the higher level of this stage. It is more difficult to achieve than the disappearance of your body. It is quite likely that you will feel that your body is already gone, but your mind and consciousness are still there, and you might have a very clear awareness of self. When self-awareness disappears, it is the stage of nature and man becoming one: you cannot distinguish nature from yourself. Since the body has "vanished," the mind then transends the boundary of the body and is traveling in the entire universe. It can expand endlessly, timelessly. Eventually it melts into the infinite, boundless universe. The process of this integration moves so naturally and perfectly. Man is nature, and nature is man. In this stage the mind is ultimately open, and self-awareness has definitely become blurred and faded.

The final disappearance of self-awareness leads to the state of Ultimate Emptiness. At the stage of nature and man becoming one, nature still exists, and man himself has melted into nature. The existence of nature means the existence of oneself; although it has been expanded and blurred, it has not yet disappeared. In the advanced state of Rujing, the feeling of nature and man becoming one will also tend to vanish. The final state of Rujing is Ultimate Emptiness, where nothing exists. This is the goal of Rujing, when self-awareness will no longer exist. As I mentioned before, in Rujing consciousness does not die. It just stops working. Otherwise, one would die. Since it has just stopped, it is possible for it to come back occasionally, just like the occurrence of ripples in a still lake. This is called "one sense is still alert." It is "appearing and disappearing, now and then." In general, inactivity and activity are relative. Rujing is a special activity of life; it constitutes a state of positive vigorousness.

FEELING OF TRANSCENDING TIME AND SPACE
Once you have experienced the feeling of having lost your ego, you will naturally feel that you have transcended time and space. This feeling begins when you start to forget the existence of your body. Space is the extension of the existence of an event. When events disappear, space cannot be created. When the body is forgotten, the space on which the body is based will also be forgotten. In the realm of nature and man becoming one, there will be no point of reference for distance. Therefore, space becomes meaningless. All you feel is infinity. When it comes to Ultimate Emptiness, nothing exists, and your feeling becomes nothing. So does space. It becomes vaguer and blurs.

This feeling of surpassing space and time usually occurs after the practice of Qigong. Sometimes you may find that time has become shortened and condensed, as in the legendary saying "When you feel that you have stayed in the cave just for a couple of hours, thousands of years have passed outside the cave." You feel that you have only practiced for a little while, but your watch tells you that actually several hours have passed. At other times, you may feel that you have practiced for quite a long time, but actually you have just practiced for 10 to 20 minutes. Time is not an isolated entity. The sense of time requires a reference for comparison. During the state when your body and consciousness are both forgotten, the sense of time is also gone. Transcendence of space and time may be said to have been attained in the process of emptiness. When you feel nothing exists, then you are far beyond time and space. "Emptiness" is everything. It transcends everything.

So far I have explained as simply as possible the main feelings and senses one has during the practice of Rujing (including perceptions such as the perception of space). Needless to say, these accounts are only examples. These are by no means standard or regulated affairs. It is not necessary to follow any models, nor should anyone seek to do so. Let nature take charge.

Experiencing Mood and Emotion

The idea of mood used here also relates to emotional experiences. Psychologists believe that mood is closely related to our biological needs, while emotion is related to our social needs. Both are reactions to the satisfaction of our needs. It is hard to distinguish between the two. In fact they are two sides and two reflections of the same event. One may experience both reflections during the state of Rujing. In the lower state of Rujing the experience of mood prevails, and when you reach the advanced level of Rujing, the emotional experience will predominate. The mood one experiences during Rujing is similar to one's daily experience of feelings. All the moods one experiences every day can be observed in Rujing, only wider and deeper.

The ancient Chinese summarized man's mood into seven types: pleasure, hate, anxiety, thoughtfulness, grief, horror, and astonishment. Modern researchers have divided mood into hundreds of types. Yet our basic moods are the following four: pleasure, hatred, grief, and terror. During the process of Rujing these emotions may not necessarily occur independently. They usually come along with, and combine with, other sensations. The most common is the mood of pleasure and comfort that appears along with the sense of relaxation and tranquillity. Many types of Qigong require you to smile as you practice. You cannot just pretend to smile. If you pretend to smile it will do you no good. But it is not very difficult to meet this requirement if you really have experienced the pleasure that comes along with the feeling of relaxation and peace during your practice of Qigong. Then the smile will result from happiness.

For those who practice Qigong to cure illness, the afflicted parts are often painful, swollen, and so on. Along with this physical experience, one may also feel depressed, worried, or even disgusted. The illusions and hallucinations one experiences in the state of Rujing are certain to be accompanied by intense emotional experiences. One may feel quite cheerful on seeing hallucinations of the palace of the deities; scared on seeing devils; worried and frightened on hearing the sounds of hell; or very comfortable on smelling fragrant flowers. If someone has the feeling of floating up off the ground in his illusion, then he may experience relief and comfort such as he has never experienced before—as if he has forgotten all his earthly worries and cares and is inhabiting a world beyond the Earth, flying towards a paradise that everyone dreams of.

The versatile emotions can be divided into two classes: pleasant and unpleasant. Rejoicing, cheerfulness, and satisfaction are all pleasant emotions. Fear, worry, and sickness are all unpleasant emotions. During the process of Rujing, emotion, though always accompanied by the senses, does not have a fixed pattern that goes along with one particular sense. The emotions occurring along with the senses can be either pleasant or unpleasant and may even shift from one to the other. This understanding of the emotional process during Rujing is important. It will help one to deal with the different senses and emotional experiences in Qigong. This is particularly important for practitioners who are practicing Qigong to cure illness, since it is directly related to trends in the development of the illness.

During the process, the shift from a non-pleasurable mood to a pleasurable one may indicate progress in recovery from illness; the reverse shift may, on the contrary, indicate worsening of the illness. For instance, if one feels heavy and blocked in the afflicted part, but then emotionally shifts from an initially anxious, scared mood to an aloof mood and is no longer concerned about the part, this may suggest recovery from illness. It is a good sign. (Of course, it would be even better if one also felt changes in the sensory experience, from feeling heavy and blocked to feeling light and transparent.) If, on the other hand, one's mood changes from carefree to very afraid, this may suggest a worsening of the illness. In the process of recovery, changes in sensation and mood may occur both at once, or separately. Both changes have clinical significance. The change in mood seems more sensitive, and often occurs as a prelude or a sign of sensory changes.

Pain is another common symptom of illness. (Whether it is a feeling or a mood is still controversial. I regard it as the former.) It is usually accompanied by a mood of anxiety, disgust, fear, and other negative moods. The more pain one feels, the less happy one will be. Of course, this is not absolutely true—sometimes pain may be accompanied by a positive mood. Sharp pain and severe swelling accompanied by a mood of happiness, pleasure, and confidence will indicate the moment when illness gives way to recovery, and are also the prelude to the decisive moment when the inner Qi is at the point of winning the battle against the illness. This can help us to better understand the relationship between sense and mood, and the clinical significance of the mood changes.

The basic feeling one should have in practicing Rujing is a feeling of slight pleasure and freedom from care. It occurs along with the feeling of relaxation and calm, which can be felt throughout the whole process. Compared to the pleasure we experience in everyday life, it involves more sensation and is clearly experienced, and it permeates through every organ, cell, hair, and pore. It is far better than the everyday experience of similar feelings. Whether or not one is able to maintain and develop this feeling has a direct impact on success in achieving the state of Rujing. It is the essence of Rujing.

Passion is an abrupt, strong, explosive, and brief emotion. It sounds quite surprising to say that one may experience passion during Rujing. If we observe that Rujing can induce spontaneous movement or even some violent action, we'll be able to understand the possible occurrence of passion. Passion in our everyday life is usually accompanied by obvious external signs, such as a dancing gesture when one is thrilled or overjoyed by something, shouting or banging the table when one becomes angry, and so on. On the other hand, when one is led to jump and dance hysterically, shout and sing at a high pitch, or present other symptoms of spontaneous movement, it may ignite passion and cause one to become very emotional and even hysterical. If not controlled properly, this will lead to severe malfunction in Qigong, and passion will only make it worse. Hence control of the occurrence of this side effect is directly connected with control of one's passion. Usually the action will gradually cease once the passion is under control and one calms down. Therefore, if the action occurs, one should first control one's emotion. So long as one is calm and emotionally stable, and not unduly passionate, the side effect of "severe malfunction" will not take place. All in all, while passion may occur during Rujing, it is better avoided.

Being hyper-stimulated is a highly intense mood that is triggered in dangerous or unexpected situations. Will one also experience it during Rujing? This is rare, but not impossible. One may develop clairvoyant ability during Rujing. One might see one's own internal organs, bones, and muscles. One might see one's skeleton first. If someone knows nothing about clairvoyance at the time, he could be horrified when he sees a skeleton in front of him. He is, to some extent, being hyper-stimulated. The sudden occurrence of a terrifying vision in Rujing, such as seeing demons and beasts, or life events that once caused hyper-stimulation, may result in a state of hyper-stimulation.

The state of arousal that occurs in Rujing is usually slight. One can recover from it very quickly if one knows how to deal with it. The illusions and hallucinations that occur during Rujing are not the same as real dangers in terms of the threat they pose for you. The severity of the state they cause is also less than the counterpoint in reality, so it is easy to overcome. It will be harmful to your health if you are frequently in a state of arousal. We should try to avoid it in everyday life, as well as in the practice of Qigong.

The experience of mood is supposed to be common to both man and animals. It is still regarded as a lower-level, simple experience. The experience of other senses, such as the sense of reason, a moral sense, and an aesthetic sense, is regarded as a uniquely human psychological experience. It is an advanced and complex human experience. It appears not to have anything to do with Rujing, but when one enters the advanced level of Rujing, those senses may all occur, even as a perfect experience of that kind. There are some things in the world that seem incredible, yet they just exist and happen.

The sense of reason is an experience that recurs in the process of man's understanding of the universe; that is to say, in man's scientific research and mental cultivation. It is associated with man's desire, curiosity, and longing to know the truth. Rujing itself is not a process of scientific research; it is not a process in which one searches intentionally for something. Nevertheless, when you reach the state of nature and man becoming one, this state consists of an understanding of nature and the universe. The subjective world and the objective world become one indistinguishable world. There is nothing for the subjective mind to perceive; or we may say that man's perception of the universe is complete. The universe is just like this! In this state, an individual will feel that he has observed the entire universe. Nothing needs to be inquired about; there is no phenomenon in the universe that needs to be perceived and understood. He feels that he is rich and fulfilled in both wisdom and intellect. All there is to know is known, and is known in perfection. He gains great pleasure from this mental satisfaction and fulfillment. We could say that in this state of happiness there seems to be no reasoning activity. The task of reason has been completed. As the ancient saying goes, "Fantasy is generated from emptiness." This is the unique, wonderful thing about it. The realization of the following two senses is also related to this notion.

The moral sense relates to experience that one applies in order to evaluate what oneself or other people say and do, in accordance with particular social norms and maxims. The moral sense occurring in the process of Rujing originates as the realm of nature and man become merged into one being. From the perspective of self-fulfillment and the purpose of our words and deeds, the ultimate goal of life has been achieved. Someone who has achieved full self-realization has accomplished his responsibility and mandate. He has set aside the heavy burden of life and is free from the mental pressure of life's battles. He is light-hearted and joyful. There is nothing to regret. A feeling of celestial being and a feeling of loftiness arises in his heart. The universe is mighty, grand, and holy. It contains all responsibilities and commitment. You feel that "I have given my whole life to the universe and joined it. I have done all I am supposed to do."

At the lower level of Rujing, one may also have moral sense. For instance, when you sit with your legs crossed and your upper body erect, you try to banish all thoughts; when you have succeeded in banishing thoughts and maintaining a calm and peaceful state, a feeling of justice will emerge from your mind, along with the feeling of awe and sanctity. The ancient Chinese scholar Meng Zi once said, "I am very good at forging my spirit of justice." He may mean the feeling we have just described. The moral sense may have its origin in religion and mythology. In the process of Rujing, they are stimulated, magnified, and re-established through the particular posture, consciousness, and the mode of breathing.

The aesthetic sense is a common sense that everyone possesses. No one is able to give a clear definition of it. Even the science of aesthetics may not be able to offer a satisfactory definition. If we say aesthetics is the experience of the beauty of an object, it sounds as if we have said nothing, because it does not explain what beauty is. The aesthetic sense emerges when we are appreciating a work of art, the beauty of nature, or harmonious events in life. In the process of Rujing, if some wonderful visual illusions appear in your mind, such as beautiful scenery or fairy buildings, it is understandable that the aesthetic sense will accompany them. The same thing happens if you hear a nice piece of music or smell a bunch of flowers during the process of Rujing. These aesthetic experiences are similar to those you have in reality. At the advanced level of Rujing, you may experience the aesthetic sense even though you have not seen, heard, or smelled anything. This beauty is deep and subtle. It is beauty out of ultimate emptiness. You could never find such beauty in real life. In the poetry of Wang Wei and Liu Zong Yuan of the Tang dynasty we find similar descriptions of this beauty. The following is from their poem "Deer and Firewood":

> No sign of man be seen in the grand mountain
> Only the voice of the traveler echoes
> The depth of woods we return to
> Only see the setting sun reflected on the lichen.

In another of their poems, "River Snow":

> No signs of the birds in the mountains
> nor of men along the trails
> nor any craft on the river but a little boat
> with an old man in rustic hat and cape
> dangling a line in the frigid waters
> a solitary figure veiled in silent snow.

These still do not describe pure emptiness; there are still scenes of one kind or another. When you reach the ultimate realm of emptiness in the practice of Rujing, you feel nature and man become one entity. It is pure, transparent, and bright. It is not eye-catching brightness, but purity itself. The transparency and brightness are purity and clarity, and vice versa. It is the brightness of pure emptiness, vacant but full of vigor. Two striking qualities of the aesthetic are "pleasurable" and "desirable." When your mind and body turn to that pure, clear, transparent, and bright state, isn't that your sense of beauty?

Here we will end our discussion of mood and emotional experience during Rujing. From our discussion above, we know that those experiences are complex and versatile. Generally speaking, if you proceed correctly, follow the natural process, and try to avoid side effects, then the experience will be pleasurable. From what we discussed in Chapter 2 in the section called "The Levels of Rujing," we can say that if the Moving and Touching stage is characterized by the experience of the senses, then the experience of mood will be the main content of the pleasure stage. As for the stage of Ultimate Emptiness, the experiences of senses, feelings, and mood all tend to fade away. They will all disappear when you reach the realm of nature and man becoming one entity.

Rujing and Motion

Stillness and movement are relative. There is no motion without stillness, and vice versa. They are interchangeable and overlapping. We have mentioned this relative feature of two types of Qigong in Chapter 1. We have mentioned that many types of active Qigong also require the practitioner to attain the state of stillness in motion. On the other hand, some types of inactive Qigong also require certain motion. Of course, this motion is not necessarily visible movement of the limbs or body, but can be the circulation of blood and Qi, or the activity of consciousness. Just as the stillness required by active Qigong does not necessarily mean inertia of the body, but rather calmness and concentration of mind, we can say that stillness leads to motion in inactive Qigong, while motion results in stillness in active Qigong. Life is the unification of motion and stillness. Active and inactive Qigong emphasize only one side of it. The two cannot be separated. In the practice of Qigong, absolute stillness means death, and absolute motion means the malfunction of over-activity.

Once we understand this dialectic relationship between stillness and motion, we know that motion is involved in Rujing. Here motion can be perceived on three levels: as psychological activity, physiological activity, and movement of the body. Psychological activity includes consciousness, senses, mood, etc. (we have discussed these in the preceding sections). Sensible physiological activity includes breathing, circulation of blood, etc. Body movement here means auto-generated motion, the spontaneous movement during

Qigong. So we can see that all the so-called movements in Rujing are still part of the three adjustments. Rujing is based on psychological activity (adjustment of mind). In Rujing, one does not need to worry about the processes of breathing and Circulation of Qi that go along with it, let alone the movement of the limbs.

As Rujing is based on the adjustment of mind, those psychological activities are regarded as normal and natural. When unexpected movements of Qi or body occur, they are regarded as unnatural, and are labeled as "internal movement" and "external movement." Internal movement refers to the feeling of Qi circulating in your body (but your limbs and body do not actually move). This kind of internal movement is quite common in the process of Rujing. Most practitioners will feel it when they reach a certain stage. For instance, an advanced practitioner of standing Qigong will be able to feel the Qi and blood circulating everywhere in his body. He might even hear the sound of this circulation. When a patient is practicing Rujing, he may often feel Qi moving towards the afflicted part of his body. The person who is sensitive to his meridian system may know the route and the direction of Qi. The Qi circulating along the Ren and Du meridians is the ultimate movement that can be sensed that many practitioners anticipate. Some types of Qigong such as Taoist NeiDanShu intentionally induce and stimulate this circulation. The occurrence of Circulation of Qi without intentional stimulation in the process of Rujing is also possible; but it does not necessarily occur every time, and not everybody will experience it; it is not the purpose of Rujing to generate this circulation, and mastery of Qigong and the physiological constitution varies from person to person. Therefore it does not much matter whether or not the circulation occurs or is sensed in the process of Rujing. Let it be as it is. The success of Rujing does not depend on it.

The type of Qigong aimed at the operation of inner Qi in a broader sense belongs to the inhaling/exhaling school, because the circulation of inner Qi is closely associated with breathing, and the operation of inner Qi circulation also begins with breathing. The types of Qigong in this school are usually non-active Qigong, such as Internal Nurturing Qigong, Strengthening Qigong, and Skill for Practicing Inner Qi Circulation; but it might also be active Qigong, such as New Qigong Therapy, Self-Controlled Qigong Therapy, etc. The relationship between circulation of the inner Qi and Rujing varies according to the type of Qigong and the individual practitioner. External movement during the process of Rujing is a kind of spontaneous movement. It is an external body movement triggered by certain factors. It usually occurs on the basis of Circulation of Qi, which causes non-controllable movements of the body. As a result, the external movement of the body promotes and clears ways for the circulation of inner Qi. So the two are mutually beneficial.

Spontaneous movement is different from that of active Qigong. Every type of active Qigong, regardless of what it is, has a postural routine. It is practiced according to the routine, with the conscious mind. Spontaneous movement has no set movement pattern. The body movement varies from person to person. One person may appear to shake his body. Another may wave his arms. Some might jump and run, while others may squat and lie down. Someone might even perform some difficult action that they could not normally do, such as a big jump, somersault, standing on their head, etc. A 70-year-old lady once performed the splits, and rolled backwards and forwards in spontaneous movement. Performance during the spontaneous movement state can be symmetrical and quite identical on each side. Sometimes the practitioner may even perform a complete martial art set that he has never learnt before. This is done in the state of unconsciousness and is quite different from movement performed with consciousness. The pattern of the martial art performed in the spontaneous movement state will be forgotten afterwards, and cannot be repeated in the next spontaneous movement state.

For those who have a particular illness, the most common action in the spontaneous movement state may be the patting and massaging of the afflicted part of the body. One might pat oneself on the head if one has a headache, or beat one's back if one suffers from back pain. Those with neck problems might shake their heads and massage their necks. The actions they perform during this time are often related to the line of the meridian associated with the afflicted organ, and the area it belongs to. Usually one would pat along the meridian line, and the action will stop once that meridian has been cleared.

Although spontaneous movement occurs without intention and consciousness is not the cause of it, it can be consciously detected and controlled. When it occurs, you should keep your mind clear and maintain your mood. You don't need to guide it, but you should be on guard. Give your body a little hint to avoid powerful action. When you are practicing Qigong in a small space, some people may be able to avoid bumping against objects in the spontaneous movement state, while others may not be able to do so. Therefore it is necessary to control your movement so as to avoid possible injury and accidents. If the relationship between Rujing and internal and external movements is handled properly, they can co-exist peacefully. It may even help the process of Rujing. If a meridian is blocked so that the Qi cannot circulate properly and Rujing is interrupted, a little movement and a slight clearance of the meridian will be very beneficial for Rujing. So long as the state of Rujing is maintained, the movement does not necessarily have a negative impact; indeed, if it helps to promote the state of Rujing, it will be very positive. However, movement occurring in the process of Rujing, regardless of whether it is internal or external, may have a negative impact if not controlled, and if the inner Qi splinters, or the external motion cannot be stopped. This is the phenomenon of "Qi chaos," as it is called. How to prevent it from happening, and how to handle it when it occurs, will be discussed in Chapter 7.

Chapter 3

The Mechanisms of Rujing

Basic practice of any kind of Qigong always involves three adjustments—mind, breathing, and body. Rujing is definitely no exception. The principle of Rujing explored in this book focuses on the mechanisms of these three adjustments, which are closely connected with the practice of Rujing. These mechanisms include the psychological, physical, and biochemical processes of the three adjustments. Since the three adjustments are different from each other, my account will also vary: At times it will focus on their psychological aspect, and at times on their physiological or biochemical aspects. In addition, our main concern will be to explore the mechanism of one of the three, namely the adjustment of mind, which is the primary one of the three.

The Mechanism of Mind Adjustment

The ultimate state of Rujing is the state of super-tranquillity and pure emptiness. The process that leads to this state is controlled by our consciousness. To understand the mechanism of the adjustment of mind in practicing Rujing is in fact to know the content and form of thought during the process of Rujing, with reference to its psychological aspect.

I have mentioned in my definition of Rujing that the form of thought will change during the process of Rujing. But how does it change? We assume that the cognitive process of mind will shift from the usual abstract, imagery thinking to the active, sensory thinking that belongs to the advanced form of "perceptual thinking."[31] Thus the essence of our discussion is to analyze the mechanism of sensory thinking. In addition, it is also necessary to give a brief account of emotional and mood thinking, which is closely related to sensory thinking.

Since the purpose of this book is to introduce the basic concept of Rujing, our discussion will selectively focus on the sensory thinking and mood thinking that are involved in the initial stage of Rujing.

The General Concept of Thinking

In order to discuss sensory thinking thoroughly, it is necessary to review the basic concepts of thinking, to help the reader to understand how the concept of *thinking* is used in this book.

What is thinking? The general textbooks of philosophy and psychology state that thinking is an indirect, idealized reflection of outside events in our mind. Thinking can be defined as an indirect, epitomized, cognitive process oriented towards problem solving. This definition is drawn from the study of the relationship between spirit and material, and suggests that thinking is primarily a reflection of the objective world in one's mind, a relatively static portrait of thinking. Here, however, we are studying the dynamic process of thinking, so that knowing only this static definition of the relationship between mind and events is insufficient. We also need to know what kind of psychological process thinking is. That is to say, we also need a definition of the dynamic process of thinking. So far, we don't yet have such a definition as a point of reference. However, study of the thinking process in terms of a psychological process is not new. For instance, the American functional psychologist William James observed that consciousness, itself, cannot be seen as fragments linked together in a chain or series. This is not its original state. Consciousness is not something that is chained. It is flowing, and the best metaphorical way of describing it is to regard it as a river or a stream. So it could be described as the stream of consciousness, stream of thinking, or the river of the subjective life.

James clearly regarded thinking as a "flowing" psychological process. The familiar expression "stream of consciousness" originated from this idea. We accept James's viewpoint that thinking is a flowing psychological process. But if we use this idea to define thinking, it is still not sufficiently clear. For convenience, I define thinking as a process initiated and purposively carried out by the consciousness with the help of images in our subjective mind. This is still quite abstract; let's elaborate it step by step. This definition states that thinking is the operation of consciousness, and specifies three aspects. The process of thinking must have the characteristics of being initiating, intentional, and evoking imagery.

None of them can be left out. First of all, thinking is an active process. A completely passive manipulation of consciousness cannot be regarded as thinking, even though it contains the other two premises mentioned above. For example, in the state of hypnosis, the subject's consciousness is still active; he can follow instructions to do things. But in this case the mind is completely passive. So it is not thinking according to our definition. In the case of sleepwalking the patient, though nobody is controlling his mind, is in a subconscious state. He might be able to do something which seems to require thought, but it is not the consequence of active consciousness. We do not take it as thinking either.

Second, thinking must have a purpose. It is the work of consciousness to solve problems. Aimless reverie is not part of our discussion. On the other hand, thinking cannot spring from nowhere. It can only proceed with the help of certain images in one's mind. This refers to the images present in our consciousness, which are the forms from which we construct the information about events in our consciousness—or we can say it is the way information about events exists in our consciousness. For instance, concepts and images are two different types of reflection in our mind. This notion emphasizes that the components that thinking manipulates and processes are various reflections in consciousness. It also emphasizes the conscious attributes of those constituents. Just as we need wood to produce a table, and steel to manufacture a locomotive, abstract thinking requires concepts, and imagery thinking requires images to work with. Marx (1818–1883) said that military weapons cannot be destroyed by means of criticism, but only by military weapons. The message we draw from this is that the spirit world and the material world function in their own respective ways. Practitioners believe not only that the process, whether spiritual or material, is undertaken on the basis of constituents with the same spiritual or material attributes, but also that changing the constituents will determine how they are processed. The saw is needed to process wood products, and fire is indispensable for processing steel components. Similarly, the manipulation of concepts requires abstract thinking, while manipulation of superficial images involves imagery thinking.

Now that we have a general understanding of the definition of thinking, let's explain what form of thinking is discussed in this book.

Let's go back to William James's observation. We have accepted James's notion that thinking is a flowing psychological process. Yet we still need to ask: What is actually flowing? What kind of water is flowing in the stream of consciousness or in the river of thinking? James believed it to be the "fluid" of subjective experiences. This is correct, but a bit too general and vague. Actually, what James meant to say is that the stream of consciousness is the stream of reflection of the objective events in our mind. The "water" in the stream is the subjective reflection in our mind. Or, in our terms, it is the way the understanding of objective events is constructed and exists in our consciousness.

Now let's analyze the possible types of reflections of objective events appearing in our mind. To summarize, the outstanding, relatively macro-subjective reflections in our consciousness can be divided into three categories:

1. reflection on abstract elements

2. reflection on imagery elements

3. reflection on concrete elements.

In other words: concept, image, and objective form.[32] We can classify thinking into three different types on the basis of these aspects with which thinking operates. Thus we have three types of thinking: abstract thinking, imagery thinking, and perceptual thinking. These are the common forms of thinking generally discussed in the textbooks of psychology. However, they differ slightly from my account here in content and definition. I will elaborate on this point later in the book. Let's move on to a brief account of each of the three forms of thinking with which we are more or less familiar. However, I will give more attention to perceptual thinking, since the sensory thinking one experiences during Rujing is actually an advanced type of perceptual thinking.

Three Types of Thinking
Abstract Thinking

This is the most familiar and common form of thinking. The process of abstract thinking relies on concepts. It is well known that concepts are labeled by words. Therefore, it is closely associated with words. Every day we are preoccupied with all kinds of problems, and we think in the form of words. The stream of consciousness in our mind is a stream of concepts in the shape of words. Someone once commented that "language is the shell of thinking," but this relates only to abstract thinking. Abstract thinking is not only the main form of thinking for problem solving, but the words with which the thinking is carried out are also the main medium for exchanging and spreading ideas. Whether you are speaking or reading, you need words. Speaking and reading actually reinforce your abstract thinking. So long as you think rationally, you cannot do away with abstract thinking. Anyone living in our society applies abstract thinking almost all the time, even in dreams. Otherwise how could we talk in our dreams?

Imagery Thinking

Apart from abstract thinking, imagery thinking is another familiar form of thinking. There have been disputes about the existence of imagery thinking. Opponents acknowledge only the existence of abstract thinking. In my view, their understanding that language is the shell of abstract thinking has been too extreme, and nowadays, the notion of imagery thinking has been accepted by most people. Imagery thinking relies on images. "Image" is different from "concept" in so far as it is man's recollection of the direct reflection of objective events; the content of the recollection has not yet been abstracted into a concept. It carries the quality of images. Generally speaking, it is mostly applied in the creative work of literature and art. For instance, when a writer is constructing a plot for his novel, what he has in mind is not (or not only) concepts in the form of words, but a vivid, lively flow of images. He can actually "see" the characters he intends to portray. Then he will find the right words and expressions to describe what he sees. Similarly, a painter may see the picture on the canvas before he starts to paint; a musician may hear the melodies he is composing. This vivid piece of painting or music, seen or heard by the artist, is still a superficial image. This tells us that images are also varied in type. They are visual, auditory, tactile, etc. In fact, in the real world, not only artists, but all of us, need imagery thinking. When you are missing one of your relatives, won't his or her image appear in your mind? When you are furnishing your room, you already have in your mind the location of each piece of furniture, don't you?

Perceptual Thinking

One element of perceptual thinking is not called by this name in general psychology textbooks; it is described as directly perceived action thinking, directly perceived behavior thinking, sensory action thinking, action thinking, and operating thinking. This is because there is no such concept as perceptual thinking in these books, which talk only about direct action thinking. Our view proposes the concept of perceptual thinking in parallel with the other two types of thinking, and sees direct action thinking as part of this. This aspect of perceptual thinking—namely direct action thinking—is, like abstract thinking and imagery thinking, a form of thinking commonly practiced by everybody. It is still not the form of thinking we practice in Qigong. As we can see, current research in psychology focuses on everyday thinking. The general psychology textbooks never even touch the other part of perceptual thinking, the part that is practiced in Qigong, so do not provide readers with a complete picture of perceptual thinking.

What is direct action thinking, then? Direct action thinking operates on the basis of the images of events. In other words, it is the direct reflection of events in consciousness, such as color, sound, and smell. To explain it in a simple way, the operating of direct action thinking is based on concrete, specific senses. So it is not a coincidence that direct action thinking is also called sensory action thinking. The psychology textbooks state that sportsmen and experienced workers are good at direct action thinking. When a basketball player is playing, his thinking follows the movement of the ball, whether it is a shot or a pass. He doesn't have time, nor is it necessary, to abstract the ever-changing movement of the ball into rational concepts. The consciousness responds directly to the movement of the ball. This is direct action thinking. On the basketball pitch, the person who really turns the movement of the ball into concepts is the commentator: in order to broadcast the match to his audience in language, he must apply conceptual thinking. A skillful worker, such as a driver or a mechanic, is always thinking in response to the actual actions in his work. The thoughts are directly associated with the changes in operation; therefore, this is also direct action thinking. We often apply direct action thinking in our everyday life without paying any attention to it. For instance, when a Chinese person is making dough for dumplings, they adjust the movement of the stick and the shape of the dough simultaneously, guided by direct action thinking. No one starts to make the dumpling dough only after a rational analysis of the path of the stick and the shape of the dough. Direct action thinking is based on objects and belongs to perceptual thinking. This is still at the initial stage of perceptual thinking. It has yet to develop to the advanced stage.

From the psychology of developing thoughts, we learn that direct action thinking develops in two ways in human infancy. First, it slowly dies out and is gradually replaced by imagery thinking in childhood. That is to say, as the baby grows, her ability to form images becomes stronger and stronger, and consciousness or thought becomes less and less dependent on the perception of events. For example, in the early stage, a bottle of milk only exists in a baby's mind when she can actually see it. Once the bottle is moved away, the objective form of it also disappears in the baby's mind. As the baby develops the ability to form superficial images, things will change. The image of the bottle will remain, even though it is out of thought. The formation of objective form is not separable from the environment containing the event, whereas the formation of the superficial image is. Therefore, initiative and freedom in the process of consciousness are far greater in imagery thinking than that in perceptual thinking. From this point of view, imagery thinking is more advanced than perceptual thinking. So it is a transformation from a lower level of thinking to a higher one in one's development of thinking, when the infant's direct action thinking is transformed into imagery thinking in childhood.

The second direction of development of direct action thinking is from its simple infantile form to the highly sophisticated forms that develop later. We can say that the highly sophisticated direct action thinking of adults, as in the example of the basketball player and skillful manual worker mentioned above, is a mature form of the direct action thinking we possess in infancy. Although it is more sophisticated than its earlier forms, this is a change only in quantity, not quality, in terms of forms of thinking.

Apart from the two developments discussed above, are there any other changes associated with direct action thinking? In our study of thinking patterns in the practice of Qigong, we discovered that direct action thinking can also develop in other directions. It can transform from its primitive stage to its advanced stage with significant changes in quality. This direction has not been discussed in any psychology textbook.

In our opinion, direct action thinking in its mature operational form of thinking belongs to the initial stage of perceptual thinking. Characteristic of the perceptual thinking at this stage is its passivity. In other words, the process of perceptual thinking at this stage is effectively the operation of the objective form in sight, and relies entirely on changes in the event it reflects. The change in the bottle in the baby's mind depends on changes in the actual bottle in reality. The image of the bottle in the baby's mind moves along with the movement of the actual milk bottle. The image in the baby's mind falls if the bottle falls. It will never happen that the image of the bottle falls in the baby's mind while the real bottle is standing. Likewise with the basketball player: the movement of the ball in the player's mind follows the movement of the ball on the pitch. The image of the ball in consciousness goes exactly as the ball goes in the real world. If the ball is not shot into the basket but the player just imagines that it is, then it is not direct action thinking but imagery thinking. In general, the change in events is the motive for the operation of perceptual thinking in its initial stage, where perceptual thinking is a passive reflection of changes in events. Therefore, we can say that direct action thinking, whether it is the simple infantile form or the mature and sophisticated adult form, is still perceptual thinking in the initial stage. Although the latter is more advanced than the former in terms of complexity and maturity, the formation of image and its alteration are still passive.

Now let's discuss how perceptual thinking works during the practice of Qigong. I'd like to exemplify it with the idea of the most common practice in Qigong—concentration on the Dantian. It is well known that the practice of most types of Qigong requires concentration on the Dantian. First of all I'd like to point out that concentration on the Dantian does not mean entertaining the concept of the Dantian. One should actually concentrate on the area one *cun* (about three centimeters) and a half below the navel. It is not important whether or not the area is called the Dantian. Thus we exclude conceptual thinking in our concentration on the Dantian.

Furthermore, how can we tell that we have concentrated on the Dantian? Does it mean we have to think of the actual shape of the Dantian? Obviously not! How can you form an image of the Dantian, which is invisible, inaudible, untouchable, and insensible? Of course, you can imagine it according to other people's descriptions. For example, it has been described as round, the size of an egg, etc. If you visualize this, your imagination of that egg is from the outside world, not your own. In other words, you are actually imagining a picture of Dantian and you are not concentrating on your own Dantian. Therefore, imagery thinking should be excluded from the practice of concentrating on the Dantian.

We believe that the operation involves entertaining neither the concept nor the image of the Dantian. You should actually evoke and construct an objective form of the Dantian. You should actually feel its existence. How can one feel it? There is a saying in martial arts: "When you are concentrating you will feel the existence of Qi; when you feel the Qi you feel the strength." This could also be applied in our practice of concentrating on the Dantian. This will enable us to understand the actual process of constructing the objective form of the Dantian. The correct way to do it is to make sure, first, that concentration brings the Qi naturally. Normally we should not consciously guide the Qi to the Dantian through consciousness. We should actually relax and let our consciousness focus on the area of the Dantian. Our innermost being will automatically sink down and settle at the Dantian. As the sunk inner Qi directed by our consciousness accumulates in the area and gathers together, a pressure or force will be felt as the Qi takes over the space originally occupied by other body tissues or organs. By feeling this force or pressure, the practitioner of Qigong has actualized the existence of the Dantian, and the area affected by this force is the range of the Dantian that one feels. It is also the objective form of the Dantian. The whole process of constructing the objective form of the Dantian is a process of engaging and operating the mode of perceptual thinking. On completion of the objective form of the Dantian, perceptual thinking on the objective form of the Dantian will develop further, along with continuous concentration on the Dantian.

What is the difference between the formation of objective form in the process described above and that in direct action thinking? The careful reader will find that the formation of objective form through concentration on the Dantian is actively stimulated by consciousness. At the initial stage of concentration, there is no objective form of the Dantian. It only comes into existence along with the operative procedure. It is not a passive reflection of the event taking place, but the product of the operation of consciousness.

The formation of objective form in direct action thinking is based on objective events, whereas the objective form generated by concentrating on the Dantian in the process of perceptual thinking is based on the existence of consciousness. Here the difference, is between activity and passivity. It is a big difference, and it's a change of quality. The significance of this difference is that it reveals another form of the interchange between spirit and matter.

Now let's come back to the effect of this perceptual thinking that enables one to generate the objective form intuitively in practicing Qigong. Again, we'll use concentrating on the Dantian as an example. Once one has formed the objective form of the Dantian, process in the psyche of concentration is not yet finished. In most cases it requires you to fill the Dantian; in this way it will become more solid, and the range of the Dantian will also change in size. These sensory changes of objective form are the consequence of the chain effect of consciousness, Qi, and strength. (Consciousness guides the Qi, and the Qi brings strength.) The practitioner can control the alteration of the objective form of the Dantian so long as he masters the art of producing that chain effect. We can say that the perceptual thinking aspect of concentration on the Dantian always initially controls the formation of the objective form. In other types of Qigong practice, such as Circulation of Qi along the Ren and Du meridians in the school of Taoism, or the manipulation of 18 touches in Buddhism, all the procedures are consequences of this type of perceptual thinking. As

THE KEY TO THE QIGONG MEDITATION STATE

this perceptual thinking that initially forms and then changes the event is more active, and has more freedom in manipulating and controlling the objective form, it is regarded as the advanced stage of perceptual thinking.

We thus classify perceptual thinking into two stages: the elementary stage and the senior or advanced stage, depending on whether it passively reflects the object or actively constructs the objective form. To obtain a thorough understanding and complete picture of perceptual thinking, however, we also need to classify perceptual thinking horizontally into sensory thinking, mood/emotion thinking, and action thinking. These categories are not based on assessment of how the objective form is actively or passively created and developed, but based on the properties and characteristics of the objects. The fundamental form is sensory thinking, because our sense of both emotion and movement can be explained as the awareness of a certain subtle sense of the internal and external world. "Feeling is the start of human perception and is a source of knowledge. It is based on the human senses that all the advanced and more complex psychological processes are undertaking" (Dictionary of Psychology).

During the practice of Qigong, all three types of thinking will be implemented, but their respective significance varies in accordance with the type of Qigong. Active Qigong emphasizes action thinking, while still Qigong emphasizes sensory thinking. There are other types of Qigong that emphasize mood/emotional thinking. In addition, each of the three types of thinking can again be subdivided into other specific forms of thinking. For example, sensory thinking can be categorized into optical thinking, auditory thinking, olfactory thinking, tactile thinking, etc., while mood/emotional thinking can be classified as positive or negative, and so on.

Having introduced respectively conceptual thinking, imagery thinking, and perceptual thinking, I should now point out that in the actual process of thinking the three modes actually interact and overlap and cannot be separated from each other. In a complete thinking process, one of them usually takes the lead while the other two simply assist the process. It is almost impossible for one single form of thinking to exist independently. If we look carefully, we may find that in any of the examples given above a shadow of one or two other forms of thinking can always be detected within the dominant form. I will not go into detail here; readers who are interested in this can explore it further for themselves.

It is necessary to discuss the difference between imagery thinking and perceptual thinking. We have already seen the difference between the two in so far as the former operates on the basis of images while the latter operates on the basis of objective form. There seems to be no great difference between image and objective form, yet it is not too difficult to distinguish one from the other. We distinguish between these two types of thinking here because perceptual thinking has not before been explored as a distinct concept in cognitive science. Part of its content has been regarded as an aspect of imagery thinking. Consequently, the notion of perceptual thinking, which requires a complete and independent description, has become non-specific and fragmented, while the content of imagery thinking has become cumbersome and complicated. As a result the character of imagery thinking has become blurred. It is therefore necessary to clarify the two different thinking processes. This is most important for the study of Qigong in relation to its learning and practice; many books that teach the theory and practice of Qigong have misconstrued the content of perceptual thinking as being part of imagery thinking. Not having a clear idea of the basic distinction between the two types of thinking will definitely have a negative impact on the practice of Qigong.

The term "perceptual thinking" has appeared in books and periodicals on psychology, art, and cognitive science, but the definition has not been generally agreed. In books on literary theory, perceptual thinking is regarded as the same as imagery thinking. The notion is used only to emphasize the corporeality of the image in the process of imagery thinking. Psychology has touched on the elementary stage of perceptual thinking, but it is not designated by the term "perceptual thinking." Instead it is called "direct action thinking." In some books on psychology the term is used to refer to imagery thinking. This turns out to be shorthand for concrete imagery thinking and sometimes it is also regarded as direct action thinking. Here, I wish to highlight the definition of perceptual thinking. In my view, it is the process of thinking based on the manipulation of objective form. This is quite different from the usage noted above.

The concept of imagery thinking is now well established and accepted by most people. There is no argument about the fact that imagery thinking is based on images; all psychology textbooks state the same. But what is an image? What content does it have? There is no unanimous answer to this question.

Some textbooks include objective form in the category of images, giving rise to confusion. Problems arise when we confuse the two notions. The key issue in solving the problem is to distinguish between the two processes.

The simplest way to distinguish between the two is to compare dreams with imagination. We take dreams to be a flow of objective form, and imagination as the manipulation of images. Everything in a dream looks genuine. You will feel hot when approaching a fire, and you'll feel cold when you dream of being in a river. In dreams one can fight others with knives and swords; lovers can caress each other. They look as real as if you were experiencing those things. You will be really scared and wake up immediately when you dream that a car is heading towards you. The feeling is so real that you feel as if you have really had an accident on the street. In the case of imagination, things are different. Although the images in your imagination are also vivid and concrete, they are not clear and genuine. Your imagination can meander freely but it will not bring you the feeling of a live experience.

The fire in your imagination will not make you feel hot, nor will the water in your imagination bring the feeling of coldness. The imagined rivals could fight, but they would not really get wounded and bleed. The imagined lovers may sit together, but still feel that they are far apart. I have mentioned that the objective form is the sense itself. The dream seems to be so real because it arouses the senses in a real way. They are obviously formed by our mind, constructed by the consciousness in the absence of direct events. So in this sense a dream has the character of advanced perceptual thinking. However, the construction of the objective form in dreams is completed subconsciously, and not consciously initiated; therefore, we still cannot say that a dream is advanced perceptual thinking, although it has the attributes of perceptual thinking. Nevertheless, dreams open a window that allows ordinary people to have a glimpse of advanced perceptual thinking. This is significant for the cultivation of perceptual thinking. Everybody dreams. To explain objective form and perceptual thinking in terms of dreams is the easiest and most understandable way to explain these concepts. The objective form is the sensation itself; the image is only the recollection and refinement of the sensation. They are related to each other, but they are different.

There are two types of images: one is the image of recollection, and the other is the image of mind. Once a man perceives the event, he has its image stored in his mind; that is, the image of recollection. The recollection is later processed, altered, split, reassembled, and transferred into a new image: image of mind. The term "image" has a narrow meaning and a broader meaning. In a broader sense it includes the image of both recollection and mind. In a narrow sense it refers only to the image of recollection. Here we can see that the image of mind is based on the image of recollection. Thus the core of the image is the image of recollection. Where do we get the image of recollection? We get it from the recollection of the objective form of event. So we have drawn a clear distinction and relationship between the objective form of an event and the image of an event.

Once we have a clear understanding of the distinction between the objective form of an object and the image of an object, we'll have no difficulty in distinguishing between perceptual thinking and imagery thinking. Perceptual thinking is based on the objective form of an object, and manipulates the objective form. Imagery thinking is based on the images of objects, and manipulates the images in the process of thinking. These are two different types of thinking. As well as the difference between the vehicles through which they operate in the thinking process, the processes are also different.

In the imagery thinking process, the main task is to change the images and construct a mosaic of images. The mind can easily manipulate those images and make them into a continuous flow of pictures.

In the perceptual thinking process, manipulating the objective form is far more difficult than manipulating images. Theoretically speaking, our consciousness works in the same way on objective form and is able to alter, cut, and paste the objective form. But to do this one must have developed the utmost competence in operating perceptual thinking, such as is not attained even by those who have reached quite an advanced level of Qigong. The practitioner must already have reached the level of Liu Shen Tong (master of the six magic skills). Thus perceptual thinking is a prerequisite in the general practice of Qigong. It is required to zoom in on the objective form or purify and refine the objective form. Difficulty in applying perceptual thinking is associated with difficulty in constructing the objective form. Construction of the image in the process of imagery thinking is much easier comparatively. It requires hardly any subjective efforts and can be constructed unconsciously.

So we can also distinguish between the two ways of thinking in terms of the process of constructing an objective form or image. Of course, when we emphasize the difference here we do not mean that the two have nothing to do with each other—they are different but also connected. This point was made when we were discussing the difference between the two.

The purpose of presenting an explicit account of the difference between perceptual thinking and imagery thinking is to highlight the former, and is also a main step in allowing it to become an independent thinking mode along with conceptual thinking and imagery thinking. It is necessary to assure the independence of perceptual thinking if we want to cultivate and elaborate its unique functions—just as the value of gold can be realized only when it is picked out of the sand.

As far as the fundamental knowledge of thinking is concerned, it is far from sufficient to know merely the modes of thinking. We should also know their origin and the reasons for their occurrence. All three modes of thinking can gain support from the study of the origin of thinking. They developed out of man's process of perception over millions of years. In the course of one's growth from infancy to adulthood, this development of thinking is replicated.

Millions of years ago when language had not yet been created, the early stage of the thinking process in primitive man could only work with different types of real practice and social activities. His understanding of the world relied on his direct communication with nature. Before language was invented, mankind could only communicate through gesture and action. This must have determined that the thinking mode was mainly direct action thinking. On the basis of this thinking mode, man's ability to memorize images formed from objects became better and better, and his faculty of imagination was built up gradually. In this way, imagery thinking developed. Later on, along with the development of social productivity, and as social interaction became more and more complicated, conceptual thinking developed. The invention of language is an indicator of the development of conceptual thinking. The occurrence and development of conceptual thinking could not take place without language. The successive occurrence of the three modes of thinking shows that man's thinking process has gradually become independent from practice. Direct action thinking cannot exist apart from practice. The contents of imagery thinking are concrete images of events, and the contents of conceptual thinking are symbols. The level of abstraction of the three modes of thinking increases along with the sequential occurrence of those thinking forms. This shows that man's mind became increasingly active and powerful. It also reveals the relationship between man's spiritual life and material life at different levels.

The origin and development of thinking in the individual reflect in microcosm the occurrence and development of thinking in mankind as a whole.

The thinking process of an infant is still in its initial stage, and at this early stage of mental development is mainly direct action thinking. The infant's consciousness and thinking rely heavily on the senses and on actions and is not independent of the concrete object. The baby can only react in consciousness or thinking to the existing concrete object. The baby can perceive the existence of a bottle when he sees it. When the bottle is removed, it does not exist any more for the infant because visually it has disappeared. The infant is not yet able to form the image of the bottle, let alone the concept of it. If the infant sees the bottle falling or moving, he will have a changing image of a moving or falling bottle in mind. This is simple, direct action thinking. The same direct action thinking is more complicated in adults. From the example of the mechanic or the basketball player, we can see that in their process of direct action thinking they need to be able not only to perceive the outside world, their own bodies, and the moving object they are working with, but also to control and manipulate their bodies and the objects in order to fulfill a particular task. The direct action thinking of an infant can hardly be compared to that of an adult. But the direct action thinking of adults is still a continuation of that of the infant, from which it develops.

In human development, imagery thinking occurs in childhood, at the age of about 6 or 7 years. As imagery thinking is based on images, it can only occur when one is able to form an image of the event. That is to say, one is able to rebuild the exact image in the mind, through recall of the event. From the games young children play, we can see that they have developed the ability to form images of events. When they are playing hide-and-seek, they are able to imagine who is hiding behind which tree, or in which cave. They can do this even when they are blindfolded. Passing through their minds are images of their friends and their surroundings. This thinking process is imagery thinking. The imagery thinking of an adult has developed from that of a child. Of course, it is more complex. The great distinction between the highly developed imagery thinking of a great artist or novelist and that of children is this: imagery thinking in children is basically a process of re-establishing the image of the event, while for artists engaged in creativity, the process of imagery thinking is basically focused on alteration of the events. For instance, in his cubist paintings, Picasso altered and rearranged objects. He could superimpose images of the same face drawn from different angles, as if to create a two-dimensional "sculpture." The novelist creates his characters and plot. Again, this is the alteration and combination in his mind of different images which have been gathered and accumulated through his own life experience.

Man develops conceptual thinking during adolescence, at the age of about 11 or 12. This is based on one's ability to form concepts. One makes judgments using concepts and deduces and concludes from these judgments. A pupil has to think by means of mathematical symbols when solving a math problem. This is conceptual thinking. A child of this age no longer needs to use his fingers to solve a math problem, or to have the image of fingers in his mind in order to complete the calculation. He can use the numbers directly to add, subtract, multiply, and divide. These numbers are actually abstract symbols, separate from concrete events. All the equations, principles, maxims, and rules in modern science were established through conceptual thinking. As humans develop this ability during the teenage years, the parents who hope that their children will become scientists, philosophers, etc. should try to train their child's conceptual thinking and ensure that it is fully developed.

Entering adulthood, man has all three modes of thinking. They co-exist and none of them "overlaps" the others. When an adult is coping with various different problems, he will choose one of the thinking modes in accordance with his actual needs. There are individual variations in the adequate development of these three modes of thinking. One person may be superior to others in conceptual thinking, which results in a thoughtful and considerate personality, while another may be good at imagery thinking and turns out to be someone with high artistic taste. Still others may be good at direct action thinking, which makes them skillful craftsmen.

Sensory Thinking

With the basic knowledge of thinking as discussed above, we can now discuss sensory thinking. Sensory thinking is a form of thinking that is fully cultivated during the process of Qigong. It is the main form of thinking during the adjustment of mind. Whether or not one has entered into the process of sensory thinking can be used as a psychological indicator for entry into the process of Rujing.

As mentioned before, sensory thinking is one type of perceptual thinking.

We all know that perceptual thinking is a kind of thinking that uses reflections of events as the material or media for the thinking process. Reflections of events are various. They may relate to shapes, colors, sounds, smells, temperature, or touch in the objective world, or to sensations one feels from outside and inside the body such as pain, itching, soreness, numbness, swelling, etc. They can also be pleasant and unpleasant human emotions, such as anxiety, irritation, happiness, etc. These are monotypic reflections. There are also polytypic reflections of the world. The action thinking we discussed before, for example, combines the reflection of the motion of the limbs and the reflection of the object the limbs can feel. We have also mentioned that perceptual thinking can be classified into sensory thinking, mood/emotion thinking, action thinking, and other types of thinking, based on different characteristics of the thought content. Sensory thinking is the thinking process that uses one's sensation of events as its thinking material or media. The sensation of events is actually man's feeling of what he senses. Sensory thinking can be further divided into optical thinking, auditory thinking, olfactory thinking, tactile thinking, etc., in accordance with the actual objects sensed.

In everyday life, visual thinking with multiple reflections is frequently used. In the stream of thought, there are both reflections of objective events and reflections of one's own feelings. Sensory thinking, like perceptual thinking, when working with a simple object, usually does not develop any further. This is because perceptual thinking in everyday life is mainly engaged in manual labor or sports that are related to movement of the body. The objects and environment in which the operation is carried out are very complicated (as in playing basketball or repairing machinery, for example).

Yet there is still some simple and lower-level sensory thinking in our everyday life. For instance, when we go to a mall to buy clothes, we often evaluate the quality of the fabric by observing and feeling it. We check its texture, its softness or hardness, and whether it shines. Our thinking proceeds along with the movement of our eyes and hands. When we do this, we can say that optical thinking and tactile thinking have developed and are a vital element in the evaluation, regardless of the fact that abstract thinking may also occur at the same time. When we are tasting something, we try carefully to distinguish different tastes on our tongue; as we follow the fragrant smell of flowers carried on the wind, and look for a particular bush or flower in the corner of the park, olfactory thinking and taste thinking become the main forms of thinking. Some occupations require the employee to develop a strong power of sensory thinking related to one particular sense. For example, a conductor must be very good at auditory thinking, since he needs to catch and distinguish the melody, color, volume, rhythm, and speed of the music. This is the foundation for his musical creativity. Needless to say, a painter must have high ability in optical thinking.

In everyday life the modes of sensory thinking can play an important role, yet they are still simple and primitive. This is because, in the process of thinking, changes in events cannot be controlled or manipulated by the thinker. The thinking can only passively follow, distinguishing the event, but without the ability to change it. It is a series of consistent and ever-changing perceptions, and recognition of those perceptions. These are not fully developed and advanced forms of sensory thinking, but can only be regarded as the preliminary stage of sensory thinking. Admittedly, it is a kind of thinking process, and more than simple perception, not just because the stream of consciousness or the stream of images has been formed during the process, but also because the process itself is involved in pursuing and identifying moving objects. These factors themselves contain the means of achieving solutions. Isn't it by touching and tasting cloth and wine respectively that we are able to tell the quality of the cloth and wine? In addition, sensing and identifying events in the process of sensory thinking relates to changes in one's feelings about the events, not in abstract perceptions of the events. It is direct experience, although sometimes abstract judgments may be involved.

Sensory thinking during the process of Rujing is quite different from that in everyday life. From the very beginning it is controlled and manipulated by consciousness. It is a somewhat creative thinking process. Thus it is a type of advanced perceptual thinking. The preliminary requirement for Rujing produces a superior condition that is hard to obtain in everyday life in the occurrence and development of sensory thinking. Rujing requires a quiet setting. One needs to close one's eyes and apply one's visual and auditory ability to the inner world, focusing attention only on oneself. These requirements subjectively and objectively help one to exclude stimuli from the outside world. One is required not to move the body when the posture is established for Rujing. One should also stop moving the limbs, and this will banish any stimuli resulting from the movement of one's own body. One is also required to clear the mind before Rujing. One needs to get rid of all distracting thoughts and concentrate the mind on the practice. By doing so, one minimizes every possible stimulus from both internal and external worlds. There will be no response, as there is no stimulus. The brain becomes a "vacuum," like a sheet of blank paper ready for drawing a new and most beautiful picture. The picture is drawn by sensory thinking activity in the process of Rujing.

Sensory thinking, first of all, must work with the senses. How could we have senses if all stimuli were excluded? The answer is that the sense or feeling one gets in Rujing is the result of subjective direction. That is why I said that sensory thinking in Rujing is creative from the time it is generated. The sensations generated in Rujing are quite different from those we experience in everyday life. In reality sensations are reflections by our sensory organs of stimuli in the outside world. When we are walking in the street, we see and hear passing pedestrians, cars, attractive shop windows, and trees. These are concrete, external stimuli. If you have a stomach ache after eating something bad, or a headache when you have a cold, the factors and stimuli that cause them to happen are also from the external world. They are real and concrete. For real stimuli, no matter where they come from, your body's sensory responses are passive. That is to say, the stimulus comes first, and the response second. This does not exclude the possibility that our mind may sometimes intuitively select the stimuli. For instance, when two people come up to us, we may selectively pay attention to one of them and ignore the other. Whatever you choose as the selected stimulus, the response is still passive.

The sensation or feeling generated in Rujing is quite different. These are not responses to real and concrete stimuli from the internal and external worlds, but the consequences of subjective direction. They are something that is generated by the thinking process alone. The initial feeling of Rujing is always of "relaxation" and "tranquillity." Although these feelings of relaxation and tranquillity have something to do with actual stimuli, such as a quiet environment and relaxed posture, they are mainly the consequence of the practitioner's own efforts of self-direction to achieve the required state. The feeling of ultimate emptiness that one aims to achieve at the advanced level of Rujing can only be obtained through the cumulative inner prompting of one's consciousness.

The genuine stimuli of ultimate emptiness are never, and never can be, the result of the internal and external experiences of reality. In general, we can see that the sense experience and feeling generated in Rujing are the result of the transformation of spirit into matter, and a transformation of psychological elements into physiological ones. Thus, it is a process that can be controlled by the practitioner herself. Our experience in everyday life is just the opposite. This is a process of matter transforming into spirit, and the physiological transforming into the psychological, and is, primarily, a subconscious physiological process.

Due to these differences, it becomes clear that the sensory thinking developed in each sphere has a different initial starting point. In everyday life it is passive and receptive from the very beginning. In Rujing it is initiating and creative from the outset.

Activity that induces the occurrence of sensory thinking in the process of Rujing applies to the practitioner's past experience of similar responses to actual stimuli in reality as a means of arousing the required feeling. This is a process of transferring from abstract or imagery thinking to perceptual thinking. Prompted by an abstract concept or the evocation of images, one finally achieves the experience of perceptual thinking. For example, one might evoke a possible superficial image of the feeling we might have in the state of Ultimate Emptiness with the help of the words "ultimate emptiness." Then, with the help of this superficial image, we achieve the virtual image of Ultimate Emptiness.

Feeling generated in the process of Rujing is only the first step in the development of sensory thinking in Rujing. In the next step, thinking will start to manipulate feeling and take it through further development in the direction required. This is actually the main work of sensory thinking in Rujing, and this is the time when sensory thinking demonstrates its power, establishment, and maturity. The manipulation of feeling is different from controlling the occurrence of feeling. To stimulate the occurrence of feeling, one may still need the help of concepts. The virtual image emerges from the superficial image, and this shows that one still needs the help of abstract and imagery thinking. As for the manipulation of feeling, sensory thinking can work independently. Thinking is free to manipulate feelings. It can alter and transform feeling into various forms. It is known that, in all perceptual thinking, there is an overlap between the development of thinking and changes in the movement of objects that thinking is working on. Thinking directly controls the virtual image of dynamic events. Therefore, in the operation of sensory thinking during Rujing, there is an overlap between the process of thinking and changes in sensation; or we can say that they mingle. Expressed in the terminology of Qigong, Qi comes along with consciousness. When Qi arrives, consciousness arrives; Qi and consciousness are one entity. Consciousness controls Qi, and Qi is employed by consciousness, as in the above-mentioned concept of concentrating on the Dantian.

Now let's look back at the development of feeling in everyday life. You may find that that feeling still moves passively along a pre-set pathway. It changes only when the external event changes. For instance, changes in the intensity of light will lead to changes of visual sensation. Changes in sound intensity will alter the hearing sensation. Once the stimuli disappear, the feeling will also vanish. As it is never an independent operation, sensory thinking on this basis is always simple and primitive. It cannot be compared with sensory thinking in the process of Rujing.

In the process of Rujing, Qi comes along with consciousness and they are the same thing. Thinking manipulates the process by which the sensory image shifts towards the high realm of Ultimate Emptiness. This is where sensory thinking is at its most active and magnificent. In the pre-set direction, it performs the expansion—strengthening and weakening, and stabilizing and transforming—of all kinds of feelings, so as to expand the realm of Rujing. This is generally a long period of time, and the adjustment of mind is mainly completed in the period between the beginning of Rujing and the end of Rujing. After that, the process of Rujing moves towards its completion, or we may say that one approaches the highest realm of Rujing where nature and oneself both disappear. Then, sensory thinking will change significantly. Of course, these changes develop gradually. Only at this point do they become more obvious. Sensory thinking changes from its active state into a passive state. This is the most noticeable change. The sensory thinking process changes from its creative aspect to a following one—that is to say, it no longer oversees the manipulation and alteration of the sensory image, but simply follows it. This is because the special state of feeling required by Rujing has now become established and fully developed. It has become stable and is no longer drifting and changing. This is called "fixed scenes" in the jargon of Qigong. Just like a baby that is born:

once it has grown up, there is no longer any need for the parents to take care of it. The creative function of sensory thinking during Rujing is now almost completed. It remains only to maintain and take care of it. Thus, all we need do is follow it. We may find that the character of sensory thinking at this stage is quite close to that of sensory thinking in everyday life. It seems to have gone back to the primitive stage.

This is still not the full picture. Sensory thinking in this inactive state during Rujing does not lose its creativity. It just stores the creativity up, ready to be used when needed. For instance, if the realm attained in Rujing is interrupted by negative factors, sensory thinking will become active again to clear out those negative factors and maintain the process of Rujing—just as when a teenager becomes an adult, the parents still have to correct him if he does something wrong. The ancient Chinese described the advanced state of Rujing as "consciousness and Qi are both silent. All disappear except one sense on alert." What is this one sense that is still on guard? It is the lookout kept by inactive sensory thinking. This lookout needs to be maintained, otherwise negative side effects may occur.

The active and inactive states of sensory thinking in the process of Rujing can also be regarded as the active and the inactive periods of sensory thinking. Throughout the process of sensory thinking, the two periods come about in turns. At the beginning of Rujing, the expected feelings are induced, and need to grow and develop later. In this first, active period, sensory thinking is active. This does not exclude relatively short inactive periods during this stage. When Rujing reaches a new level that is still building up and needs to be further stabilized, the operation of sensory thinking proves to be quite plain and smooth. At the advanced level of Rujing, sensory thinking is inactive, although some relatively active operation may also occur. Thus there is no absolute division between active and inactive sensory thinking.

At the advanced stage of Rujing, one of the changes in sensory thinking is that it becomes a subconscious process: there is a shift from the conscious to the subconscious. Every thinking process is observable and within the scale of consciousness. Each has to show observable signs, whether they be abstract, concrete, virtual, moving, or flowing—otherwise the process cannot be regarded as thinking. At the subconscious level there are no observable signs. Our observation of the subconscious is achieved by re-establishing that it has reversed back into conscious activity, as made evident in the form of a sign or image. We still do not know the exact process of subconscious activity. Thus it cannot be regarded as a thinking process at all. When we say that sensory thinking turns into the subconscious, we are actually referring to the transformation from existence to non-existence. Sensory thinking fluctuates between conscious and subconscious. It comes and goes in our mind. But why don't we say so? Why should we adopt the notion of a transformation from conscious to subconscious? This is because, although the psychological process that forms the "scenery" has ceased, the physiological process has not. Sensory thinking is the unification of both psychological and physiological processes. The inactivity of one does not lead to inactivity of the other. When we are walking along the street, we may not look at or see passers-by approaching, but this does not mean they do not exist. They are going about in their own way.

Similarly, in the advanced stage of Rujing, when the consciousness ceases to experience physiological activity that is strong enough to generate a feeling, it does not mean that those activities are no more. They are still operating in their own way. When the results of their operation are sensed as they occasionally return into consciousness, the feelings will have changed compared to what they were before. Besides, the reason why we regard them as the continuation of sensory thinking is mainly that these non-sensed physiological operations are still going on in the pre-established manner when they are not controlled by the mind, just as they are sometimes manipulated by sensory thinking in consciousness. For instance, in the realm of ultimate emptiness when sensory awareness comes and goes, this realm does not cease along with it. Each time the feeling returns, the realm of emptiness is still there as before. It may even develop further and become more magnificent; therefore, although sensory thinking has ceased to make any impact, it is still there, though it is right to say that it has become subconscious.

Sensory thinking tends to weaken when the advanced stage of Rujing is reached. It changes from being active to inactive, from being conscious to subconscious. This is the general tendency of the thinking.

We have learnt that the highest level of Rujing is "complete oblivion" during which all consciousness becomes inactive, and so does the activity of sensory thinking. It withdraws once it has completed its task in stimulating the sensory experience of Rujing.

The above discussion outlines the process of sensory thinking during Rujing and its origin and development. It needs to be re-stated that during the process of adjustment of mind, as well as sensory thinking, there are also some other types of thinking. But sensory thinking sits at the center and is the main stream of thinking. As I mentioned before, the three modes of thinking (abstract, concrete, and virtual) cannot be totally separated. Thus, in the process of Rujing, abstract thinking and imagery thinking are also involved, albeit not in the leading position. From the order of the occurrence of these thinking modes, the practitioner usually starts with abstract and imagery thinking, as in everyday life, and then transfers to the sensory thinking of perceptual thinking. This is a regression of the thinking mode. This regression is somewhat "back to nature" with reference to the origin of thinking of human beings. For each individual, it is the return to childhood thinking. It is known that the concepts of "back to nature" and "return to childhood" are the guidelines in many schools of Qigong, particularly the Taoist school. The regression of thinking mode in the process of Rujing seems to coincide with what the ancient scholars and philosophers sought. Astonishingly, this regression in thinking is reflected not only in form, but also in content. In his work on perception, Piaget states that an infant associates everything with his body, as if his body were the center of the universe—a center that cannot be perceived by itself. It is a wonderful footnote to the realm of Rujing, where nature and man become one single entity, and the world and self have been forgotten.

Is this only a coincidence? The advanced realm of Rujing is just the same as the realm of infant consciousness (from form to content). The twentieth-century scientist's account of the infant's mind coincides with Laozi's and Zhuang Zi's description of the realm of Qigong, and we can see that it shows that mentally returning to nature and to childhood is possible from the standpoint of cognitive science. Our thinking, whether in form or in content, will be able to return to infancy in the process of Rujing. Of course, this regression is not a simple retreat but rather a spiral forward. It is the opposite of negative. The content of perceptual thinking such as it is in the early conscious activity of man and infant can only be used to balance and coordinate the simplest link between man and his environment (and the relationship between subject and object in infancy). The advanced perceptual thinking mode (sensory thinking and action thinking that are highly developed by this stage) will enable one to achieve the self-adjustment and control necessary to complete the most complicated and delicate operations. The difference between the infant thinking mode and the advanced perceptual thinking mode is vast.

Compared to other thinking modes, does the main thinking mode in the process of Rujing and sensory thinking require any special conditions in order to be realized? Not at all. If you think carefully, you can see that other forms of thinking also have relatively special conditions of existence. The father of Chinese cognitive science, the famous scientist Qang Xuesen, once said that there are three types of state in our life: the waking state, the sleeping state, and the state of Qigong. If we match the thinking modes to man's functional states, we find that abstract thinking dominates man's thinking in the waking state, and visual thinking recurs frequently in our dreams, during the state of sleep. In the process of Rujing, when one enters the state of Qigong, sensory thinking becomes the main thinking mode. These divisions are only for ease of reference. But they show that, like other events in the world, thinking modes also require certain conditions of existence. If that is so, can we still say that the conditions for sensory thinking are special?

Mood/Emotion Thinking

The study of mood and emotion is one of the least developed areas in modern psychology. Up to now it still has no commonly accepted definition. There is still controversy as to whether mood is an independent psychological process or state. There are many theories on mood/emotion, such as those regarding mood as a perception, act, physiological process, etc. This diversity actually shows us that one theory will be able to provide us with a satisfactory answer; otherwise one or two theories would be sufficient. This is just like the medication for a particular disease: the more remedies there are, the less effective they will be. If there is any special, effective medication, one or two remedies are enough.

What is a mood or sentiment? It is a sort of experience, a response, an impulse, and a reaction. The mood must consist of three aspects: experience, presentation, and the physiological aspect. It is a combination of one's mental and physical state. Our studies of the mechanism of mood change during Rujing focus mainly on its quality as an experiential process. We will take advantage of the definition of mood as a sort of experience, just as we used the definition of stream of consciousness for thinking. We have already discussed this definition of mood in Chapter 2, and saw there that this experience is often accompanied by sensory experience.

The reason why we treat mood as a kind of experience is because, in the process of Rujing, all that mood thinking can control is the experiential component. It may also be able to control a little bit, maybe only a tiny part, of its presenting component (such as smiling). We cannot control the physiological component. This is just the same as in sensory thinking, where the mind can only control changes in the sensations experienced but is ignorant of the physiological function. Mood thinking is perceptual thinking based on the experiencing of mood—that is to say, using events in mood experiencing as the material for perceptual thinking.

The mechanism of mood/emotion thinking during the process of Rujing is quite similar to that of sensory thinking. The generation and development of mood/emotion thinking is also the consequence of subjective induction and manipulation. It involves the process leading from abstract thinking to imagery and perceptual thinking. This may even start in the preliminary stage of Rujing. For instance, standing Qigong requires one to be calm and to stand for a few minutes in silence before one closes one's eyes to start the practice of Rujing. Of course, this also involves the adjustment of mind and breath. But most important is to calm down and stabilize your mood, and the way to achieve this is to have your consciousness tell yourself to calm down and stimulate a stable mood. Once the feeling is established, you should try to reinforce it. This process in which consciousness manipulates mood is just like the process in which consciousness manipulates the senses. It is easy to comprehend with reference to the account already given of sensory thinking. In this section I'll talk mainly about the difference between mood/emotion thinking and sensory thinking, and how they interact.

First of all, there are certain characteristics that differentiate the two. For instance, sensory thinking can be associated with either part of the body or the entire body. For example, you feel pain in your back or feet, or your finger feels numb. These are local experiences, but the senses of losing weight, of self-forgetting, and of balancing are all experiences associated with the entire body. So are the feelings of thirst, hunger, and other feelings of your body or organs.

Mood experience is different. It is never partial. Nobody ever said that his hand or foot felt scared, or his back felt very happy. Fear and happiness are always related to the whole body. The integral feature of this mood experience does not seem like the sense of balance or motion, which more or less has the feeling of the limbs. It is more like the feeling of the organs. Therefore, in the process of mood experiencing, the mind will not expand or scale down the content of the mood. It operates only by increasing or decreasing the intensity of the mood experienced. For instance, trying to maintain a state of lower intensity and avoiding being excited and stimulated.

In mood/emotion experience, the differences among different types of mood are not as clear as sensory differences. Pain, itching, soreness, numbness, and swelling are all easier sensations to identify, even when subtle and slight. No one will confuse pain and itching. Mood/emotion experiencing is not like that. It is, of course, easier to distinguish between strong emotions such as rage and happiness. But subtle moods and emotions can be more difficult to distinguish between, such as slight regret and disappointment. We tend to classify the experiences of all mood/emotion into two categories—pleasant and unpleasant—because the boundaries between the subtleties of different moods is vague and blurred. Thus, although we do not need to make the same precise analysis and identification of the different types of mood as we do with the senses in sensory thinking, with a more precise identification we will find it easier to manipulate the transformations of various moods. Besides, in the adjustment of mood, facial expression, breathing, and even posture and relaxation of the limbs can have a direct impact on the adjustment. The widening brow, smooth breathing, and comfortably settled limbs can all directly promote the production of a pleasurable state, though they do not have any impact on the senses. If you have a headache, the widening brow does not help you to reduce the headache. The organic association of mood and the above-mentioned action presents its own action profile. Thus the adjusting of mood and action during the process of Rujing is also the necessary means to help with the process of Rujing. It is not just the operation of mood/emotion thinking that we should rely on to help the process of Rujing.

All in all, the operation of mood/emotion thinking is a little easier than sensory thinking. All you need to do is to control and manipulate the type and intensity of different moods. In addition, it can be assisted by action adjustment.

Although the basic mechanisms of the two types of thinking are the same, there are considerable differences in content and detail.

Now let's see what special function this has in helping the process of Rujing.

Mood is closely related to abstract and imagery thinking, the latter in particular. We may become thrilled when we listen to an exciting lecture or see a magnificent scene. We may still feel our blood boiling, even when we just recall scenes from our memory. Conversely, unstable mood can also quicken the pace of our thinking, disturb our logic, and result in a chain of endless thoughts. Therefore, in the process of Rujing, the uncertainty of mood is more or less associated with the number of distracting thoughts. Those thoughts emerge when one is in the mood of excitement, and will disappear when one is calm and peaceful. We may say that, to this extent, the stabilizing of one's mood itself will exclude distracting thoughts. This has been proved by the practice of Rujing. Getting rid of thoughts and clearing the mind by stabilizing your mood will enable you to achieve the goal with less effort. If you try to get rid of distracting thoughts just by stopping thinking after they have occurred, but do not try to cut off the emotional factors that may actually help the generation of those thoughts, you are unlikely to succeed. Besides, it is known that a light-hearted, pleasant mood plays a vital role in the construction of Rujing. It is just like a background color that supports sensory experiencing and lays a foundation for the realm of Rujing. If we take the entire realm of Rujing as the dark, mysterious night sky, then the mood experience is the vast, dark blue hemisphere, and the sensory experience is the sparkling stars and the cool moon in the sea of clouds.

The mood with its behavioral aspect can directly affect the adjustment of breathing and mind. It will affect the process of Rujing in both respects. For instance, control of one's mood will also lead to control of one's breath. Mood thinking, though independent, is mostly associated with sensory thinking. In the process of Rujing, mood experience and sensory experience are mixed up and together form the experience of the realm of Rujing. The stars of sensory experience emerge in the night sky of mood experience, melting and evenly scattered, and gradually mingle into one being. In the initial stage of Rujing, "relaxed" and "tranquil" are the most frequently used terms to induce consciousness. This is a wonderful choice of words. Why? Because they can refer to both feeling and mood and help bring peace into both, akin to killing two birds with one stone. This also shows that mood thinking and sensory thinking are twinned at the very beginning. The ultimate realm of Rujing is also the combination of two states: ultimate emptiness and oblivion of both nature and oneself. Thus, in the process of Rujing, mood thinking and sensory thinking are generally more linked than separate. When we discuss one of them, we are at the same time discussing the other.

As sensory thinking is more complicated than mood thinking in the process of Rujing, and change in sensory experiencing is more obvious and colorful than it is in mood experiencing, I have taken sensory thinking as representative in discussing the operation and process of thinking in Rujing. I regard mood as a companion of sensations and mood thinking as a companion of sensory thinking. This is not to suggest that I am degrading the value of mood thinking, or upgrading the value of sensory thinking, but to help avoid repetition and redundancy.

Biochemical and Physiological Functions of the Brain

The brain is an organ that controls man's psychological world. Man's psychological activity is part of its function. Now that we have explored the subjective operation of the adjustment of mind during Rujing, namely the processes of sensory thinking and emotional thinking, let's look at the predictable and observable physical and biochemical changes in our brain during that process of thinking. This will enable us to understand the nature of Rujing, during which the body and mind become one entity, from a new point of view, so as to increase our understanding of the essence of Qigong meditation.

Physical and biochemical changes of the pallium (the layers of gray and white matter that cover the upper surface of the cerebrum) during the process of Qigong meditation can be observed using electroencephalography (EEG). Generally speaking the graph will show that the α wave becomes more active, the amplitude of the wave increases while the frequency of it slows down, and the rhythm is stable. The α waves from different parts of the pallium tend to be synchronized. In some cases, θ and δ waves may also occur. On the EEG diagram, the α wave reflects the state of peacefulness of the pallium. It is a kind of intermediate-speed wave. Usually it occurs when you are at rest with your eyes closed. The θ wave reveals a reinforcement of the natural constraining nature of the pallium. This is the wave that occurs when we are in a state of sleep. We may find it when sleepy or in a trance. The θ wave is slower than the α wave. The δ wave is the wave that occurs when our brain is inhibited. It occurs in sleep, and is even slower than the θ wave.

It is clear that the waves that occur during Rujing are quite similar to those that occur in rest, sleep, and hypnotic states, but there is also something unique about them.

For instance, the amplitude of the α wave in relaxation is lower and less stable than the α wave in the state of Rujing. In the state of hypnosis the θ wave usually occurs when the α wave becomes weakened or disappears, while in the state of Rujing it occurs when the α wave is reinforced and is not accompanied by a dazed condition. During sleep, the EEG diagram changes periodically. The amplitude of the α wave is rather low and the cycle is shortened. Then the α wave vanishes and the spindle wave occurs; then comes the synchronized δ wave. One enters the period of slow wave sleep. After a period of time, one enters the period of synchronized fast wave (β wave) sleep. For quite a long period of time, fast wave sleep and slow wave sleep come about in turns for several times, and finally transfer into the wakening state. Although the δ wave may also occur in the state of Rujing, it is mainly the α wave that is continuously activated. The occasional occurrence of the δ wave is still based on the reinforced α wave. If the δ wave prevails and the α wave occurs occasionally, then the practitioner is quite likely to have fallen asleep. Thus we can conclude that the brain is in a unique state during Rujing, quite different from the brain in the state of relaxation, sleep, and hypnosis.

The significance of analyzing the EEG graph of the brain in the state of Rujing is that it enables us to know that the cerebral cortex is in a process of subjective inner repression. This restraint of the cerebral cortex during Rujing differs from that during sleep, which is the result of a comprehensive repression passively induced on the basis of the restraint of the upwards stimulating system in the reticular formation in the brain stem. Rujing is the state of subjective repression while the upwards stimulating system of the reticular formation in the brain stem is still functioning. This restrained state of the brain during Rujing is quite helpful for the adjustment, improvement, and recovery of brain function. Analysis of EEG shows that the changes in the α wave during Rujing are the most significant and characteristic alterations. These alterations suggest a reduction of energy expenditure in the central nervous system within the brain, increase of negative entropy, improvement of synthesized function, and improvement of harmony in the system.

Based on the improvement and reinforcement of brain functions, there will be a series of effective changes in the system of the lower cerebral ganglion–pituitary–adrenal axis in the process of Rujing, with an integral effect on the whole body. The lower cerebral ganglion is the central controlling center nerve of the autonomic nervous system. Its function directly affects the sympathetic and parasympathetic nervous system. In the practice of Rujing the parasympathetic nervous system will be physiologically strengthened. This reinforcement is beneficial for the reduction of energy consumption and readjustment of the body such as to protect the body and improve the state of health.

From a biochemical point of view, Rujing causes a change in the secretion of a certain substance in the central nervous system. Practitioners have found that secretion of 5-hydroxytryptamine (5-HT) will increase in the process of Rujing. This change is related to man's experience of the senses and emotions. This can be illustrated by its link to LSD. It is well known that those who take ergotamine and marijuana will experience illusions and such pleasurable sensations as bright colors, beautiful music, or sometimes even past experiences and the hallucination of heaven. They become very excited and joyful. At this time their minds are still clear, to some extent. These experiences are quite similar to what is experienced at a certain level of Rujing. It has been reported that some Native American tribes ask their members to take a herb containing the substance LSD during some religious ceremonies. They thought this would remove them from the world and enable them to talk to God. This is quite strange. LSD is very addictive. To some extent, Rujing is also addictive. Those who have experienced the happiness of Rujing are unlikely to stop practicing Rujing. Of course, this kind of addiction is not the same as the experience of drugs. If you stop practicing, you will not suffer any uncomfortable symptoms, such as a drug user would.

Why does LSD cause hallucinations? The study of pharmacology shows that the structure of LSD is quite similar to that of 5-HT in the central nervous system. The structures of many drugs are at least partly similar to the structure of 5-HT. Once you take LSD, it operates on nerve cells like 5-HT, since they have a similar chemical structure and our body cannot tell the difference. This "increased" 5-HT certainly leads to a diversity of heightened sensory and emotional experience. The increase of 5-HT during Rujing is physiological, while the increase of 5-HT after taking LSD is virtual. It may actually lead to reduction of 5-HT and result in depression and other symptoms that occur when one tries to come off drugs. This offers us a glimpse of the hazards of LSD.

From what we have discussed above we can see that brain function and its changes are very complicated in the process of Rujing. Its power is also multidimensional. Study of the biochemical and physiological changes in the brain during the practice of Rujing is continuing. We look forward to exciting results from the research, which may provide us with a better understanding of the mechanism of Rujing and a new objective test for the process of Rujing. Up to now we have not been able to set up a reliable objective standard to test the process of Rujing.

The Mechanism of Breathing Adjustment

In ancient times people regarded a complete cycle of inhaling/exhaling as one breath. The adjustment of breathing is to modify the movement of your breathing, and it is one of the most important activities in the process of Rujing. Whether or not you are able to adjust your breathing has an immediate impact on Rujing. We can see the importance of this from the term "Qigong" itself, where "Qi" means air. Of course, the concept of Qi is far more than the concept of the air we are inhaling/exhaling every day.

Better Understanding of Breathing

The vitality of an event is not necessarily always noticeable, and an event that attracts people's attention is not necessarily vital. This is a common but profound concept. Breathing is essential to living creatures, but we hardly notice it. Even the scientific world seems not to have paid enough attention to it, otherwise the treatment of air pollution would be more effective. A man can survive hunger and thirst for several days but would die at once if he stopped breathing for only a few minutes. This is a down-to-earth fact that everybody knows. Breathing is too easy. The air is infinite and it is effortless to inhale; therefore, it is ignored. It is a common phenomenon that if something is too easy to get, it is not explored and cultivated. People will not know more about it if they never explore it. The things people do not know much about are sometimes the easiest and simplest things, such as breathing. However, the ancient masters and founders of Qigong showed more concern about breathing. The adjustment of breathing in Qigong takes breathing as a most significant activity in human life and lays great emphasis on it. The ancients knew that it was possible for a tiny adjustment of one's breathing to have a profound impact on the whole of human life, since it is vital for life. This understanding is supported by the practice of Qigong.

Modern scientific study of physiology also shows that breathing is far more than the inhalation of oxygen and exhalation of carbon dioxide. It has been reported in the media that scientists in the former Soviet Union discovered in their research that the tribesmen of an island in Papua New Guinea absorb less than the amount of protein they consume every day, probably only half as much. Yet they look very healthy and do not have any diseases caused by lack of protein. It seems that the protein they absorb every day is no less than that they consume. Then where do they get the necessary protein? The study shows that the secret is in their breathing. They can take in nitrogen from the air as they inhale. Their bodies synthesize it into protein, just as soybean gets nitrogen from the air and its rhizobium synthesizes it into protein. The stomach of the Papuan contains certain bacteria that can produce protein with air. This ability is not found among other ethnic groups. Yet if Papuans can do this, why not other ethnic groups in particular circumstances?

In ancient China, a book, *Yi Wen Ji*[33] (The Diary of Anecdotes), records the following story. A man named Zhang Guang Din wanted to flee from a rebellion happening in his county. He found it hard to make the final decision because of his four-year-old daughter. Finally he decided to leave home, and abandoned his daughter. He put her in a big ancient tomb near his village. Three years later he returned to his village, as the rebellion had been suppressed. He went to the tomb to collect his daughter's body. To his surprise, his daughter was sitting in the tomb alive. He thought it was a ghost. He just did not believe his daughter was still alive until she recognized him and called him Daddy. He asked his daughter how she had been able to survive without starving. His daughter replied that she was indeed very hungry for the first few days, until she saw something stretching its neck and breathing but not eating anything. So she imitated that creature and stretched her neck and breathed. Day after day she no longer felt hungry. Zhang began to search for that creature and found a big turtle. So his daughter had learned from the turtle's breathing and survived. In this story, the little girl's ability to absorb nutrition from the atmosphere by breathing is far superior to the Papuans', and she actually learned this skill. This may suggest that the ability can be obtained through training. Of course, no one knows if the story is true or not. If we associate this with the phenomenon of "BiGu" (stop eating; see below), the story sounds quite possible. We all know that turtle breathing is one type of breathing in Qigong. "BiGu" is learned through practice of Qigong, isn't it?

The book *Gui Bao Zhi Guang*[34] (The Light of Treasure) records another story. A young girl learned Qigong after attending some lectures of a Qigong master. From 3 October 1987 to 12 February 1988, she did not eat for 133 days. For 106 days she did not eat a single meal or any other food. She did not drink any water for 87 days. She would feel sick and her stomach and whole body would feel uncomfortable if she tried to eat any fruit or drink a little soup. Yet she was energetic and strong. Sometimes she appeared even stronger than before. She still did the chores every day and slept less, since she was so energetic. For several days she would only sleep for about ten minutes. She would feel uncomfortable if she slept more. In the chill of winter, she did not feel cold when wearing only a sweater. Later on she started to eat, because she wanted to end the state of BiGu. Otherwise she could have continued in this state of BiGu. Her experience leads us to believe that Zhang Guang Din's daughter had entered the state of BiGu while observing the turtle's breathing. So she could survive starvation for three years.

The so-called "BiGu" refers to the phenomenon of being very energetic without eating and drinking anything for a long time. It usually occurs during the practice of Qigong. The phenomenon has been frequently reported in recent years. So its occurrence is not rare during the practice of Qigong. However, if you stop eating and your health is getting worse, it is not so-called BiGu, but rather a state of illness.

There are only a few assumptions and hypotheses and primary observations about the mechanism of BiGu and no detailed study on it. Research on this issue could take the following two considerations as a starting point: the reduction of energy consumption; and the intake of nutrition from sources other than food and drink. The first approach could try to prove that, during Rujing, energy consumption is at a very low level, even lower than during sleep, by measuring changes in the rate of basic metabolism, pulse and heartbeat. It could draw an analogy between the state of Rujing and that of an animal in hibernation. In hibernation, animals live for months not eating and drinking anything. Thus far, it is quite similar to the state of Rujing and BiGu. The second approach would be similar to the study of the Papuan taking in nitrogen through breathing to synthesize protein.

The concept of breathing in Qigong has broadened and the technique has also been studied in various ways. It is said that there are hundreds of breathing modes in Qigong, such as breathing imitating a turtle or snake in hibernation; sonic breathing; and breathing imitating the sound of a cricket. There is also action breathing; five sounds breathing; seven emotions breathing; environment breathing, etc. If we get as far as navel breathing, observable breathing has actually stopped. It appears that the whole body is metabolizing directly with the universe. It is questionable whether those special types of breathing could absorb nutrients other than oxygen from the air to satisfy the needs of the body. Judging by the story of the man's daughter in the book *Yi Wen Ji*, there may be types of breathing that have this function, and this may be one of the causes of the phenomenon of BiGu.

In short, our understanding of breathing is gradually becoming deeper. Besides the study of the common breath, the variety of types of breathing during Qigong has aroused great interest among scientists. Some breathing methods in Qigong are associated with extraordinary power. The relation between breathing and life is complicated and multifarious. Research into how we breathe, and the mystery of breath adjustment, will certainly be one of the main approaches to reveal the mystery of Qigong, or even the mystery of life.

Alteration of Breathing Forms in the Process of Rujing

Modern physiology tells us that normal breathing is lung breathing. Oxygen and carbon dioxide are exchanged in the alveoli, and then the air passes through the windpipe and bronchi and out through the mouth and nose. Physiology also has the concept of cell breathing or internal breathing. Lung breathing is also called external breathing.

All the types of breathing associated with Rujing are external breathing. Those who have reached the level of navel breathing, or body breathing, in practicing Qigong will experience internal breathing—in other words, they can feel the cells breathing. But this can only be achieved by very few Qigong masters. Most Qigong practitioners can only practice external breathing.

Modern physiology and Chinese traditional medical science both regard the lungs as the organ of respiration, but there are still some differences. Traditional Chinese medicine (TCM) believes that all blood vessels lead to the lungs. This concept coincides with modern physiology's theory of metabolism, in which blood flows through the lungs for the exchange of air. TCM also believes that the lungs are associated with the skin and hair, and the opening and closing of the pores. This explains the possibility of body breathing. Since the lungs are responsible for the opening and closing of all the pores in one's body, it is possible that they operate body breathing through those pores, not the mouth and nose. Actually, when body breathing is just developing, you experience air exchange through the pores. It seems as if you have stopped breathing through your mouth or nose and you feel the air flow in and out consistently through the pores, as if the skin is no longer a barrier but a boundless channel. Undertaking body breathing, which is impossible from the standpoint of modern physiology, is quite likely to happen from the standpoint of TCM. The various breathing forms during Rujing are more than just body breathing. The explanation of body breathing by the theory that the lungs control the skin and hair does not undermine the main role of the lungs in the respiratory system. Some breathing forms during Rujing are quite different from lung breathing, the most common being Dantian breathing. The differences we have emphasized here relate mainly to the different mode of operation—that is to say, the difference of subjective experience and manipulation.

The practitioner who has developed Dantian breathing will feel that the supporting point (where the air finally comes in and out) is the Dantian, not the lungs. Inhaling/exhaling depends on the opening and closing of the Dantian. It has nothing to do with contraction of the lungs. It seems that the lungs have stopped working and their work has been taken over by the Dantian. You feel that the windpipe extends down to the Dantian and the air flows directly and smoothly from the mouth and nose to the Dantian. Where is the Dantian? From the experience of inhaling/exhaling and the opening and closing of the Dantian, we can say that the location of the Dantian is the condensing point of the force exerted on the abdomen when it contracts inwards. It is the supporting point of breathing. Now you feel that the center of breathing is the Dantian and you feel the same way as if lung breathing.

There are other types of breathing during Rujing, such as the Baihui breath, Mingmen breath, breathing through the heels, etc. In each type the acupuncture point becomes the supporting point of breathing, and the breathing is controlled by it.

As far as the operation of breathing is concerned, Qigong regards breathing as an activity that can be varied in its form. That is to say, the control center and the passage of breathing can be changed in accordance with the condition of your body (for instance, a sensitive point in your body) and the requirements of the practice. Any part of your body is able to be the center of breathing. This seems incredible, doesn't it? Indeed, this cannot be explained or acknowledged by modern physiology. From modern physiology's point of view, all experiences of changes of the breathing center and passage are illusions and hallucinations, because there is no concrete proof of changes in the organs of respiration. As for breathing activity in Qigong, we have to acknowledge these experiences, and then carefully analyze and manipulate them. Otherwise we will not be able to practice Qigong.

As already mentioned, the different forms of breathing in Qigong have different functions. This may give us a hint that they might have certain connections with some particular physiological phenomenon beyond the scope of breathing. It may not necessarily be an illusion or hallucination. Therefore, to make some breakthrough in research, the study of the special forms of breathing during Qigong should take into consideration both the practitioner's personal experience and the biochemical and physiological mechanism behind this experience.

The Mechanism of Inhaling/Exhaling in Rujing

In the study of the mechanism of breathing in Rujing, the changes of the lungs' function in inhaling/exhaling during Rujing are the first issue to be studied by modern physiology.

The breathing in Rujing is usually deep and slow. Compared to normal daily breathing, the amount of air exchanged during each inhaling/exhaling increases dramatically, from 500 milliliters to 700 and over. However, as the frequency of breathing is far lower than in normal breathing (about 3–6 times per minute in Rujing, compared to 14–16 times per minute in everyday breathing), the total amount of air (the air exchanged per single breath frequency of breaths per minute) exchanged during Rujing is quite reduced: from the normal 8000–10,000 milliliters to 5000 milliliters or below. Under these circumstances the concentration of carbon dioxide in the blood will be very high. The increased carbon dioxide in the blood will stimulate chemical sensors in the central nervous system and the associated nerves. This will result in the asphyxiation response, to speed up the rate of breathing so as to take in more oxygen. In the process of Rujing the slow, deep breathing goes on continuously and the content of carbon dioxide in the blood is always higher, but no asphyxiation response ever occurs. This shows that the central nervous system is to some extent in a state of suppression. This will have a series of impacts on the brain and the whole body.

The respiration center is located in the medulla. During deep, slow breathing, the respiration center has a profound effect on the motor neuron clusters in the cerebrum (such as the facial nerve ganglion, hypoglossal nerve ganglion, and trigeminal nerve ganglion). Experiments show that as the concentration of carbon dioxide in the blood increases, an electrical discharge in time with the rhythm of breathing may occur in the motor muscles controlled by those nerve clusters. The discharge of electricity is synchronized with the rhythm of breathing, and affected by the depth of inhalation. The deeper one inhales, the stronger the discharge of electricity.

The function of the respiration center also affects other parts of the brain. Scientists have detected the phasic electricity discharge associated with inhaling/exhaling from neurons in the diaphragm area of the brain's brim system and the back side of the hippocampus area. It is quite likely the site of the respiration center. According to nerve activity, in the diaphragm area of the brim system there is a passage leading to the front core of the lower cerebral ganglion and bow-shaped core. The bow-shaped core has the function of excrete neural hormones. The back side of the sea horse area is associated with man's memory function. Both the diaphragm area and sea horse area are connected with emotional reactions. We can infer that the rhythmic discharge of electricity in those local nerve neurons, correlated with the activity of breathing, may influence the body's function of homeostasis. Control of breathing during Rujing may directly affect this homeostasis. In addition, the activity of the respiratory center may also affect the function of the cerebral cortex. It plays an important role in maintaining the active state and tensility of the cerebral cortex, and sustaining the degree of agitation of the brain. The breathing rhythm has been observed by EEG.

The activity of the respiratory center has a considerable impact on the autonomic nervous system. Agitation of the *inhalation* center can be transferred widely into the *sympathetic* system, while agitation of the *exhalation* center can be transferred into the *parasympathetic* system. We all know that the autonomic nervous system balances the work of many organs; it may directly affect the functions of the heart, lungs, stomach, and intestines, and also the endocrine system. For example, the movement and secretions of the stomach are controlled by the autonomic nervous system: the vagus nerve, as part of the parasympathetic system, will *stimulate* stomach movement and secretions, while the stomach nerve, which is part of the sympathetic system, will *restrain* stomach movement and secretions. Thus inhalation will reinforce stomach movement and secretions, while exhalation works vice versa. Stomach movement and secretions are directly related to digestion, so adjustment of these will actually adjust the function of digestion.

The work of the respiratory center also directly affects the sympathetic and parasympathetic nervous systems associated with the brain, heart, and blood vessels. Thus it will also affect man's heart and circulation, causing changes of heartbeat, blood pressure, etc. Control of the autonomic nervous system through breathing enables a person to promote homeostasis in organ function, making non-controllable organ function controllable. This will greatly enhance the ability to self-regulate and adapt to various environments.

Apart from the function of the respiratory center, which directly and indirectly influences the brain and body, the mechanical movement of deep, slow breathing during Rujing may also have a broader impact on the body. It is well known that the pressure inside the thoracic cavity is negative, and is lower than the air pressure outside the body, allowing one's breathing to happen smoothly. The deep, slow inhalation and exhalation will increase the variation in negative air pressure inside the chest. In the case of a natural breath, the negative air pressure from the end of the exhalation to the end of the inhalation changes from −3 to −5 and −5 to −10mm Hg. In the case of deep, slow breathing, it can reach −20 to −40mm Hg. These changes of negative air pressure will function as a pump and affect the veins in the chest. This causes the veins to dilate and increase the amount of blood flowing back to the heart, thus enhancing blood circulation. So we can say this has a direct impact on the heart and circulatory system. When you make a deep exhalation, your blood pressure may drop by 5–15mm Hg. It will recover or slightly rise when you inhale. During this time the heart can work in a massage rhythm. In addition, rhythmic changes in blood pressure, on a small scale, will result in the same rhythmic contraction of blood vessels, producing a positive adjustment of the contracting function of the blood vessels, particularly during deep, slow breathing, when the blood vessels mainly dilate.

The deep, slow movement of breathing may also enhance movement of the diaphragm. The diaphragm is located at the bottom of the chest, under the lungs. The range of its movement is about 3cm on average. In the state of Rujing, it can reach up to 9cm. The diaphragm divides the chest from the abdomen. When it moves downwards, it presses the liver, stomach, pancreas, and other organs down, and causes the abdominal wall to expand. When it moves upwards, the abdominal wall springs back, and pushes the internal organs up. This rhythmic up-and-down movement actually massages the organs in the belly. In deep, slow breathing this massage action is reinforced and strengthens the functioning of these organs. Increased secretion of stomach juices results not only from the influence of the autonomic nervous system, but also from the reinforced massage function of the diaphragm.

Deep, slow breathing will also benefit the respiratory organs and passages. It will improve the range of functioning of the lungs, adjust blood flow through the lungs, and promote the release of prostaglandin in the lungs. (This can assist in dilation of the blood vessels.) This mode of breathing also has a positive effect in coping with resistance in the airways.

We have discussed above some recent outputs in the study of breathing physiology during Rujing. This research was undertaken on some of the main features of breathing in Rujing, such as depth of breathing, slow motion, stable rhythm, etc. There are still many aspects of breathing in Rujing awaiting further study. Further explanation for the simple mechanism of changes of breathing rhythm is needed, let alone the more complicated principle concerning changes in the various breathing modes, such as Baihui breathing and Dantian breathing. The breathing rhythm in Internal Nursing Qigong is exhaling–pause–exhaling, inhaling–pause–exhaling–pause. The breathing rhythm of New Qigong Therapy is inhaling–inhaling–exhaling. The practice of those breathing modes shows that different rhythms of breathing have a medical effect on different illnesses. Yet little is known about how these breathing modes achieve such effects. Modern study of the mechanisms of breathing in Rujing has only just begun.

Breathing and Vital Energy

As far as the inner Qi is concerned, we should first explain the notion of Qi sensation. Remember, Qi is not the air we breathe, but the inner quintessence. The "feeling" of Qi refers to the feeling of this quintessence being produced, filled and spread throughout your body. Qigong masters can also sense the Qi from other human beings or from animals or plants. That awareness is also a feeling of Qi.

The feeling of Qi is closely related to the experiences we have discussed so far. There are some differences. Some experiences are caused by the inner Qi, while others do not have any direct connection with it at all. For example, the feelings of numbness or itching are often caused by the movement of Qi; the feeling of losing weight and shape is often the consequence of the inner Qi filling up and pervading the body. The illusory feelings, hallucinations, and other similar subjective experiences seen have nothing to do with the inner Qi. Generally speaking, we may say that the sensation has little connection with Qi, while the physical feeling has a considerable connection with Qi. Because the experience of inner Qi is interwoven with other feelings and experiences, it is not easy to clearly distinguish between them. And from the practical point of view, it is not necessary to make this distinction. In a narrow sense we can also regard the feeling of Qi moving along the meridians as the sense of Qi. In a broader sense, any feeling that is beneficial to Rujing and tends to lead to the realm of Ultimate Emptiness can be regarded as the sense of Qi. At the macro level, this more general, blurred definition of the sense of Qi is useful.

The generation and development of inner Qi are closely related to breathing. The relationship consists of three parts. At the initial stage of Rujing, the adjustment of breathing has a key function in the formation of inner Qi. It starts after Dantian breathing has been established. The operation of Dantian breathing is the process of transferring and exchanging inner Qi and the air one breathes. From the subjective point of view, the Qi that reaches the Dantian along with the movement of breathing is the inner Qi. The movement of Qi toward the Dantian in time with the inhaling/exhaling is like this: the Dantian closes when you inhale. The inner Qi needs to fill the Dantian. The Dantian opens when you exhale, and the inner Qi moves down and enters the Dantian. Thus, with the help of breathing, the Dantian gradually becomes filled with Qi. When it is filled to a certain extent, the Qi begins to spread out. It may run along the meridians or just meander around the body. When it moves along the meridians you may be able to feel Circulation of Qi, or the Qi may reach your afflicted organ as it spreads out. You may feel that your body is light and bouncing.

The relationship between breathing and inner Qi is pushing and being pushed. That is to say, breathing provides power for the movement and spreading of Qi. For example, when Qi is circulating in your body, it is quite likely that it will go up along the Du meridian when you inhale, and down the Ren meridian when you exhale. It cycles round like this. In the case of the inner Qi spreading around, breathing works like a pump pumping up a balloon. The balloon becomes bigger along with the movement of the pump. In a similar way, the Qi spreads around with the rhythm of breathing. Just as the filled balloon will float, when the inner Qi fills your body, you will also feel light and bouncing. You will get a feeling of loss of weight. Furthermore, when the inner Qi spreads outside your body and mixes with the Qi of the universe, your feeling of shape will also become blurred.

When you reach the higher levels of Rujing, the relationship between breathing and inner Qi becomes relatively less. This is for two reasons. For one thing, the inner Qi has already become enriched and strong. It can function independently of breathing. At the same time, the breathing becomes weaker and weaker. The air going in and out through your mouth and nose becomes imperceptible. The breathing tends to cease, let alone affect, the inner Qi.

In general, breathing promotes the generation of inner Qi and nurtures its growth. When the inner Qi becomes independent, the breathing becomes much less important. Modern physiology has conducted many studies on the process of breathing. The difference in composition between the air we inhale and the air we exhale has also been clarified.

Modern research has not yet made any significant progress in the study of the true nature of inner Qi. According to the classic theory of Qigong, it is the origin of the vigor of life, of genuine Qi and basic Qi. It is also believed to be linked with the genuine Qi of the universe. This is the ultimate significance of "returning to nature." For the ancient Chinese, man's relationship with nature is the essence of being, and entirely necessary. It is magnificent. Deepening this relationship will result in a healthy body and mind. Rujing is just one of the aids to realizing this communion. Modern psychology and physiology believe that the feeling of inner Qi occurring in the practice of Qigong is the comprehensive perception by consciousness of the mechanical changes of breathing, changes in the nerve/endocrine system caused by the work of the respiration center, and the change of the functional state of the entire body. These changes are not usually noticed, or cannot be noticed, in our everyday life. The ancient Chinese understanding of inner Qi is still a macro viewpoint. It contains some reasoning but lacks detail. Our understanding of inner Qi is just the first step. We have command of some details, but are still not quite clear about its overall essence. To find out the real meaning of inner Qi is obviously very important for the practice of Qigong and Rujing, and for the entire development of Qigong. The understanding of the basis of inner Qi will lay a sound foundation on which to build the science of Qigong.

The Mechanism of Body Adjustment

Body "adjustment" means adjusting and rearranging the posture and movement of the body during Rujing. The principles involved in terms of body adjustment focus mainly on the impact of different postures on Rujing.

The Common Postures in Rujing

There are several options for practitioners. Generally speaking any posture that is steady and natural is the right posture for Rujing. Practitioners can choose any that fulfill their needs. The most commonly used postures include standing mode, sitting mode, and lying down mode, and each has its variations.

STANDING MODE

This is the basic posture for standing Qigong. It includes variations in the position of the limbs.

1. ***Three Rings Posture (Ball-Holding Posture)***

   Standing with your feet shoulders' width apart, and pointing forwards, place the toes of both feet slightly closer to one another, with the heels a bit further apart than the toes. (This is not a very strict requirement. Sometimes you just need to have your feet parallel to one another.) The toes should slightly bend downwards, as if you want to grip the Earth. Bend your knees a little, but ensure that the knees do not extend beyond the tips of the edges of your toes. Stretch your wrists and place your bottom as if you are sitting on a high bench. Straighten your upper body. Draw in your chest a little and open your back. Hold your arms in a semi-circular shape, as if you are holding a round balloon. Drop your shoulders, lower your elbows, and keep your armpits open. Your hands should not be more than 33cm away from your body. Spread your fingers, and point the fingers of both hands towards each other with a space of 27–30cm between them. Bend all your fingers slightly and maintain a finger's-width space between all your fingers. Hold your head up straight and close your eyes. Place your tongue in a natural position. Move your lower jaw a little bit backwards. When all this is settled, relax. The "three rings" are actually the ring of the fingers and toes, the ring of the arms, and the ring of the hands.

2. ***Ball-Carrying Posture; Holding and Pressing Posture; Pulling and Embracing Posture***

All three of these postures are developed from the Three Rings Posture. They are interchangeable during practice, but you should not change position too often as it may affect the process of Rujing. The Ball-Carrying Posture is the same as the Three Rings Posture, except for the following: You raise both arms slightly and stretch them forwards. Keep your hands about 33cm away from your body, with your palms facing upward. Open your fingers, as if you are carrying a balloon in your hands. (When you start to practice the Three Rings Posture as a beginner, you may feel tired after a short time. If this happens, you can turn your arms so that your palms are facing upwards, and stretch your arms forwards. This will bring you into the Ball-Carrying Posture, to ease your fatigue.)

The requirements for Fu An Shi (Holding and Pressing Posture) are similar to the Three Rings Posture. The only difference is that when you stretch out your arms, turn your arms with your palms facing downward and the fingers open, as if you are holding the back of a chair or putting your hands on the table, or as if you are pressing your palms on the surface of water. This posture can also be used as a substitute for the Three Rings Posture when your arms feel sore. When practicing the three rings for the first time, if your arms and shoulders are sore, then you can move your arms down below the navel with your palms upwards and the fingers of both hands pointing towards each other at a distance of 30cm. Keep your hands 20cm away from your body, as if you are pulling a balloon. Make sure that you do not have your arms close to your body, but a bit away from your body, and leave some space under your armpits.

3. ***Three Enclosures Posture***

Stand with your feet one behind the other. The space between the two feet will vary according to the height of the person. So long as you can stand firmly and comfortably, the space will be right for you. Usually it is about 66cm. The toes of the front foot are pointing forwards and the toes of the back foot are turned at a 45° angle outwards from the front foot. The front leg is straightened slightly, and the back leg a little bent. Place your body weight on the two feet, so that the front one holds 30 percent of your body weight, and the back one 70 percent of your body weight. If you have your left foot in front, let your left arm and elbow bend at an angle of 135°. The elbows are raised and your left elbow is turned outward. Have your middle finger, index finger, and little finger (pinkie) bent towards your palm in the shape of a tiger's paw. Make a semi-circle with your thumb and forefinger and move the forefinger up a bit, to eye level. Put your right arm down and back, at about 8cm from your body. Position your right elbow and right arm at a 90° angle. Hold your right hand 5–8cm away from the right side of your body, as if to protect the right side of your chest. The fingers of your right hand should also be in the shape of a tiger's paw. If you have your right foot in front, just reverse all the positions mentioned above.

This posture requires you to keep your head up and your waist expanded. You should try to achieve the three-fold coordination of shoulders and pelvis, elbows and knees, and feet and hands. This posture is a bit more difficult to practice than the Three Rings Posture. I suggest you practice it only when you have mastered the Three Rings Posture. This posture is easy for those with some training in Chinese martial arts.

4. *Relaxed Posture*

This is the same as the Three Rings Posture, except that you let both arms hang down with the elbows bent slightly backwards. Place the backs of your hands on your pelvis. This posture requires little energy and lets you rest from the fatigue of practicing other variants. Hence it is called the Relaxed Posture. You can also place your hands in your jacket pockets with the thumbs on the outside. The rest is the same as for the Three Rings Posture.

SITTING MODE
This is the most common posture in Rujing. It has a number of variants. There are four types of sitting mode: Normal Sitting, Cross-Legged Sitting, Supported Sitting and Kneeling Posture (Seiza).

1. *Normal Sitting*
This is the most common posture for beginners. You sit on a bench or a wooden chair. Sit on just the front third of the bench or seat. The height of the bench should be the same as the length of your crus (lower leg). Keep your legs shoulders' width apart and level. Have your lower legs perpendicular to the ground, with your knees bent 90°. Have your feet shoulders' width apart from each other. Hold your head and waist as in the standing mode. You can let your buttocks stretch backward a little. Position your arms in the ball-carrying mode. You can also let your elbows turn outwards a little, with your palms facing downwards, and put them on the crease at the top of your legs; or you can let your arms hang down naturally and rest your hands on your thighs.

2. *Cross-Legged Sitting*
Sitting with the legs crossed is the most suitable and "official" posture for Rujing. I'll discuss it in detail. Cross-Legged Sitting consists of three types: Natural Sitting Posture, Single Cross-Legged Posture, and Double Cross-Legged Posture. In Buddhism Cross-Legged Sitting is sitting with your legs folded and crossed. It can be further divided into sitting with both legs crossed, and sitting with one leg crossed on the other. For the former there is also the so-called Conquer the Demon Posture and the Happy and Harmony Posture. In the Conquer

the Demon Posture, you place your right foot on your left leg, then place your left foot on your right leg. It is the same order with your hands. Your left hand is on top of your right hand. You have your left hand and left foot over your right hand and right foot respectively. In the Happy and Harmony Posture, you just do it the other way round.

The place where you sit could be an ordinary bed, a kang,[35] or a square bench specially designed for meditation. This square-shaped bench is usually bigger than an ordinary bench. A cushion is also needed. If you practice Qigong sitting on the ground, the cushion must be extra thick.

- *Natural Sitting Posture*
  Hold your head up; close your mouth and eyes; and relax your shoulders and elbows. Straighten up your chest a bit. The waist stretches naturally as a result. Sit with both legs crossed; it does not matter which leg is over which. Put your feet on the chair, each one under the knee of the opposite leg. Let your arms hang down. You can place your hands on your legs, or bring them together on your Dantian. You can put something under your bottom to raise it 3–5cm.

- *Single Cross-Legged Posture (Dan Pan)*
  The position of your head, upper body, and arms is the same as in the natural sitting mode. Sit with only one foot over the opposite leg—the right or left foot, according to your preference. In this posture there is only one foot on the bench.

- *Double Cross-Legged Posture (Shuang Pan)*
  Again, the position of the head, body, and arms is the same as in the natural sitting mode. Put either foot, right or left, on the opposite leg, then do the same with your other foot. Turn the soles of your feet upwards. In this posture neither foot is touching the bench. This is the posture monks use in their meditation practice.

3. **Supported Sitting**

Lean back slightly against the back of the chair or sofa. The rest of your body will be sitting in the same way as for the other variants of sitting. As your back is leaning a bit backwards, you can stretch out your feet a little. Remember to try to keep your waist stretched, in spite of the fact that you are leaning on the back of the bench. It is best to have your back leaning against the chair, not your waist. Once your waist is leaning on the back of your chair, you will not be able to stretch it straight.

4. **Kneeling Posture (Seiza)**

The Japanese always use this posture to practice Qigong. You kneel down, with both knees and the backs of your feet on the chair. As the soles of your feet are facing upward, you are naturally sitting on your feet. You may hold your hands lightly together and put them on your Dantian. Requirements for your head and body are the same as for other sitting postures.

LYING DOWN MODE

This is also a frequently adopted mode. It consists of several types of lying Posture, such as Lying on Your Back, Lying on Your Side, and Half-Lying Posture. When you practice this mode, make sure that the height of your pillow is right, and that your bed is not too soft. A mattress may not be suitable for this practice.

1. **Lying on Your Back**

This is the most common posture of the lying down mode. Lie on your back on the bed and with your head straight. Close your eyes and mouth. Naturally stretch out your limbs. You can have your legs slightly apart or close together, depending on your personal preference. Turn your feet outwards to the sides, or stretch your toes forward. Let your arms lie naturally at the sides of your body, with your palms against the sides of your legs—or you can bend your elbows and put your hands with palms down on your Dantian.

2. *Lying on Your Side*

The basic posture is lying on your side on the bed. Either side will do. The more common posture would be the right side. Slightly lower your head. Close your eyes and place your legs one on top of the other. Bend your knees naturally. The top leg (let's say the right leg) can bend a little more than the other, so as to have both feet on the bed. Stretch out your right hand and lay the palm on your pelvic bone. Bring your left hand up to your head, with the palm uppermost and the fingers together, next to your ear. You can also stretch out your left leg straight. Raise your right knee, bent at an angle of 90°, and then put it down on the bed. Now you no longer have your legs one on top of the other. The sole of your right foot should be resting against your left knee. Now reach out your right arm and place the hand on your right knee; then raise and bend your left arm, and place your left hand on your right elbow. This posture is also called the "Three Connections" mode.

3. *Half-Lying Posture*

Lie on your side with something under your body or head to hold them up, so that you are resting on the bed in a sloping position. This posture looks like half sitting and half lying. You can stretch out your legs. You can also put something under your knees to raise your crus (lower leg).

The modes we have covered are the most common and typical used in the practice of Rujing. Beginners can follow the description above for their practice. They can also make adjustments according to their own needs. Among the three adjustments in the process of Rujing, requirements for the adjustment of the body are not very strict relatively and emphasize the realm of Rujing rather than the shape and posture. Thus, for Qigong masters, posture is not something they have to consider. They can reach the state of Rujing regardless of what posture they use. For beginners it is necessary to take posture into consideration, since, after all, it will affect the process of Rujing, even though the impact of it is weaker than that of the adjustment of mind and breath.

The Postural Mechanism

As the physiological mechanism for maintaining a particular posture will vary, the different postures can have different impacts on Rujing, mainly on its depth.

In our account of the relationship between Rujing and the three adjustments, we have discussed how coordination of the muscles of your waist, legs, etc. is needed in order to maintain a standing posture; as a result it will reduce the level of your body relaxation. To prevent yourself from falling down, your mind must be alert and on guard. Your consciousness will also be intense. So the state of Rujing will certainly be affected. This is not the only impact the standing posture has on Rujing. It also affects the breathing process in Rujing. The standing posture makes abdominal breathing a little more difficult and it is relatively hard to manipulate the Qi down to the Dantian. This is because the abdominal muscles become tense and the center of gravity is higher in the standing mode. Nevertheless, the standing posture also offers some unique and significant advantages.

First of all, standing is a unique posture that distinguishes man from animal. It obviously demonstrates the power of self-control and maneuverability. From an evolutionary perspective, it is natural that we should have adopted this posture for practicing Qigong. Our biological structure is adapted for standing. In this posture the whole body can benefit from the practice. Furthermore, while standing, man is smart and decisive, and has a strong power of self-control. When we are making an important decision, we often stand up, don't we? It is relatively easy for man to adjust his mind in standing. The standing posture is not limited by space. One can practice it anywhere. This is especially convenient for office workers. In addition, in the standing posture there isn't any restriction on your body and limbs. If spontaneous movement occurs during the practice, the standing posture allows the body to move to its full capacity. This helps Circulation of Qi. Therefore, most types of Qigong aimed at stimulating spontaneous movement have adopted the standing posture.

The standing posture consumes relatively more energy. For a healthy person, it will help them to build up strength and physical fitness. It is not suitable for those who are physically weak.

As far as Rujing is concerned, the standing posture can be used as a preliminary posture for practice, as it cannot bring you into the deep level of Rujing. You can stand anywhere and any time before you practice Rujing. It can help you to lay a strong foundation for the practicing of Rujing afterwards. When you start to practice Rujing, it's better to use the sitting posture.

The sitting posture is, first of all, very stable. Whatever type of sitting posture it is, you do not need to be on guard against the possibility of falling over. Your legs will not need to support your body, and the level of relaxation will be much better than in the standing posture. Besides, in the sitting posture your center of gravity is lower and your abdominal muscles are relaxed, so it is easy to practice abdominal breathing, and easy for the Qi to move down. Apart from these advantages, which all the types of sitting posture have, the Cross-Legged Posture has another unique advantage. In this posture you have your legs crossed and your feet close to the root of your thighs. The whole leg is folded tightly. The body becomes compact at the base, and loose at the top, which is just the opposite of the standing posture. This is very beneficial to enable the Qi to find its way towards the Dantian. And at the same time, since the legs and buttocks are jointly supporting your body weight, a stable triangle is formed on which the whole body can stand firmly. In this posture your upper body is held a little forward. This helps you to keep your upper body straight and to tuck your jaw in a little. It keeps the spine fully stretched, which is very significant during the process of Rujing.

It is known in the science of TCM that the Du meridian goes along the midline of your back. Thus the effect of stretching the spine is to expand the Du meridian, which controls all the routes of the Yang element and is also called the "sea of the routes of Yang" in Chinese medicine. Flow along the Du meridian has a direct impact on the many routes of Yang related to the feet and hands. Although Rujing does not pursue the sense of Qi circulating around the body, or even notice it, the circulation of Qi along the meridians exists objectively. The extension and stretching of the spine is taken into consideration by many types of Qigong. Some of these may require a movement of your spinal column, one vertebra at a time, before practicing Rujing, so that flow through the Du meridian will be easy. The Cross-Legged Posture naturally provides a stable base, compactness of the lower body, and a straight, relaxed upper body, which has a positive impact on the activity of consciousness. Since the Qi can move down and the weight point is lower, it comes naturally to let your consciousness concentrate on the Dantian. It helps to exclude other thoughts and reach the state of Rujing easily.

Among the cross-legged postures, the one with both your feet crossed is the best.

This posture is rather difficult to master. Along with the increasing pace of modern life, people are less accustomed to lotus sitting. This is more obvious among city dwellers, who are often less accustomed to taking exercise in the course of their daily life, with consequences for the suppleness of their joints. One cannot learn the Double Cross-Legged Posture quickly. It's better to start from the nature posture, then the single leg mode, and finally the fully crossed mode. For an adult who does not have the habit of sitting with crossed legs, it may take several years to learn. At the beginning, he may even find it difficult to learn the natural type. The habit of sitting with the legs crossed probably disappeared with the invention of chairs and benches. If we did not have the "interference" of those inventions, if everyone were just used to sitting on the ground with their legs crossed, it would be easy and convenient to sit that way.

The kneeling position, to some extent, has the same advantage as lotus sitting. It is not as stable as lotus sitting. The crus (lower leg) will have to support a good deal of pressure from the body, as the buttocks are resting on the soles of the feet. It is not easy to be fully relaxed. The main reason why most people do not like using this posture is the difference in culture and habit. The Japanese are used to kneeling, so when they can choose between lotus sitting and kneeling, they choose the latter. Apart from those cultural factors, another reason for choosing the kneeling position is that it is easier to get up from than the lotus position. In our everyday life we constantly have to be standing and sitting. So of course we like to choose the way that is the most convenient.

Plain sitting is quite close to the standing posture, except for those aspects such as relaxed legs, lower weight point, and stability. The disadvantage of this posture is that the upper body is likely to be leaning backward. This will be no good for stretching the spine. Therefore, one is required not to sit on the full area of the chair seat but on one third of it, with the buttocks stretched backwards so that the upper body naturally comes forward a bit to compensate for the defects of the plain sitting posture.

Supported sitting is designed in particular for those who are physically very weak or can only lie in bed. Other people are advised not to use this posture, or to use it only as a supplementary aid before practicing Rujing. The good part of the Supported Sitting Posture is that it enables one to practice abdominal breathing and lets the Qi move down to the Dantian easily. Of course, your body is also relaxed, but you might become too relaxed.

The total energy consumed in the sitting posture is certainly less than in the standing posture. Therefore it is good for lengthy practice. It is impossible to practice in the standing posture for the whole night, or even several days or months, which it is possible to do in the sitting posture.

The lying down posture is perhaps the most stable, as the body has already "fallen down." It is also the most relaxed, and the limbs may even be very loose. In this posture abdominal breathing comes naturally. When someone is lying down, natural breathing is usually the abdominal breathing mode. In the side-lying posture the abdominal muscles are relaxed and this is very good for abdominal breathing. The biggest drawback with the lying down posture is that it makes the adjustment of mind difficult. In this posture, one may be carried away by various thoughts, or fall asleep. It is too easy to be mentally undisciplined and indulge in fantasy. All these are harmful to the process of Rujing. Falling asleep may not be bad for your body, but it is far from the practice of Qigong. It is a totally different state compared to the state of Rujing. To avoid these pitfalls, one needs to maintain a certain concentration, mentally and physically, and be relaxed but not loose. Of course, if you don't intend to use the lying down posture as the regular posture for practice, but just to clear your mind and relax before you fall asleep, you should feel free to use it.

The second type, the side-lying posture, has a certain medical effect, since the hands, knees, and feet are all connected with acupuncture points. It is suitable for patients who are lacking in vital energy and are weak.

Now we have discussed the impact of various postures on the process of Rujing. Generally speaking, the sitting posture, especially the Cross-Legged Posture, is the most suitable posture for Rujing. The standing posture and lying down posture can be used as preliminary postures. For any individual practitioner, there are other factors to take into consideration in the choice of posture. This will be dealt with in Chapter 6, "Rujing and Its Components."

Chapter 4

The Benefits of Practicing Rujing

The realm of Rujing is wonderful. Indulging in this world of Rujing is a superb yet not luxurious delight. How does this experience affect one's body and mind? This chapter is going to discuss the benefits and advantages of Rujing.

Will Rujing cause any negative side effects? If it is properly carried out and if you follow your instinct in the rule required by the practice, there will be no such side effects. Negative effects experienced in Rujing are all due to violation of the principle of "following nature" and flawed practice, and are therefore not side effects of Rujing. I'll discuss this later, in Chapter 7. In this chapter I will talk mainly about the positive effects of Rujing—as the chapter title states: the benefits of Rujing. There are many anecdotes or legends, ancient and modern, demonstrating the magic effects of Rujing. All of them are related to Qigong, regardless of their narrative variants: being cured of illness, building up a strong body and mind, or becoming a god. To summarize, Rujing has four basic benefits: curing disease, improving health, cultivating one's latent potential, and understanding the universe.

Curing Disease and Illness

For beginners of Qigong who have a particular illness, the first benefit they can gain from practicing Qigong is to cure their disease. Within the Chinese medical tradition, the final goal of any medical therapy, medicine, operation, and injection, no matter what it is, is to mobilize and strengthen patients' capacity for self-recovery and enable them to resist and defeat the illness. In TCM the slogan "Aid the positive, wipe out the negative" expresses this concept. Life has the capacity for self-preservation. If it is fully cultivated and mobilized, it will help one to recover from illness much sooner. Qigong therapy does not rely on medicine, surgery, and other means from outside of one's body. It relies on the patient's inner ability to overcome the illness. In general, this power does not work to its full potential, due to the influence of various factors. Therefore, it is to some extent a "potentiality." Qigong will certainly mobilize this power so that it can function to its full capacity. Rujing is one of the most important methods for achieving this goal. In the state of Rujing, stimuli from the outside world will be minimized as one concentrates on the inner world, and the best place for practice is usually somewhere quiet and clean. The subjective consciousness also reduces its impact on the individual, as one tries to exclude distracting thoughts and aims at achieving the Ultimate Emptiness. The original, natural state within the body begins to increase and enable one to resist the invasion of disease, as the body has been kept away from internal and external interference. Man's power of recovery from illness is just the demonstration of the natural state fighting against the illness.

The mechanism of Rujing as a medical treatment is quite different from that of regular medical treatment. It is effective not just for one particular disease. It has an effect on many diseases, even those caused by contradictory factors such as high blood pressure and low blood pressure, diabetes and low blood sugar, etc. Modern medical science has a particular interest in medicine that has a special effect on a particular disease. Once the medicine is taken, the illness is cured. For any particular disease, if a special medicine is invented, there will be no difficulty in curing that disease. Guided by this concept, modern medical science has invented many medicines that turn out to have a special effect on particular diseases—for example, penicillin, quinine, etc. Yet that effective medicine is still not sufficient to meet man's needs in fighting against all kinds of diseases that are constantly changing and coming out in new forms.

If we regard Rujing as a kind of medicine, then not only is it a medicine for multiple diseases, but also its effectiveness depends on success in "taking" the medicine. That is to say, it depends on success in getting into the state of Rujing, and on how skillful you are in practicing Rujing. This is quite different from taking pills. To take the medicine of Rujing, one needs to take it by producing it.

Why is Rujing effective in curing many diseases, even those with opposite physiological mechanisms? This is because Rujing provides a comprehensive, integrative adjustment of the whole body, unlike the conventional approach, which only focuses on the parts that have been affected. Rujing improves the affected part by adjusting the whole body. That's why Qigong is regarded as a "whole-body therapy."

This whole-body therapy consists of both psychological and physiological treatments, and they are also interrelated. A comprehensive psychological adjustment of the patient is the vital and main factor for the effectiveness of Rujing. As man is a unified organism, psychological improvements certainly have a positive effect on his physiological functioning and state. Thus the patient receives treatment for both mind and body. This aspect of Rujing may just fill the gap in modern medical treatment. Current medical science still sees diseases in terms of organic or functional changes in particular organs. It still regards illness as something purely physiological, and neglects the psychological changes it brings for the patient. In fact, many illnesses are related to psychological factors, causal or consequential. Whatever they are, they are part of the illness in terms of the symptoms or process. No patient will be happy with his illness. The illness makes the patient depressed. This depression is the least of the patient's psychological symptoms, let alone other negative feelings associated with the discomfort the illness causes in the body, and the psychological problems caused by the depressive emotion and severe mental pressure.

Since all illnesses contain certain psychological problems, the solving of these problems is part of the treatment. For the most part, Rujing as a means of treatment takes the solving of those problems as its starting point. The state of Rujing requires the practitioner to maintain a relaxed and pleasant mood. This mood has a direct healing effect on many psychological problems. It turns anxiety into peace, and irritation into calmness. It reduces or eliminates the symptoms of discomfort, such as soreness, numbness, swelling, and pain. It can also relieve mental pressure. It will enable the patient to build up his confidence in recovery and deal with the illness in a straightforward manner. A good psychological mood will also affect the patient physiologically, and will improve the functioning of the nervous system and other internal systems. It will enhance the immune system. The ability to resist illness will be strengthened, and the power of self-recovery will be at its highest level. Some scientists in the former USSR believed that the brain can produce millions of nerve peptides. These endocrine products transport messages between the two brain hemispheres and to the different parts of the body so as to affect the endocrine glands and organs in the body and thus carry out the brain's instructions. This is the process during which the psychological elements result in physiological changes.

This factor is the reason why Rujing as a medical therapy has its own particular requirements. One of the requirements is that the user must find out if this therapy is suitable for him. Although Rujing can cure many diseases, its effectiveness has a particular range and is more applicable to certain diseases than others. Unlike drugs and medicines, the range of application is limited by factors such as the patient's physical condition, profession, living environment, etc. rather than the kind of illnesses.

One's physical constitution includes the type and condition of his body. No matter what disease one has, if one is constitutionally very weak, Rujing is a suitable form of help. For certain diseases it might be better for the patient to choose an active Qigong. If the patient has to stay in bed, he can only choose still Qigong. All still Qigong requires Rujing to some extent. For instance, if one is diagnosed with cancer, the best choice is "New Qigong," "Crane Qigong," "Wild Goose Qigong," and other types of active Qigong. Many patients may not be able to practice them at the very beginning, as they are still physically too weak. They need to restore their energy by practicing Rujing. They can practice one of the active Qigong later, when they have the strength to walk again. Of course, if the patient's condition is good at the very beginning, he can start with active Qigong. Usually it requires the practice of both active and inactive Qigong. One should also consider practicing and resting in turn. It is more difficult to judge the type of one's physical condition than the strength of one's physical condition. According to traditional Chinese medicine, assessment of one's health constitution is an overall evaluation of the balance and contrast between Yin and Yang in one's body.

There are chapters in *The Medical Canon of the Yellow Emperor*[36] about physical conditions. These were classified into 25 types in the theory of Yin Yang Wu Xin (the Five Elements and their relationships: Metal, Wood, Water, Fire, and Earth). It is very helpful for selecting the right Qigong for someone if one knows the type that he belongs to. For instance, the book states that if one belongs to Wood, he looks dark, has a small head, long face, broad shoulders, straight back, and small hands and feet, likes money, works hard but is not strong, and has many things to take care of. A Fire man looks red, has a small head with a triangular jaw, with shoulders and back well built and small hands and feet, is quick-tempered, and bounces while walking. He looks fat around the shoulders and back, does not think much about money, is mistrustful, likes to worry, is smart but likes to annoy people, and may die early. According to these descriptions, the Wood man tends to be quiet and mild, which is good for practicing Rujing. The Fire man may not be able to calm down and be patient enough to practice Rujing. He's better off choosing active Qigong to start with. Active Qigong seeks quietness through activity. After practicing for some time, he may develop a peaceful and quiet mind and find it easier to practice Rujing. If he tries Rujing at the very beginning, he may not be able to get rid of all the distracting thoughts, his emotion state will not be stabilized, and he will not achieve satisfactory results.

In general, the Wood man has a balanced Yin and Yang. The Fire man usually has a strong Yang. Yang is related to activity, and Yin is related to inactivity. So the Wood man will find it easy to enter the state of peace. In addition, be aware also that the man in whom Yin prevails tends to be inactive. Although he can easily enter the state of Rujing, it is not suitable for him just to practice Rujing. He needs to do some active Qigong. Otherwise, there might be some negative effects and things could even go wrong. A healthy person should have a balanced Yin and Yang. Moreover, the psychological and physiological changes reflected in different age groups are another factor. Adults and the elderly have a strong power of self-control and are not rigid. Rujing is quite suitable for them. Active Qigong is less suitable for children and adolescents. They are active and not good at self-control. It may be hard for them to practice Rujing.

To consider someone's physical condition when deciding whether Rujing is suitable for them to practice is to teach on the basis of different personalities. One can also choose the type of Qigong depending on the illness. Qigong therapy is in fact a whole-body therapy. Every type of Qigong can treat many different diseases. There is probably no type of Qigong that is only good for one type of disease. At the same time, each Qigong may have its own characteristics and effectiveness for treating particular kinds of diseases.

This way of selecting a suitable Qigong is worth considering, but it is only for general guidance. We should not take it to the extreme. From the clinical perspective, Internal Nursing Qigong and Strengthening Qigong are known to be good for diseases of the digestive system. Void and Bright Qigong, which focuses on Rujing, is another choice. For patients with high blood pressure, glaucoma, and tonsillitis, some types of relaxed Qigong will be good choices. I have earlier recommended some types of Qigong for patients with cancer. Rujing is good for patients with gynecological diseases and diseases of old age.

The patient's profession and living and working environment are other factors in the selection of Qigong. Sedentary workers should choose active Qigong, while those whose work involves more action could practice Rujing. This can help one to become more interested in practicing Qigong, and maintain a good balance of Yin and Yang. As far as living conditions are concerned, the size of accommodation has a remarkable effect on Rujing. Many families' living conditions are quite limited and not spacious. When the whole family is living in only one room, it is certainly not good for practicing Rujing. Family members' reactions will become an annoying distraction for the practitioner.

Season is another factor to take into consideration. In spring and summer the Yang element is rising, so it is good for practicing active Qigong. In autumn and winter the Yin element prevails, so it is good for practicing Rujing. This matches the saying in *The Medical Canon of the Yellow Emperor*, which states that spring and summer bring about Yang and autumn and winter bring about Yin.

To summarize, whether or not to choose Rujing as your main therapy depends on a thorough consideration of all factors, including your physical condition, time, illness, location, etc.

The second requirement is that you should not be always thinking about your illness, pondering about what kind of disease you have, or which part of your body is afflicted. This can only do you harm. We have mentioned that Rujing mobilizes your power of self-recovery to cure your disease. The life force is "smart." It knows where the illness is, and how to deal with it. It does not need any guidance from one's subjective consciousness. If you keep thinking about your illness, you are doing two harms to yourself. First, you will not be able to reach the deep level of Rujing, as you have not excluded all other thoughts. You will not be able to enter the state of Ultimate Tranquillity. Second, the practice of Qigong requires you to direct the Qi with the guidance of consciousness. The process of consciousness has a great impact on the circulation of inner Qi. If you are always thinking about the afflicted part of your body, you are actually guiding the Qi with your consciousness to that part; the Qi will remain at that part and be unable to move smoothly. If you do this again and again, you will actually strengthen the illness instead of curing it. Rujing as a medical treatment takes the approach of affecting the object by not working on it subjectively. You should not worry and obsess about it. Stop all the active interference to create favorable conditions that will let your innate powers work.

The third requirement is never to take Rujing as the sole treatment for your illness. You should also apply other treatments according to your actual condition. For instance, active Qigong should be combined with still Qigong. Every day you should practice both. Medicine and other means of medical treatment should be used if the illness gets serious. If you have been taking medication, you can cut down the amount of pills you are taking when you take up Rujing therapy. You should never stop your medication all at once. Qigong therapy takes time to cure your illness. It does not have an immediate effect on your disease.

Rujing has a good level of medical effectiveness on many diseases. Yet it does not work on all diseases, nor can it cure disease in a short period of time. The effectiveness of this therapy in terms of speed and visibility is related to one's success in entering the Rujing state and one's power of self-recovery. An old Chinese saying goes that a doctor cures your illness but does not necessarily save your life. This maxim has meaning in it. Whatever therapy one has, it all comes down to the mobilizing of one's own life force to resist disease. Therefore, the final result of the treatment depends on the vitality of one's life. Some patients with a serious illness may find Rujing therapy quite effective because they are physically strong and vigorous, while other patients who are not seriously ill may find Rujing therapy does not work for them because they are physically weak and lack vitality.

It is not only Rujing therapy that needs vitality in patients, but also other medical treatments and medicines. The external elements affect the object only with the help of its internal elements. No medicine will work, not even the most powerful one, if the patient is too weak to use it. This is perhaps why a doctor can cure your illness but not necessarily save your life.

Staying Healthy

For patients, Rujing is regarded as a medical therapy. For healthy people, the benefit of practicing Rujing is maintaining good health, and the improvement in your health will slow down the process of aging and extend your life.

Adjusting Body and Mind

Rujing as a means to improve your state of health will also achieve this goal by mobilizing your life force and a thorough, integrative adjustment of your body and mind, just as it does in coping with illness. It starts from a direct psychological adjustment which gradually leads to a physiological change in your body.

If we say that in the case of curing illness the psychological adjustment achieved through Rujing focuses mainly on overcoming worries, loneliness, and other negative emotions, releasing pain and other uncomfortable feelings, throwing off mental pressure, and setting up the right attitude towards your illness—that is to say, working on the level of overcoming psychological barriers—then psychological adjustment goes far beyond this level when Rujing is used to improve health rather than to cure a particular disease. It works at the level of adjusting human essence and drives at a more advanced level. Thus it has a profound impact on one's personality.

What are these adjustments on human essence and drives? The ancient Chinese said that "One will not seek sexual fulfillment when he is full of Yin. One will not feel hungry when his Yang is full. One will not feel sleepy when he is full of energy." Once you reach the higher level of Rujing, you will naturally feel full of life, energy, and Qi, and you will be able to eat less, sleep less, and regulate your sexual life.

The current study of psychology, physiology, and medicine is still unable to provide us with a scientific explanation of this effect of Rujing. I can only comment on the phenomenon *per se*. As for the effect on one's eating habits, not only can it reduce the amount of food a person consumes, it may also happen that they enter the state of BiGu (stops taking any food and drink). There are many reports on this, as I mentioned earlier in the book. The state of BiGu may last from several days to 200–300 days.

Those who have good mastery of Rujing often sleep less. They often replace their regular sleeping hours with Rujing. Around midnight (23:00pm to 1:00am) is a good time for practicing Rujing. Generally speaking, people who practice Rujing always continue past midnight and finish by 1:00am or 2:00am. It will soon be dawn by the time they have had three to four hours' sleep. They get up as soon as it is light outside, never lying in bed once they are awake. They do this year after year, not sleeping much, yet are very alert and full of energy, and never feel sleepy during the daytime. They have a high level of sleep efficiency, seldom dreaming, not even turning over in their sleep. As for their sexual life, many of them do not have sex, as they are monks. Of course, many Qigong masters get married, but their sexual appetite is controlled and they have intercourse less frequently. Buddhism requires a Ju She (a religious person who does not live in a temple) to control and restrict their sexual life when their children are grown up. Once their children are married, they should stop having sex with their wives.

Those who have little idea about Qigong will find this hard to understand. They assume that it must be very difficult and painful to control and forbid human drives. When they see monks in the woods, far away from society, sitting all day long, eating simple meals, wearing plain clothes, having no money while they are alive, and leaving behind only a heap of earth when they die, they suppose this life to be boring and dull. They don't know that, for Qigong masters, living away from society is their choice for peacefulness. They have found an infinite world in their isolation. They eat simple meals because they find rich food disgusting. They may even feel sick at the smell of meat and fish. They do not lie down but rather sit, because they are not sleepy. They do not want to sleep, and are afraid of going blind if they sleep too much. They are not forced to live like this, and they do it voluntarily. They feel a psychological and physical need to do so. For them, living in this way is so natural that they would suffer if they did not do so. In general, their desires and drives have changed, compared to those of ordinary people. The advanced level of Rujing dissolves that ordinary desire and drive. It brings to you a superior happiness, super-pleasure, and even a feeling of returning to your eternal home. It is in this sense that we no longer regard those Qigong masters as ordinary people but as saints and divines.

This change in man's essential needs for food, rest, and sex will certainly have an effect on one's personality and attitude towards life and society. Monks who have practiced Qigong all their lives do not think much of materialism, power and prestige, secular joy, sorrow, parting and reunion, and not even death. Their so-called "having seen through the secular world" is just this attitude to life. Doubtless, the monks' attitude to life is greatly influenced by the doctrine of Buddhism, independent of the practice of Qigong. As religion has a close connection with Qigong, it certainly has a strong influence on one's outlook on the world and life. It is not a coincidence that monks choose to sit in meditation for self-fulfillment. It is actually the practice of Qigong within religious clothing.

Is it a good thing to rearrange man's essence and drives, and even one's personality? Let's look at this from a position diametrically opposite to the normal point of view. We should realize that man's various needs and desires provide the energy for social and economic development. In a certain sense, it is man's ever-expanding desire that has created our glorious civilization. As man was not satisfied with primitive forms of agriculture, he invented the plow, hoe, and sickle, and later even the tractor and combine harvester. When man no longer enjoyed eating raw food, he started to study cookery, which has resulted in the luxurious feasts we have today. All that modern society offers is directed to satisfying man's needs and desires. However, these needs and desires are endless. The satisfaction of one demand will lead to another. This bottomless pit of desire can never be filled. Man's desires can never be completely satisfied; and this urges man to create and to invent, which actually promotes the development of society. Yet everything has its negative side. The infinite expansion of man's desire has led us to destroy the ecological balance of nature, which in turn threatens human existence. Environmental pollution, population explosion, AIDS —none of these global catastrophes is unrelated to man's ever-swelling desire and lust. As for an individual, his overrated desire will cost him tension in his relationships with others. If there is a conflict of interests between two nations, war may be the outcome.

All of this tells us that man must control his desires. Otherwise, he is destroying himself. Modern society is inadequate if it exists only to satisfy man's desire and lust. Man's desire can only be restrained by the powers of the external world and by law, moral standards, and education. But this is still passive, and depends on complete or partial reinforcement from the external world. Qigong functions differently. It does not force anyone to give up their needs and desires. It makes you do it voluntarily. Thus it has a unique value and effectiveness in the control of man's desire and the forging of morality. No wonder the ancient Chinese all liked to do Qigong as a means of forming one's character, and admired its moral values. Confucianism, which had a strong influence in the feudal society of ancient China, always regarded Qigong and Rujing as the means of tempering one's body and preserving one's morality.

In talking about restraint of our desires, I am not asking you to become a Puritan. I do not want to see lots of people leaving their homes and hiding in the woods or trampling around. That would be going too far. Without those desires and lusts, mankind would lose its power of creativity, and society would not move forwards. Throughout history we can see that in Eastern cultures religion seems not to contribute much to social productivity. This may be due to its philosophy of indifference to society, and the expectation of reincarnation. A healthy mind keeps desires in proportion, empowering us to develop and seek for what is better, and living in harmony with nature and the environment at the same time. The World Health Organization states in its charter that "Healthy does not only refer to a man as physically strong and not struck by illness but also to a state of physical, psychological and social perfection of man." That is to say that a healthy person is one who is not sick, but is also a physically and psychologically well human being with the ability to adapt to society. What we want to achieve through Rujing precisely matches these requirements.

If we compare Qigong and Rujing with modern sports, it is quite amusing. The healthy body one obtains through the practice of

Qigong is quite different from that of the sportsman in appearance. We can all recall the ideal gymnasts who look strong and heavy, with bulky, cast-iron muscles. The Qigong masters, on the contrary, look like thin, weak scholars or elders, but their eyes are shining, they walk lightly and springily, and their voices ring like a bell when they speak. Not many outstanding sportsmen have lived a long life, but the monks who practice Qigong have a record of longevity. This shows that the two are quite different in terms of training methodology, content, and the theory that guides their training and practice. To put it simply, Qigong and Rujing aim at the practice and training of the inner Qi, while modern sports aim at the development of one's physical body and skill. Which is better? It is hard to say. They should be mutually complementary; and they can be. Most of the masters of Chinese martial arts are trained in both ways. There is a saying among them: "You will achieve nothing if you only practice your skill in fist fighting without practicing the inner Qi." They all know the importance of practicing both. You may also be wondering about the advice I gave earlier in the book about doing active Qigong alongside still Qigong. Active Qigong is also different from modern sports, despite many similarities.

From the difference between Qigong and modern sports we can see that Qigong is not only a unique method for improving health by means of psycho-adjustments, but also an incomparable way of maintaining one's physical balance. It shows us that being healthy does not necessarily mean having a big, well-built body. One should not be judged by appearance only. This is also true for the practitioners of Qigong.

Delaying the Aging Process

Health is always associated with longevity. If we talk about improving one's health without mentioning the issue of longevity, the listener will feel the lecture is incomplete. Many lovers of Rujing are willing to spend a lifetime practicing. Yet it is not easy to give a clear and thorough explanation of the matter. It is still a controversial question, whether or not Rujing and other types of Qigong will actually make one live longer. From the historical archives there are many records of those who lived a long life after practicing Qigong. Peng Zhu (a legendary figure) lived for 800 years. This is perhaps nonsense. But the doctor and Qigong master Sun Simiao of the Tang dynasty lived to 101. HuaTuo, the creator of WuQingXi (a type of Qigong imitating the action of five animals), lived to over 90. Their birth and death dates can be checked in the archives. Their life was really quite long, even by today's standards.

They all lived 1000–2000 years ago, when living standards were far lower than today. It is likely due to the practice of Qigong that they lived such long lives. They must have been good at Qigong and health care. In modern and contemporary times, there have also been many Qigong practitioners who have lived long lives. For instance, the so-called "world monk," a Japanese national, lived to the age of 97. There are also reports of Qigong practitioners who lived shorter lives. There are reports of some well-known practitioners, including monks and Taoists, who did not live long lives. Many of them died in their 60s or 70s. So if anyone is suspicious about Qigong's effect on longevity, I should say that their suspicions are not unfounded. There are fewer convincing outcomes of the systematic, scientific study of Qigong's effect on life expectancy. Generally speaking there are long-lived Qigong masters and short-lived ones as well. There is no sound evidence to show that the long-lived masters owed their longevity to Qigong. Yet from the research, we can say that Qigong tends to improve one's life expectancy.

If we are not sure about the effect of Qigong on life expectancy in terms of quantity, we can be sure that it does help to maintain quality of life. The words "YiShou" and "YanNian" are each formed from two words: Yi Shou (help to live a longer life) and Yan Nian (extend your life and delay aging). Originally both words had the connotation of extending one's life. In order to explain Qigong's effect on life expectancy in terms of quantity and quality, we need to reinterpret the word "YiShou" as "good for improving the quality of life." Therefore, the purpose of practicing Qigong is not merely to live longer but, more important, to gain a better quality of life. Some articles have stated that Qigong can resist or delay the process of aging. This is a suitable explanation, since it covers both life expectancy and quality of life.

Many people who practice Qigong, no matter what type of Qigong they have chosen, do not seem to have lived long lives. They have died at about 70 or 80 years old. If we examine the quality of their lives we can see that they have successfully resisted the aging process, as they have always demonstrated vigor and enthusiasm. They are younger among their peers in the aged population. Though they are 70 or 80 years old, they maintain the vigor of those 20 or 40 years younger than them. By the age of 70 or 80, those who do not practice Qigong often show symptoms of aging, such as loss of hair and teeth, a bent or humped back, and weak knees. By contrast, Qigong practitioners usually look much younger, having the face of a child, with their original hair colour and excellent mobility. As one's physical condition affects one's psychological mood and vice versa, those who are old and physically weak can easily display a negative, depressed attitude towards life, and be full of complaints. Older people who are healthy will turn out to be optimistic, ambitious, and enthusiastic.

Man does not live for the sake of living. He must work and do something interesting. He should be able to enjoy happiness in life. So quality of life is no less important than life expectancy. For seniors who are over 70, the quality of life is even more important. Many seniors who are physically and mentally weak would rather die than lead a lifeless existence, waiting for their last moment. Life for them is more suffering than pleasure. If Qigong can help them to obtain sufficient vigor to be happy for the rest of their time, isn't that wonderful, even if it doesn't necessarily extend their lives?

It has been proved by many seniors that Qigong does have an immediate positive effect on quality of life. A well-known Qigong master once declared that as long as he kept practicing Qigong, his eyesight was never blurred and his hearing was sharp. He would feel very energetic and full of strength. If he stopped practicing for only three days, his eyesight would get worse, and so would his hearing ability. He was only able to hear you when you shouted at him. He would also feel lazy and not want to move. His experience shows that practicing Qigong makes a real difference. Do it, and you will be full of life; do not do it, and you will be indolent and lack vitality.

Life expectancy is one of the issues that people are most concerned about. Everybody wishes to live a longer and better life. It is a major concern for people all over the world, and an issue waiting year after year to be solved. From the findings of research on Qigong, we can already see that Rujing has a great deal to offer.

Cultivating Your Latent Potential

Cultivating one's latent potential or preparing to develop it is one of the benefits of practicing Rujing. "Latent potential" refers to psychic power or extraordinary power. This is mostly the concern of young practitioners of Qigong. Unlike the elderly, who tend to relate Qigong to longevity, the young definitely hope Qigong will bring out and develop their psychic powers, such as clairvoyance, psychokinesis, etc., so that they will become a kind of superman.

The effect of Rujing in developing one's psychic power varies from person to person, due to variation in people's natural gifts. Some individuals have the "HuiGen" (wisdom root), an innate gift of wisdom and intuition. Once they enter the state of Rujing, certain psychic powers may manifest themselves automatically. The commonest one is clairvoyance. One is able to see his own or another's organs or skeleton with his naked eyes. The image might be blurred and vague to begin with and become increasingly clear along with an increase in one's Qigong power. Others may show signs of the possible development of psychokinesis. For instance, a man who had been practicing standing Qigong found that light objects around him would move or some slight sounds could be heard, such as the sound of a waving curtain or tablecloth, or a clicking sound like tables and chairs moving.

In general these phenomena are still at their preliminary stage. They are far from being a stable, controllable power. Fully developed psychic power cannot be generated by practicing Rujing alone. It requires other special training.

For the majority, Rujing is only the preparation for the cultivation of psychic power. At this stage, "magic power" may not yet emerge, but this is still a vital period for the development of psychic power. At this stage the practitioner's sensitivity to Qi will be raised dramatically as he focuses on the adjustment of his inner environment, directing his vision and hearing back into his internal world. It is possible that some part of the body where the potential psychic power might develop will respond in one way or another. For instance, the area around TianMu[37] (an acupuncture point between the brows) may become tight and swollen, and even a bit painful. Even though the clairvoyant power has not yet appeared, the swelling and painful response from the TianMu point suggests the possibility that it will develop.

There are many sensitive points on our body. One must pay particular attention to these sensitive parts, which are most likely to develop psychic power later. Clairvoyance may not necessarily develop at TianMu. We have reports of people who are able to identify Chinese characters with their ear, foot, or palm. Qigong places great emphasis on intuition. It means one should be sensitive to changes in anything inside or outside the body. The more sensitive you are, the better understanding you will have. Of course, being sensitive is only the beginning. Rujing creates a better environment for you to refine your sensitivity and your ability to identify sensitive points quickly. It all depends on whether or not you are good at finding and pinpointing them. Except for those who are born with a psychic power, most of us have to experience the process of developing psychic power, from zero power to final acquisition. The turning point is usually the time when the sensitivity in part of your body improves dramatically; therefore, being alert to the slightest change in your body at any time is an important step for developing and stimulating psychic power.

Rujing is a vital step in the development of one's latent powers. Practitioners who wish to develop psychic power should look for an experienced Qigong master as a guide at this stage. At the initial stage when psychic power is being stimulated, it may be very vague.

It may appear and disappear, and be difficult to identify. But this is the critical moment. If you misinterpret the evidence, you might give up practicing further to develop it, and consequently either get no results or keep subjectively chasing after something non-existent, with consequent side effects. At this stage an experienced master's guidance will help you to settle the matter. What if you cannot find a master when you reach this stage in your practice? Generally speaking, you should not give up easily. Remember, once you give up, the power will never come back. You should not subjectively seek after it, either. Just let it be as it is and observe it for a period of time. No decision should be made until you can identify it.

The practice of Qigong is closely associated with latent potential. It is an effective, scientific means of cultivating man's latent potential; yet it is not the only means. Many people with extraordinary power actually obtained it at birth, not through practicing Qigong. For example, a well-known Chinese army doctor has clairvoyant power. She can break a steel needle and kill a goldfish just by staring at it. She was born with this power, which was discovered later in life. Even the extraordinary power one develops after birth may be obtained by other means than Qigong. One may acquire extraordinary power after being struck by lightning, or it develops after an illness. Someone may wake up in the morning and find that the world around them has changed a bit—extraordinary power has developed. All in all, nature provides the opportunity for the development of latent potential. In addition, there are various approaches in Qigong for cultivating it. Rujing is only one of them. There is a report of an experimental training in which children were guided to read words by ear or fingers with the help of Qi emitted by a Qigong master. In one case, 40 percent of the children were reported as being able to develop this power. According to the report, this method is most effective for children aged 6–12. The older one is, the less effective the method will be. Yet there are also examples of middle-aged people who have developed the same power by this method. Some experiments concluded that girls are able to cultivate it more easily than boys. This is perhaps due to the fact that girls are more sensitive than boys.

Now let's talk about the categories of extraordinary power. There are generally two categories, that is, clairvoyance and psychokinesis, in parapsychology terms. Clairvoyance includes all non-visual powers of "seeing" events in space and time. Psychokinesis includes all the powers of altering the state of objects by thought and consciousness, without actually touching them, such as breaking the stem of a flower, moving an object, clearing away clouds, etc. The forms of extraordinary power vary, but whatever they are, they belong to the two above-mentioned classes. With this understanding of extraordinary power, the notion of extraordinary power becomes much more clearer. It is slightly different from the notion of latent potential. "Extraordinary power" refers to the paranormal aspect of someone's latent potential, but latent potential also includes uncultivated ordinary powers such as the power of recovery from illness, the power of memory, etc.

Understanding the Universe

Understanding the world is one of the provinces of Rujing, as I have mentioned in Chapter 2. It will lead you to a profound perception of the universe because it touches on the basic elements and the origin of the universe. The knowledge one acquires during Rujing is closely related to quantum theory, the most sophisticated theory of modern science. No wonder many high-energy physicists such as Robert Oppenheimer are seeking support from ancient oriental scholars. The new knowledge that comes from atomic physics is not totally unfamiliar; even in our own culture it has its history. In Buddhism and Indian culture, it is located at the center and is only an example—an advanced refinement of ancient wisdom.

Now let's illustrate the state of perception during Rujing. These examples are by no means exhaustive. They are just a small part, a drop in the ocean. We have given a brief account of the experience of time and space during Rujing. Entering the higher state of Rujing, one becomes aware that time and space are all one. Gao Binda, a

Tibetan lama, once said in a talk on meditation in Buddhism (similar to the idea of Rujing) that "If we are asked about the sense of space during meditation, we are dealing with a completely different area. In this way of experiencing space, the sequence of time turns out to be synchronous, it is the synchronization of events...and it is not still, it is a dynamic, concessive system in which time and space become one."

Daisaku Suzuki[38] also states:

time and space permeate each other. A main feature of Buddhism's sudden awakening is the experience of this osmosis. It is well known that the notion of an inseparable relationship between time and space has already been accepted by relativity physicists. In relativity physics, time is added to the three-dimensional coordinates as the fourth dimension. Each dimension connects with the others and forms a four-dimensional time/space continuum. Therefore, the concept of time and space one gains from Rujing is consistent with the concept of time and space acquired through modern science. This uniformity again reveals the profundity and effectiveness of Rujing in understanding the universe.

The ultimate state of Rujing is XuWu (emptiness). As mentioned in previous chapters, here the idea of Wu (emptiness) is alive and dynamic, an emptiness containing infinite energy, not death and silence. The practitioner's mind is this, due to the notion of nature and man becoming one, and such is the universe too. This emptiness that is full of life and energy is the origin of the universe. Nothing exists, yet everything exists. Everything can come out of nothing; it can be generated and transformed.

This experience and the concept of emptiness are quite similar to the concept of vacuum in quantum theory. The theory states that the vacuum contains all the potential forms in the world of particles, and that these forms do not exist in physical isolation, but as the instant's demonstration of emptiness, which is the basis of the vacuum. All in all, "vacuum" is a living emptiness. It is an emptiness of rhythmic pulse, infinitely generated and extinguished. This is the same as saying "Se Bu Yi Kong, Kong Bu Yi Se, Se Ji Shi Kong, Kong Ji Shi Se" ("Physical existence is no different from emptiness, and vice versa; Physical existence is the emptiness, and the emptiness is physical existence"). Moreover, the state of Rujing can provide profound and dynamic experience in perceiving both the fundamental unity of the universe and the infinite movement of the dynamic world.

It might not be appropriate to label what one gains during Rujing as one's perception. It is actually an experience. Perception usually involves cognitive thinking, and involves an abstract thinking process, which is quite different from experiencing. Nevertheless, when one is in the advanced state of Rujing, everything and its counterpart tend to be extinguished, and so is the difference between perception and experience. The two terms have become synonymous; therefore, we can still describe this knowledge as "perceived" during Rujing.

In spite of the fact that what one gains during Rujing is similar or equivalent to what we obtain through modern technology, we should be aware that each is obtained by different means. Modern science and technology rely on precise experiment, which manipulates objects and concludes the results through abstract deduction, while in Rujing the results are obtained through the practitioner's own sensation and experience, relying on the transforming of oneself, and on one's instinct to know the world. If we borrow language from modern psychology or parapsychology to define the state of Rujing, we can say that the state of Rujing is equivalent to the state of concise alternation. In other words, the practitioner completes his perceiving of the world by changing his consciousness into a particular, unusual state of consciousness.

Here the two different approaches come to a more or less similar conclusion about many fundamental concepts. This may illustrate that the effectiveness of the two approaches occurs at the same level. The perception of the world obtained through direct experience during Rujing is no less valid than what we gain through precise experiments in modern science. I am not suggesting that personal instinct and experience can replace or exclude scientific experiment, or vice versa.

Although the two approaches arrive at the same conclusions, they each have a different focus. In other words, the practitioner often knows the essentials without knowing the details, while the experimenter knows the details but not the essentials. They cannot substitute for one another. A complete understanding must include both the essentials and the details. Thus they should mutually promote, prove, supplement, and stimulate one another, for us to reach an adequate understanding of both the universe and ourselves as human beings.

Without doubt the two approaches should support each other; yet the function of knowing the world through the practice of Rujing is far from being fully cultivated nowadays. The significance and benefits of Rujing are yet to be recognized and studied. I hope that this special approach to knowing the world will stimulate much public interest in the near future, especially among scientists and philosophers.

Chapter 5

Preparatory Work for Rujing

Preparation for Rujing includes adjustment of body and mood in everyday life and routine practice before starting Rujing. The daily adjustment of body and mood is very important, but most people often ignore this. In fact, anyone seeking to master Rujing should begin with a good daily adjustment of his body and mood, just like a good poet whose perfect poems are the result not only of his writing skills, but also of his everyday experience.

Daily Adjustment of Human Body and Mood

On the subject of adjusting body and mood, it is easy for people to associate it with all sorts of psychological and physiological approaches and therapies relating to health and medical care. However, the principle of daily adjusting the human body and mood means keeping to the natural mode of practice, not intentionally taking up all kinds of keep-fit methods. This adjustment includes both mental and physical training.

Psychological Aspect

Regarding daily mood adjustment, Qigong masters often draw attention in relation to self-cultivation on morality and sentiment. For example, taking morality as a priority: let practitioners be charitable, respectful, and unselfish, to purify their hearts and reduce their desires. As for daily behavior, they should be open-minded, not preoccupied with their personal gains and losses all the time, and willing to help others. Morality is best understood in the active sense as being open-hearted and optimistic, but if we looked at it in terms of a passive attitude, it is something like seeing through the vanity of the world.

How should we actually review these requirements? People often ask whether the requirements about morality and sentiment are a kind of sermon influenced by religions, that has nothing to do with exercise or the mode of cultivating one's moral character that is necessarily linked with the practice of Rujing.

To answer this question we have to take both views into consideration.

We have no wish to deny that the requirements are influenced by religion and by the passive attitude of seeing through the vanity of the world. As already mentioned, Qigong basically has countless ties with religion; therefore, it is not at all surprising that some self-cultivation modes of Qigong are related to religion. However, it is more important to address it on its own terms when we are evaluating the requirements. It is not important to discuss its connection with religion. We must take a dialectical view of the issue.

Regarding the notion of seeing through the vanity of the world: it is obviously very negative. It makes people lose confidence and give up trying to make progress. Is there really nothing positive? Yes. Seeing through the vanity of the world means maintaining an attitude of detachment from the world, regardless of one's personal gains and losses. This attitude appears objective and not influenced by subjective human moods, so it helps one to see clearly the internal principles that are deep-rooted in matters of the world, so that people can deal with them in the proper way. Mao Tse Tung once wrote in the poem "Climb Lu Montain":

I scan the world beyond the seas with frosty eye;
The warm winds sprinkle raindrops from the river's sky.

Precisely because of his "frosty eye," the poet had a wide view and saw clearly. He got a bird's-eye view of the whole world, and the changes of the Earth were clear for him to see. If he had "hot eyes," perhaps he would not have seen the world so clearly. The poem suggests the view that the poet is standing on top of the highest mountain, that he despises the world and has an attitude of detachment from real society, and has not thought for himself. Sometimes it is necessary to adopt this attitude of being aloof from the world. As for morality and charity, it is much more helpful to observe the standards they set for relating with other people. Statistics clearly show that the crime rate among people of all religious faiths, including Buddhists and Christians, is lower than it is among non-believers. We could say that the crime rate has a direct link with the factor of religious tenets. In brief, the requirements for self-cultivation of sentiment and morality have something positive to offer us in our lives as social beings.

To study the necessary relationship between self-cultivation and meditation in Rujing, we have to place them against an even wider background which is beyond social life—in other words, to concentrate on the essential links between man and nature.

In traditional Chinese medical science these links are described as follows: the human body is a microcosm of nature; a human being is a microcosm of the universe. In traditional Chinese medical science we often use the method of analogy to compare the activity of human life with the movement of nature. Take the *Medical Canon of the Yellow Emperor* as an example. It says:

> Nature has the sun and the moon; man has two eyeballs. Earth has nine states; man has nine Qiao (orifices). A year has 365 days; man has 360 joints. Nature has four seasons: spring, summer, autumn, and winter, and these make the weather cold, hot, dry, and humid. Man has five main organs to digest the internal changes, and man has happiness, anger, sorrow, worry, and fear related to these.

Ancient astrology also pointed out that the movements of the sun, moon, and stars are directly linked with man's character and fortune. Ignoring any elements of forced analogy and subjective conjecture in this theory, we find that its essential emphasis is on the unity of man and nature.

Ancient Qigong theory took Qi as the root from which everything grows, and revealed the ties between man and nature on a very basic level. The theory shows that Qi constructs everything in the universe. Man is one of these things, and is also made up of Qi. Therefore, man and nature come from one source. On this level, if we are talking about the human body as a microcosm of nature, we are not merely talking about the similarities in character between man and nature, but rather the way they are interlinked in nature. It is also said that people who have never practiced Qigong may not be able to see these links, in spite of the fact that man and nature are essentially linked in nature. Only through the meditation of Rujing can people be aware of and return to these links. In modern society people have become more and more aware of the close ties between man and nature, since environmental pollution and the destruction of the ecological balance are directly threatening human existence. Realizing this does not mean experiencing it personally. If people really try to understand what it is for man and nature to become one, perhaps they still need to know it by practicing Rujing.

As mentioned before, the key to adjustment of body and mood before practicing Rujing is to follow nature. We can only fully realize this when we reach the level of man and nature becoming one. On this level, the unity of man and nature is not only in form but also in character. The universe is vast—it conserves infinite matter and energy. It is boundless in space and has no beginning and no end in time. Everything in the universe grows, changes dramatically, and is a unified entity. Its character is wide, inclusive, creative, and coordinated. These characteristics are reflected in man as being open-hearted, unselfish, full of vigor and vitality, and glad to help others. All this can naturally appear when the state of man and nature becoming one arises during the exercise of Rujing. Therefore, there is indeed a fixed relation between self-cultivation in morality and the exercises of Rujing.

Why do Qigong masters ask practitioners to make a psychological adjustment, improving self-cultivation and being kind in their everyday life? The purpose is to make people actively get to know the links through practice, so as to lay a basic foundation for a gradual entry into the higher level of Qigong. We may say that the lower level of Rujing meditation is not much linked with moral self-cultivation; however, when entering the higher level of Rujing, people cannot separate the exercise of Rujing from self-cultivation. It's like the relationship between fish and water. Therefore, it has been said that, by observing a Qigong master's morality and deeds, we can get to know a good deal about the skills he has developed. And this sounds reasonable.

Physiological Aspect

In daily physiological adjustments, the principle of following nature is realized in the congruity between people's life routine and natural laws. This requires a knowledge of both yourself and others. You need to not only understand the characteristics of your own physiological activities and control your own biological clock, but also to recognize the changeable characteristics and movements of nature. Then you can coordinate the two and get your work, studies, and life well organized.

People have particular habits in life. The development of these habits is due to their physiological nature, as well as to social and personal reasons. The physiological reasons are hidden and we are unaware of them. For example, some people like to go to bed early, while others prefer to sleep late. It is actually related to their tiredness and laziness. Furthermore, it is also closely linked with the variations in people's sleep–wake cycle. An organism, on average, has periodic cycles on all different levels. The frequency is different on different levels of periodicity. For the smallest organism, a cycle might take one millisecond, whereas for the biggest it might take several years. We can observe the biological rhythm of the human body on three levels. One is the cycle at the *cellular level*, such as the initial rhythm of the heart and the pulse of a cranial nerve. Another is an *organic system* such as blood circulation, cycles of secretion in the internal system, the menstrual cycle, period of ovulation, etc. The third is the regular, *whole-body cycle*, such as sleep–wake cycle, or the biorhythms of energy, intelligence, mood, etc. It is very hard for ordinary people to be consciously aware of the cellular cycles; some people can feel the cycles of the organic system; and as for the biorhythm of the whole body, people cannot only feel it, but may also be able to control it to some extent. However, it is not easy to control the biorhythm, because it is necessary to diligently observe, practice, compare, and summarize before you can achieve this. It is not something that you are born with.

To follow one's bio-periodicity reflects the principle of following natural laws. If you do this well, you can remarkably improve efficiency in your work and studies, as well as feeling a sense of ease and well-being. For example, someone may be very tired after supper. According to his biorhythm, if he takes a nap for, say, 10 or 20 minutes, he may be full of energy for the whole evening, until midnight, and be able to do a lot of things. But if he does not understand this, and starts to work after supper, he will not get good results for the entire evening. He will also need to go to bed early, and he will definitely not sleep soundly. To take another example: perhaps someone gets used to sleeping late, and he can work efficiently at night. This habit matches his biorhythm. If this is the case, he need not regard it as a so-called bad habit and try to change it.

So we can see that it may not be easy for ordinary people to arrange their schedule in coordination with their own biorhythms, especially when their biorhythms do not match social conventions. Suppose it is good for a person to have four meals a day to match his digestive system. It may be a problem, because most people's eating habits are not like his. When he is ready to eat dinner is probably the time when other people are concentrating on their work. Not only are the dining halls and restaurants not open for business, but also he himself may not be able to get time away from work. Therefore, we may have to look for other ways of solving the problem. For example, we may have to provide him with an extra meal at work, and so on.

In their everyday life, people's biorhythms are often overridden by all sorts of life habits. Most people do not use their own biorhythms as the basis for a cycle, but instead follow their own habits—although their habits may not match their own biorhythm. Therefore, if they are to try to discover their own biorhythms, usually they need first to get rid of their old habits—whether good or bad. But everybody knows it is really hard to change your habits unless you have an indomitable will, which makes it even more difficult to subjectively control your own biorhythm.

We can see from this that we have to press forward and overcome both subjective and objective difficulties if we are to have a full understanding and control of our own biorhythm. Furthermore, one's biorhythm is not fixed for ever. As one grows older, biorhythms will change on different levels, so long-term exploration is required for mastery of our biorhythm. It can never be done in just one attempt that results in permanent benefit. If a sick man is practicing Qigong, he must have a sound knowledge of the cycle that indicates when his illness gets worse or better, and of the effective period of the medicine he takes. This is very significant for the speed of recovery.

Is what we have discussed above relevant to Rujing? Yes; to practice Rujing is to return to nature. To follow your own biorhythm in ordinary living is to return to your own nature. They are connected to each other and differ only in background and level. Therefore, following your own biorhythm has an imperceptible effect on your practice of Rujing. If the concept of Rujing is explained in the broadest sense, the act of following one's biorhythm can be regarded as part of Rujing, as well as going back to nature in everyday life.

Man and nature are essentially one. The biorhythm of the human body is a microcosm of nature's cyclical movement. They are closely linked. For example, sleep–wake cycles are correlated with the passage of day and night; the menstrual period is also linked with the phases of the moon. In the final analysis, man's biorhythm is affected by the changes of nature, and restricted by the cyclical movement of nature. Thus, if we want to have a better understanding of the biorhythm of the human body, we must gain more knowledge of the movements of nature and follow the laws of its movement conscientiously.

The ancient Chinese paid great attention to this concept. In *The Medical Canon of the Yellow Emperor*, there is a brilliant exposition on how people should follow nature. There are perhaps no statements better than this one. The following is from that book:

- In spring time (we call it "Fa Shen"), everything on Earth wakes up and starts to be full of vigor. Go to sleep late and get up early. With their hair loose, people take a leisurely walk in the courtyard in order to have aspirations. To grow and not to kill; to give and not to take; to reward and not to punish. This is how we should follow nature in spring time. It is also the way for a creature to grow up.

- In summer time (we call it "Fan Xiong"), the essence of ground and air meets and everything on Earth grows rapidly. Go to sleep late and get up early. Enjoy the sunshine; control your spirit; nurture the green and the essence of things; exclude the stale. Everything you love is outdoors. This is how we should follow nature in the summer season. It is the way for a creature to keep growing.

- In autumn time (we call it "Rong Ping"), the autumn sky is clear and the air is crisp. Go to sleep early and get up early, together with the roosters; do not have too much ambitions and keep a clear mind in response to the severe changes of autumn. Reserve your energy and spirit and respond smoothly to the hastiness of autumn. Preserve your spirit and keep your lungs clear. This is how we should follow nature in autumn. It is also the way to keep fit.

- In winter time (we call it "Bi Chang"), the world is frozen with snow and ice and it is quiet everywhere. Go to sleep early and get up late in order to get more sunshine. You may have some spirits or you may not have them. This period is to clear away the cold and keep warm and hold your own energy inside. This is how we should follow the nature in winter. It is also the way to hide your vigor and energy inside your body.

Is it too negative for us simply to follow nature step by step? The answer is no. Human beings can definitely replicate nature to some degree. But the transformation can only be made on the basis of our understanding and abiding by the laws of nature. We cannot contradict them in law. In brief, our remaking of the world is, after all, a creative adaptation to nature. Since man is creative, adapting himself to nature involves not just copying nature mechanically, but following its changes in development. For example, normally people tend to sleep more in winter than in summer. In winter we go to sleep early and get up late, while in summer we go to sleep late and get up early. When we put this life routine into practice, it does not mean that we have to go to sleep late and get up early every day in summer, and go to sleep early and get up late every day in winter. All we need to do is to follow the general trend, and sleep a little bit more in winter than in summer. Generally speaking, we don't need to do it deliberately. In winter, people will naturally sleep more than in other seasons. It is all right—people are not going to go against the laws of nature.

To match our own biorhythm to the periods of nature is to return to nature and merge the individual with the whole. Compared with one who merely follows his own biorhythm, the process really goes deeper. It is a step towards the state of man and nature becoming one in everyday life. There is no doubt that it is beneficial for the practice of Rujing.

Now let us talk about the effect of the four seasons on Qigong exercise.

There is a picture describing self-cultivation in the White Cloud Temple in Beijing; it shows 24 solar terms or periods[39] in the traditional Chinese calendar corresponding to man's 24 spinal vertebrae. Of these:

- the five lumbar vertebrae correspond to five divisions: Winter Solstice, Great Cold, Slight Cold, Beginning of Spring, and Rain Water

- the 12 thoracic vertebrae correspond to 12 divisions, from the Waking of Insects to Hot Summer

- the seven cervical vertebrae correspond to seven divisions, from White Dew to Heavy Snow.

We really do not know whether this match is scientific, and as yet there are not many studies on the subject. Actually, some practitioners of Rujing do have certain feelings in their spine, associated with the 24 solar terms. The time they feel, and the associated vertebrae, are a close match with the depiction in that self-cultivation picture. For example: 20 January 1987 was the 21st day of the last month of the year 1986 in the Chinese lunar calendar. The solar term DaHan (Great Cold) commenced at 22:41 of that evening. One practitioner recalled his experience while practicing Qigong that day:

> My wife and I started to sit cross-legged in meditation at 22:30 at home. After sitting there for about ten minutes, I began to feel heavy and sore all through my low back. Soon afterwards, it gradually became worse, and later on the discomfort became concentrated on my lumbar vertebrae. It was perhaps the third lumbar vertebra. Suddenly I got a pain in my third lumbar vertebra, just like a doctor giving me an injection, and also had the sensation of obtaining Qi (vital energy), and my body had a tingling sensation. No other feelings. After finishing the exercise, my wife said, "I felt more pain in my low back when sitting in meditation this evening than other evenings. I could hardly bear the pain."

The practitioner said that the reason why his wife got low back pain was because her right side had suffered from the cold earlier, and Great Cold was the coldest period of the year. Thus, his wife's response could be seen as evidence for this. He kept a record of his responses to the seven solar terms from the last month of 1986 in the Chinese calendar to April 1987. Each time he had a response in the corresponding vertebra. From our knowledge of astronomy, we know that the 24 solar terms are decided by the angles between the sun and the orbit of the Earth around the sun. They indicate the distance between the sun and the Earth, and also the angles at which the sun's rays fall on the Earth. According to the theory of Chinese traditional medical science, the movement of the sun is directly related to the generating and vanishing of Yin and Yang in the human body. We know that vital energy moves along the Du meridian, circulating around part of the spine and controlling Yang in the body. Therefore, the movement of the sun may affect the Qi circulating along the Du meridian; and practitioners may be able to feel the effect.

Not only can the movement of the sun affect your practice of Qigong, but the movement of the moon can too. Many practitioners have their strongest feelings of vital energy during mid-month during the lunar year, as full moon approaches. However, this feeling will diminish after the twentieth day and drop to its lowest point by the twenty-eighth day of the month. It will recommence and increase in the early days of the next month. As stated in the book *The Lunar Effect: Biological Tides and Human Emotions* by the American psychiatrist A.L. Lieber, every cell of the human body, like a mini-solar system, possesses a weak electromagnetic field. Great electromagnetic power produced by the moon can affect the complex balance of hormones, body fluids, and electrolytes in the human body. Eighty percent of the human body is liquid. Lunar gravitation can have an effect on the fluid in the human body, just as it does on sea tides. This is the so-called biological tide. The full moon has the strongest impact on the human body. During this period there is a big difference in electrical potential between man's head and chest; man is extremely full of vigor and has the strongest energy in his internal body, and also easily gets excited. Lieber explains from a modern scientific viewpoint why people have a very strong sense of Qi (vital energy) around the middle of the lunar month.

In the science of TCM, we describe the phenomenon in terms of Yin and Yang, of positive Qi and negative Qi. For example, it says in *The Medical Canon of the Yellow Emperor* that in the early part of the month man's vital energy and blood start to be produced and circulate; in mid-month, man is full of energy, with strong muscles;

and at the end of the month his muscles become slack, and his main and collateral channels grow weak. We have been talking about adjusting man's vital energy and blood in step with the calendar. Now we can see that the explanations from both modern science and TCM science are not contradictory.

It is easy for practitioners to explore their latent potential when they have a strong sense of Qi during Qigong practice. Therefore, some practitioners with extraordinary power may demonstrate a strong function around the middle of the month, and their function weakens at the end of the month. Also, it is thought that it is easy to get one's Qi circulating in summer. The reason is that man's positive energy in summer is extremely full.

It is very important for sick people who are trying to cure their diseases by practicing Qigong to be aware of the effects of the four seasons on disease. The onset and development of many diseases are closely linked with the seasons. For example, in spring, people can easily get respiratory tract disease, as well as alimentary canal disease in summer, while in winter, people quite often have heart attacks. Patients need this kind of knowledge to consciously control the expansion of disease.

Preliminaries to Practicing Rujing

It is necessary to make full preparations before exercise if one is really trying to make much progress during Rujing. The preparations have two aspects—the objective and the subjective. We will consider each separately.

Objective Concerns

The objective preparations before the practicing of Rujing mainly involve selecting the proper environment for exercise. Here are some of the most important.

TIME

Our ancestors had a special time requirement for practicing Qigong. They preferred to do exercise around noon and midnight because these two periods are the moments when Yin and Yang interchange. The period from 11:00pm to 1:00am is the time when Yin turns to Yang; the period from 11:00am to 1:00pm is the time when Yang turns to Yin. Practicing Qigong during these two periods will enable you to realize the shift of Yin and Yang naturally and most effectively. Another suggestion is to do Qigong during the six Yang periods. These are midnight, 2:00am, 4:00am, 6:00am, 8:00am, and 10:00am. You should avoid exercising during the six Yin periods, that is, at noon, 2:00pm, 4:00pm, 6:00pm, 8:00pm, and 10:00pm. The six Yang periods are full of positive energy. Yang is live and can assist the movement of vital energy in your body. It is no good choosing the six Yin periods from 11:00am to 11:00pm, because they are periods during which Yin will grow. These periods are less beneficial for practicing, as Yin is lifeless. Of course, these ideas are for reference only. We should not apply them mechanically.

Nowadays time arrangements for most people are limited to their work, study, and living conditions. People cannot change them casually. Take the two periods of 11:00pm to 1:00am, and 11:00am to 1:00pm, for example: although they are theoretically the best times for practicing Qigong, most people are actually sleeping and having lunch during these two periods, so it is hard to practice Qigong then. Taking circumstances into consideration, it is not appropriate to mechanically arrange a time for practice. Everyone should arrange their time for practice according to their own circumstances. If possible, it will be good to practice at midnight and noon. If not possible, you may find another relatively fixed and acceptable time for practice. A conditioned response will be easily established if you practice at a fixed time: every day when the time comes, practitioners will automatically relax their bodies and mood. This is quite helpful for Rujing. Generally speaking, it is appropriate for practitioners to practice Rujing before going to bed, as one becomes quiet and the environment is also less disturbed in the evening; on the other hand, the morning will be the best choice for practicing active Qigong. Practitioners may practice once or twice per day, for about 30 or 60 minutes each time. Of course, it is better to practice a bit longer.

PLACE

Practicing outdoors is better than practicing indoors. Not only can people breathe fresh air outside, but they also have flowers, grass, and trees around them. Fresh air benefits practitioners. That is the reason why monks choose to live in the depths of the mountains. Apart from their wish to be away from the noise of populated areas, the fresh air and plenty of trees are also what they want. In the cities, hundreds and hundreds of cars, buses, and trucks come and go on the streets at rush hour in the morning and in the evening. They discharge a lot of toxic exhaust. So it is not a good idea for practitioners to practice in city-center parks during rush hour. Places like lake shores, coastal beaches, and forests provide the best environment with fresh air for practitioners. In so far as those places are within the reach of ordinary people, practitioners may be able to choose a place that is far away from streets, chimneys, and places full of dust. Choose places surrounded by pine trees, flowers, and grasses.

Practitioners' choice of plants should be compatible with their health conditions. It is suitable for a healthy person to exercise beside pine trees, but it is not necessarily a good place for sick people. For example, for patients with lung disease, it would be better to exercise next to poplar trees; patients with liver disease should practice near date trees. We know that all living organisms have their own biotic fields. Man has one, and so do trees. Some practitioners with extraordinary power can see these biotic fields. They can see different-colored light around different organisms. The light surrounding poplar trees is white. According to TCM science, lung energy is a white color. According to the principle that Qi of the same kind attracts each other, the energy produced by poplar trees can supplement a practitioner's lung Qi. It is therefore beneficial for patients with lung disease.

In the practice of Qigong it is important for people to have the knowledge to opt for the appropriate plants for their exercises, but it is more important to be aware of their own experience. After practicing Qigong for some time, practitioners who are sensitive can sense whether the biotic field around them is congenial for them or not, even though they are still not able to see it with their own eyes. Beginners in Qigong should develop their ability in this respect from the very beginning. Practitioners should have a sense of what environment to opt for, and carefully observe their experience of how the environment affects them. When one is able to feel comfortable or uncomfortable under different trees, it shows that one has the essential ability of psychic communication with the outside world. This reflects a practitioner's progress in Qigong.

Although outdoor practice has so many benefits, it is not easy to find a suitable place to sit in meditation, and normally practitioners can only practice the standing mode, so it is not easy for them to enter the deep state of Rujing. Therefore, the best way for them is to practice Qigong twice a day. Practitioners should practice the standing posture outdoors in the daytime, and sitting postures indoors at night. In addition, if possible, they should open their windows when they are practicing indoors.

SOUND

Practitioners should choose surroundings that are as tranquil as possible. Noise greatly affects practitioners who practice Rujing. Very noisy places (such as construction sites) definitely do not suit practitioners. Can practitioners practice Rujing on a passenger ship, or on trains, during their journey? There are noises on ships and trains, and loud noises may occur, such as the sudden sounding of a horn, which hinder people who are practicing Rujing. However, on a journey, people have plenty of time to practice Qigong, as there is nothing else to do on a ship or train. During a trip practitioners may practice Qigong, but they should not enter the deep level of Rujing. They must be mentally alert for sudden noises and events, so as to avoid accidental disturbance.

Practicing Rujing requires tranquil surroundings, but this does not necessarily mean the quieter, the better. One might assume that a sound-proof room is the quietest place, and that practitioners can get the best results there. Actually, this is not the case. As soon as he enters that silent room, the practitioner will have swelling in his ears, his whole body will feel uncomfortable, and he will spontaneously start to feel nervous. He can never ever practice Rujing in there. It is obvious that things turn into their opposites when they reach an extreme. Extremely tranquil surroundings do not really benefit practitioners. It is necessary for Qigong practitioners to hear birds singing and the wind blowing, or the sound of vehicles from a long way off. During this time practitioners will have a deeper understanding of relatively peaceful circumstances, compared with total silence.

LIGHT

Practitioners should not choose a place that is too bright to practice Qigong. During the practice of Rujing, practitioners are required to slightly close their eyes, thus preventing the light from entering their eyes directly.

Practitioners have asked if they can face the sun when practicing outdoors. Different types of Qigong have different requirements. For practitioners who practice Rujing, they can face the sun only during sunrise and sunset, because the sun is less than blazing at those times. If the sunlight becomes intensely bright, practitioners will get a dazzling brightness, even though they close their eyes while practicing. So it is no good for practitioners to face the sun at these times. Practitioners should practice under trees, and avoid direct sunlight.

It is also not suitable for practitioners to practice under very bright lamps indoors at night. They should switch off the light, or turn on a small lamp.

ORIENTATION

Choosing the orientation for practice has been the norm ever since ancient times. In *The Medical Canon of the Yellow Emperor*, it says that all sick people who have a long history of kidney disease should face the south during the period from 3:00am to 5:00am, clear their minds, and hold their breath seven times; then swallow air down their throats seven times, just like swallowing food. After that, their mouths are full of saliva. What we have here is a type of still Qigong characterized by inhaling/exhaling. Practitioners are required to practice with exposure to the South during the period of day from 3:00am to 5:00am. Facing South during practice was highly praised by our ancestors. There is scientific evidence for this, even from the viewpoint of modern science. It is well known that the Earth has a powerful magnetic field. As proved by scientific research, if man can stay in alignment with the axis of the Earth's magnetic field, this produces a bio-magnetic effect on the organism which adjusts and improves the functions of the human organs. During the practice of Rujing the physiological functions of our organs are in a state of adjustment and reinforcement. During this time, if practitioners are aligned with the Earth's magnetic field, it will produce a greater bio-magnetic effect on them. The Earth's magnetic field has a South–North axis; therefore, it is good for practitioners to practice Qigong with exposure to the South.

However, there can be anomalies in aligning with the Earth's magnetic field, due to the physiological variations in each individual. For example, when a patient with liver disease does Qigong, no matter which direction he faces when he starts his practice, he always ends up facing West after the occurrence of spontaneous actions. This may be related to his disease. In TCM science, Liver belongs to Wood and stays in the East. When the patient sits facing West, the Earth's magnetic field may have a therapeutic effect on his disease by virtue of its impact on the patient's own bio-magnetic field. Besides, the Earth's magnetic field is not the only choice of orientation you should rely on; there are other resources, such as the directions of sunrise and sunset, the positions of the moon and stars, etc. Thus facing South to practice Qigong is not an absolute imperative.

Just as they are able to feel the bio-magnetic field of the right plants around them, sensitive practitioners will also be able to feel which direction suits them. Once they get used to facing in a set direction, they will feel uncomfortable if asked to change it. Just like someone sleeping with their head facing South, if they suddenly change orientation, they may suffer from insomnia. The reason is that their own bio-magnetic field is already used to the South–North orientation. The sudden change causes a temporary imbalance in the person's own bio-magnetic field, which will lead to physiologic malfunction and insomnia. After a while, when he has adapted to the new magnetic field, he will sleep well again.

Beginners should not often change, or suddenly change orientation once they have decided on it, unless they have a negative reaction to that direction.

WEATHER (CLIMATE)
Practicing Qigong on a stormy day, either outdoors or indoors, is strongly discouraged. Besides possible disturbance from thunder, there are other injury defects that thunder and lightning can cast on human bodies, just as they can interrupt broadcasting from TV and radio stations. In addition, practicing Rujing during this time is not consistent with the state of nature, given the view of man and nature becoming one entity. Foggy days are not suitable for outdoor practice, due to high humidity and dust particles in the air. It is harmful to practitioners to inhale them. You should also not practice Qigong outdoors on windy days. In TCM, wind is regarded as the source of many diseases. There are six sources of unhealthy trends in the world. They are wind, cold, heat, damp, dryness, and fire. Wind is the first; therefore, we should keep in mind what *The Medical Canon of the Yellow Emperor* says: be in time to avoid the sudden attack of wind.

Hot weather makes practitioners agitated. It is difficult for them to practice Rujing in these conditions, but relatively easier on cool days. While practicing Rujing, people are better able to adapt to cold and heat than in ordinary living, so that colder or hotter weather will not disrupt their practice of Rujing. Anyway, cooler weather is still the best for practitioners of Rujing, so they should intensify their practice on cool, autumn days.

SOLITARY AND GROUP PRACTICE

Should one practice Rujing by oneself, or should practitioners get together for practice? Which way is better? This is a hard question to answer. We cannot make generalizations.

Generally speaking, for beginners, practicing Rujing in a group is certainly better than individual practice. In addition to the atmosphere of the setting, the interplay within practitioners' biotic field also needs to be taken into account. Practicing in a large group will establish a larger biotic field, which will affect and reinforce each individual's own biotic field so that each person can experience a sense of Qi far quicker than when practicing alone. Furthermore, it is helpful for practitioners to have discussions and share their experiences with each other before and after practice, so as to deepen their understanding of Qigong and their interest in the practice.

Positioning is very important when practicing in a large group. Practitioners should not form casual groupings, the way they would for general keep-fit exercises, or as seniors do for morning disco dancing in the Beijing parks. They should also avoid changing position randomly each time. This sort of approach will result in an imbalanced distribution in the biotic field, and poor team coordination. Some practitioners may have strong feelings, some may have weak feelings, and some may have none. Facing inwards in a closed line-up is better for group practice. Practitioners can assemble in a circle, square, or cross formation. When lining up, the number and sex of practitioners should be taken into consideration. The posture of each person should be comparatively fixed. At the beginning, each posture can be assumed temporarily, and after trying a few, readjustments should be made for practitioners who do not feel at ease. Postures should then not be changed again, once the majority have adapted themselves to the set-up. This will bring good results. Currently some special studies are being done on set patterns for collective practice, with some interesting results. For example, practitioners could assemble according to the First and Second Heavens of the Eight Trigrams, or according to the patterns in the texts *He Tu* or *Luo Shu*,[40] or by arranging the numbers and positions of males and females in accordance with the principle of Yin and Yang.

Through practice based on groupings like those mentioned above, practitioners can obtain a strong sense of vital energy in certain positions, and it is very effective at curing their diseases. In addition, studies have shown that some practitioners with better mastery of Qigong should be placed in particular positions, otherwise the entire biotic field will be affected. So we can see that positioning for collective practice is quite mysterious, and should not be done without careful thought; while practitioners can be self-taught for individual practice, collective practice needs to be done under the guidance of teachers, and it cannot be just a disorganized cluster of practitioners.

As a practitioner in group practice, you should constantly be aware whether the position as arranged suits you or not. If you really do not feel right, bring this up as soon as possible and ask to change your position. If everyone is in the right position and there is a powerful and evenly distributed biotic field, all the practitioners will feel warm, comfortable, and at ease.

After practicing for some time, you may have stable feelings of vital energy, and will have made some remarkable progress. You should then seriously consider whether collective practice still suits you. Collective practice may continue to be suitable for some, and not for others. The reason is that when you are a beginner, the influence from the collective biotic field can easily improve your personal biotic field, but when your personal biotic field is strengthened to some extent, its individual characteristics need room in which to gradually develop their own uniqueness. As we know, the collective biotic field is formed by all of the practitioners. It may strengthen one person's biotic field, and at the same time interfere with others' biotic fields. For example, if you have just begun to develop the power of clairvoyance, it may be very weak to begin with, and is easily upset by all kinds of interruptions. It will disappear when you are in the collective biotic field, which does not help to reinforce your power of clairvoyance. It may occur if you practice alone in a quiet place without any interruption. Therefore, if you find your extraordinary power occurring, collective practice is not the best choice for you. Opting for collective or single practice should depend on your own specific circumstances. Of course, the best way is to find a Qigong master to practice with you.

Alternating group and single practice is an efficient approach for practitioners. You can benefit from collective practice, as well as developing individual uniqueness. This is suitable for the majority of practitioners. Someone can do collective practice as their primary practice, and individual practice as secondary. Or they could give priority to single practice, with group practice as secondary. When you opt for alternating collective and single practice, be alert to the experience of different feelings in each, and try your best to keep improving through the process of comparison.

SELF-TEACHING AND SEEKING A MASTER

No matter whether it be group or individual practice, the ideal way to learn is certainly under the guidance of teachers, but due to limitations in all kinds of conditions, not everyone can find a teacher.

The practice of Rujing is different from practicing other types of Qigong. It is comparatively easier to learn by yourself. It is hard to master any kind of active Qigong without the guidance of masters. However, you can master Rujing by following instructions or finding teach-yourself books.

One thing is important to pay attention to when seeking a master. That is the mutual selection between teacher and student. Teachers should choose the right students, and students should choose the right teachers, too. Teaching can go smoothly only when both sides feel satisfied with each other. People vary psychologically and physiologically; one way of practicing does not suit everyone. It is the same when it comes to Rujing as the purpose of practice. Some people may find it helpful to start from the adjustment of mind, whereas others prefer to start from the adjustment of breathing. So teaching methods need to be versatile in order to meet the needs of different students. The teacher should select students who are used to his teaching methods and have a good understanding of what he teaches; students should select a teacher they trust and are willing to listen to. In learning Qigong, and especially in learning Rujing, there is nothing visible and concrete to teach and learn. Students need to learn with their whole hearts. It all depends on the sensitivity of practitioners in understanding and grasping the essence of Rujing. Therefore, it is really important to have mutual understanding and cooperation between teachers and students. Teachers place high demands on students, as do the students of their teachers.

No matter whether Qigong is self-taught or taught by masters, in order to learn it well it is necessary for practitioners to make great efforts in practice, as well as having a good understanding of Rujing. Nobody can master it very quickly. We are against the attitude of "going fishing for three days and drying the nets for two."

Subjective Concerns

Before practice, the subjective preparations to be made are to clear the mind and get rid of all burdens, mentally and physically. The subjective preparations must follow the objective ones. Here are some of the key points.

CLOTHING

Light, loose-fitting clothing is suitable. Different from gymnastics and martial arts, a skin-tight outfit is not appropriate for practicing Rujing. If practitioners wear clothing that fits tightly around the waist and legs, what it will do is hinder relaxation and affect the circulation of vital energy and blood. Monks and Taoist priests often wear wide, voluminous robes; you will not find a figure wearing skin-tight clothes among the clay sculptures typically found in large temples. The Buddha Sakyamuni also wears loose clothing.

Nowadays young people like wearing jeans, which are not suitable for the practice of Rujing. It is difficult for people wearing jeans to sit cross-legged. If they do not sit this way, jeans are still too tight for them. Also, as regards wearing loose clothing for practice, overcoats are not appropriate. Of course, if it is too cold outdoors, that is a different matter.

If possible, practitioners should not wear hats, shoes, gloves, glasses, watches, etc. when practicing Rujing. It is perfectly convenient for practitioners to sit cross-legged without any shoes on. They can wear slippers when they are siting on chairs or standing. If it is not convenient for them to wear slippers, they can wear felt shoes when they practice in the park. As for seniors, due to the lack of elasticity at the bottom of their feet, they can wear shoes with low heels, so as to keep steady on their feet. It is not appropriate to wear high-heeled shoes for practice. It can affect the standing posture, and make practitioners stiffen their bodies and tighten their bellies. This is contrary to the requirement of toning up the back. In addition, you should wear cloth shoes for practice. Leather shoes and tennis shoes are good for insulation, but they obstruct the exchange of electrical charge between the human body and the Earth. It is a joyful thing for practitioners to practice on the soil with bare feet on a fine day. Wearing glasses can have some effects on Rujing. The area between the middle of the eyebrows and the alae of the nose is quite sensitive, and wearing glasses may reduce the sensitivity. In addition, that part is also close to the point of Shang Que Qao, a key point for the minor circulation route of Zhou Tian, which should never be pressed. Therefore, practitioners should take off their glasses when they are ready to practice. Wrist watches should also be taken off. The place on the wrist where you wear your watch is on Guan Xue (an acupuncture point). Pressure on Guan Xue will affect the main and collateral channels of the heart. Furthermore, most watches are made of metal, which will disturb human bio-magnetic fields. For the same reason, some Qigong masters will request sick people to take off their watches before they will emanate their vital energy for them.

The main principle of practicing Rujing is to follow the way of nature. Practitioners should eliminate all factors that might interfere with their relaxation and comfort.

CLEANLINESS

It is obvious that anyone with disheveled hair and a dirty face, or soaked with sweat, is not in a fit state to practice Rujing; nor is a woman who is richly attired and heavily made-up in the right state. It is easy for practitioners to practice Rujing when they have clean skin and their bodies feel pure and fresh. Practicing Rujing after a shower at night certainly meets the requirement for cleanliness.

Practitioners should first relieve themselves before starting to practice Rujing. This is not just for the sake of cleanliness, but also gets rid of waste from the body, reduces the bad stimulation inside the body, and lets the vital energy pass smoothly through the body.

Our ancestors put great emphasis on cleaning the body before practicing Qigong. For instance, they would take a bath, abstain from meat, wine, etc., light sticks of incense, and purify the body. What they did was not only to clean their bodies and beautify the environment, but also to cultivate themselves and restrain their desires. In addition, it expressed their great veneration for Qigong. What our ancestors used to do has been accepted by many modern Qigong masters. For example, the first of the five requirements in standing Qigong (esteem, care, attention, precision, harmony) incorporates the meaning of veneration.

FOOD AND DRINK

Here are three points to be aware of: eating time, quality, and quantity of food. In short, practicing time and eating time should be separated; practitioners do not eat too much before they practice Rujing, and they should eat little or no meat.

There should be a one-hour interval between dinner and practicing Rujing and it is no good for practitioners to practice soon after dinner. As we know, the practice of Rujing requires abdominal breathing.

This breathing mode may cause the movement of the diaphragm to fluctuate within a wider range, and result in increased abdominal pressure. If practitioners practice Rujing soon after dinner, it may cause the contents of the stomach to move back up into the esophagus due to the increased abdominal pressure. All of this will bring about symptoms such as heartburn, etc. One hour after dinner is the period when the stomach discharges rapidly, with copious secretion of bile and pancreatic juice. It is also the peak period for digestion. If in this period you practice anything that increases abdominal pressure, it may reduce the speed at which the stomach pushes undigestable matter into the duodenum. This can cause gastrectasia or even make alkaline substances from the duodenum move back up into the stomach. This will cause gastric ulcers; therefore, it is not good to practice Rujing within one hour of dinner, as the results may not be good, and possibly even harmful to health.

Nowadays we usually have three meals a day. In order to separate eating time from practicing time, it is simple enough to arrange to practice before breakfast and after supper. In addition, practitioners can also change their eating time. Although three meals per day is the norm for most people in most areas, this is not appropriate for everyone. People can change their meals to four a day, two a day, etc., according to their actual state of digestion and hunger. This will be beneficial for their practice of Rujing, and consistent with their own biotic regulation.

Practitioners should not eat too much at each meal, and even less for the meal just before their practice of Rujing. A full stomach will hinder the movement of the diaphragm, making it difficult for practitioners to adjust their breathing in Rujing. Generally, practitioners are advised to eat to the point of being 70 percent full. Then they will feel content and relaxed when they start to practice an hour after the meal. If they eat too much, they will still feel full an hour later, and unable to practice Rujing. On the other hand, it is also not suitable for them to practice when they are hungry. How can someone practice Rujing if he feels upset because he is hungry? Of course, there are some types of Qigong that are designed for resisting cold and hunger. These are types of Qigong that do not take Rujing as their purpose.

Now let's talk briefly about losing appetite during the practice of Rujing. Many practitioners do get to the point of eating less than before, after they have been practicing for some time. Some practitioners have less to eat per meal, and some have one meal a day or one meal for several days. This is not the phenomenon of BiGu, but it is the same as BiGu in principle. In this circumstances, we should follow nature and let it last for as long as we are full of vigor, and not hungry or thirsty. Practitioners should not force themselves to eat, or not to eat. Not everyone will enter the state of BiGu, but eating less will occur in almost everyone. This is the self-readjustment of our body, and it is not necessary for practitioners to interfere. Qigong masters are usually light eaters, and no one eats and drinks too much at one meal. Eating less reduces the burden on our stomach and demands less energy for digestion. This is one of the factors in longevity.

On eating meat and fish: I think that whatever one likes to eat, either meat or vegetables, people should not force themselves to change their own eating habits, but it is better for practitioners to eat vegetables in the meal before they start the practice of Rujing. Compared with meat, vegetables are easier to digest, and may reduce the burden on the stomach. Furthermore, the reason for encouraging practitioners to eat vegetables is not only that mentioned above. A vegetarian diet is intrinsically linked with the practice of Qigong, which still can't be explained by modern nutritional science. Good practitioners who have practiced for quite a long time opt for a vegetarian diet naturally and spontaneously. They even feel sick when they eat meat. Some people worry that a vegetarian diet over a long period of time may lead to malnutrition. Doctors have done research on the nutrition of monks living in remote mountains. The conclusion was that they were malnourished. But the question is, why are those supposedly malnourished monks full of vitality and living a long life? Is there something wrong with the monks, or with the theories about nutrition? That is still the question.

WORK AND REST

Practitioners should not practice Rujing straight after work. During this time their muscles cannot be relaxed, and their vital energy and blood have not been adjusted. They should have a rest first, and they can take a walk or read newspapers and magazines, so as to relax fully—and then practice Rujing. In other words, we cannot slam the brakes on a fast-running car or suddenly rein in a running horse. The functional transfer in the human body needs a buffer.

It is not suitable for someone to practice Rujing when he is extremely tired, either. Due to drowsiness and fatigue he may go to sleep during the practice. In this case he'd better take a nap first, and practice Rujing afterwards. Some practitioners try to use the practice of Rujing as part of their sleep regime. It is possible for good practitioners, but impossible for beginners. They have to go to bed when they feel sleepy. They can practice Rujing to replace part of their sleep only after their skills have improved. Yes, some masters use Rujing as a substitute for sleep, but they are a tiny minority. Beginners can practice Rujing when they are feeling only a little bit tired. It can help practitioners to rest well, but it cannot replace sleep.

If practitioners are in high spirits and are trying to do sporting activities, the conditions are not right for Rujing either. According to the principle of following the way of nature, they should do some sports exercises or try some active Qigong. To preserve our health we need a balance of Yin and Yang, and between activity and keeping quiet. We should join in sports when necessary. It is biased and inadequate to concentrate only on Rujing.

According to our general arrangements for work and rest, the best time to practice Rujing is in the evening. Practitioners may feel tired after a whole day's work or activity, but they are not so tired that they need to go to bed immediately. It is just the right time to practice Rujing.

MOOD

People should be prohibited from practicing Rujing after being in a towering rage. Practitioners should also not practice Rujing just after they have been in a state of great joy, sorrow, or fear. The mood directly affects the movements of vital energy in human bodies. In *The Medical Canon of the Yellow Emperor* it says:

> Anger stops Qi (vital energy); joy makes Qi run slowly; sorrow makes Qi disappear; fear makes Qi go down; cold makes Qi go back to the original state; flexibility makes Qi discharge; fear brings Qi into disorder; tiredness consumes Qi; thinking makes Qi blocked.

When someone practices Rujing in a state of excitement, Qi may be in a state of disorder and very difficult to control, and this may lead to deviations and malfunction.

As for Qigong masters, they are not moody people, and remain unruffled whatever happens, but once they fly into a rage or become narrow-minded, their bad mood will cause more harm to their health than it does to ordinary people. The reason is that Qigong masters have a high capacity for merging their bodies and thinking into a single entity. As we know, the practice of Rujing adjusts human physiological conditions through a psychological impact. As a result of long-term practice, the psychological impact on physiological conditions is greatly intensified. The connection between the two becomes much more sensitive and direct. When the impact from the mind is positive, your health will be greatly improved, and vice versa. During the ten-year turmoil of the Cultural Revolution, many famous Qigong masters passed away prematurely as a result of being badly upset. The direct reason was that their mood produced a much stronger impact on their health than it would have done in ordinary people.

Therefore, we should avoid being over-emotional before our practice of Rujing. Indeed, we should avoid this all the time and everywhere. Being overjoyed is included here, as joy makes Qi (vital energy) concentrate slowly. In TCM it says that being overjoyed can consume Qi from the heart. Furthermore, extreme joy begets sorrow. Extreme joy often makes people forget themselves and do silly things.

THINKING

Just as with mood activities, it is not appropriate to practice Rujing soon after extremely intensive thinking, such as when making a main decision, taking an examination, or playing chess. At times like this the practitioner's mind is still intensively active. Even if they have sat down, they still cannot enter the state of Rujing. All they can do is to recall and mull over what has just happened, one thing after another. So they should relax themselves first; they could play table tennis or have a chat (but not about a topic that makes them so excited). When they calm down, they can start practicing Rujing.

In addition, as usual, before they do Rujing, all life and work matters should be temporarily put aside. Practitioners should avoid being worried about anything or thinking about something during the practice of Rujing. If they are really worrying or thinking about something, they cannot reach the state of Rujing, and may get into bad habits: later on, as soon as they start to practice Rujing, they will start to think of something; thus, they will never, ever make any progress. In short, we must get rid of all sorts of ideas in our minds. That is very important in preparing for Rujing. If you are really trying to practice at a time when you definitely have something on your mind, you can do a "working practice." That is, concentrate on one matter to be dealt with and get rid of other ideas while you are practicing Qigong. This is one method used by the Japanese. It is said that it gets good results in problem solving. When you are in the state for practicing Qigong, you may be able to clear up a problem that you could not see through before your practice. You may even get the inspiration to solve the problem. Everybody can try, if they are interested in this method, but it is beyond the subject of Rujing.

There is another very important preparation in thinking before Rujing. That is to bring the purpose of Rujing to mind.

Some people practice Qigong in order to clear the Ren and Du meridians. Some are trying to cultivate extraordinary power, and some to cure their diseases. Our purpose in practicing Rujing is to reach the realm of emptiness and to forget both oneself and the material world. This purpose must be defined and held in mind before practicing Rujing. One thing to mention here is that "holding in mind" is not to imprint on human consciousness, but to transfer the aim to the subconscious via consciousness. When practitioners are in the process of Rujing, the ultimate aim does not always appear in their minds. Their thinking activities will be done step by step. Each step is directed towards the goal, and each step has its own special contents. Just like someone driving a car somewhere, the direction of the car depends on the destination, which only appears at the end. It never, ever appears midway.

Do not look down on this preparation for practice. It is key in the guidance for the whole Rujing operation. It plays an essential role in the whole procedure of Rujing. Without this clear guidance, it is just like a ship sailing on the sea without a rudder, just floating before the wind.

The actual advice on setting up the guidelines for Rujing is as follows: Before Rujing, practitioners should think of the purpose of Rujing. Only think of it quickly, and do not think of it again and again and for a long time. The purpose of doing this is to have the guidelines for Rujing engraved on our subconscious, and not in our mind. If it remains in our mind, it will be hard for it to enter the subconscious. Most practitioners have actually done this preparation, but they have done it subconsciously and not consciously. Perhaps they will get better results if they do it consciously. Besides, it is not necessary for practitioners to consider the purpose in very concrete terms; simply think of it as entering into the emptiness and the state of Rujing. You don't need to figure out what exactly the emptiness is. It's just like traveling by taxi: we tell the driver where we are going; there is no need to describe in detail what the scenery is like in that place. When we arrive there, beautiful scenery will naturally appear before us. Of course, there is one thing that has to be said: the driver must be familiar with the place where we are going. It is no use telling him the name of the place if he really does not know where it is. It is the same with the ideas discussed above: If we try to define the guidelines for Rujing, we first need to know what Rujing is. If we know nothing about Rujing, we are in no position to define the guidelines.

Chapter 6

Rujing and Its Components

Rujing comprises the whole process of practice. It includes three parts: adjustments of mind, breath, and body. The three adjustments are independent and integrated as well. Together they form different levels of Rujing.

The Basic Principles

The first principle is to maintain the conditions of relaxation, quietness, and naturalness. *Relaxation* means being loose, not worrying, being open-hearted and not in a hurry; *quietness* means being calm and good-tempered; *naturalness* means being at ease, being neither pretentious nor reluctant, and handling everything in its own way. During the process of Rujing, practitioners should mentally and physically satisfy the three conditions listed above.

Among these three, relaxation and quietness are manifestations of naturalness. When people are mentally and physically free from all burdens, their minds and whole bodies will naturally be at ease. Therefore, the key point of the three is naturalness. Following the way of nature is the essential principle that one should fulfill through the entire process of Rujing.

The fundamentals of relaxation, quietness, and naturalness can be applied in all the three adjustments of mind, breath, and body. Since the contents of the three adjustments are different, the requirements of those fundamentals for each adjustment are of different importance.

For the adjustment of mind, quietness is the most important aspect. Relaxation and naturalness both serve the purpose of achieving this, and we know that relaxation is closely related to quietness. During the practice of Rujing, mind relaxation is the starting point and the only way to reach quietness. Now, relaxation serves only for the purpose of quietness and it is the means of being quiet. For example, when you banish distracting thoughts from your mind, you must first reduce your attention to them. That is, relaxation in mind. In short, during the adjustment of psychological activities, relaxation is a capable assistant to quietness.

Quietness and naturalness are linked together, too. You can become quiet only when you are at ease. In other words, you cannot calm down when you are forced to do so. Just like relaxation, the fundamentals of naturalness are also to serve quietness during the adjustment of psychological systems. Rujing must be processed naturally. Practitioners enter the state of Rujing spontaneously when all conditions are ripe. They should not intentionally chase this. Yet naturalness does not mean freedom from any control. There are still certain constraints. The bounds are the guidelines within the mind set up in the preparatory period of Rujing. During this time the guidelines have taken root in the subconscious and start functioning. It is not conscious. What exists in the consciousness is relaxation, quietness, and naturalness.

With reference to the adjustment of breath, the principle of naturalness is key. Both relaxation and quietness make practitioners breathe more naturally. Inhaling/exhaling during Rujing will deepen gradually, from regular breathing and abdominal breathing, to navel breathing like a baby. Practitioners must complete the deepening processes spontaneously and smoothly and should be able to do this without much difficulty. During this process of one mode of breathing transforming to another, any overreaction will cause stagnation of the circulation of vital energy. The stagnation will make practitioners feel unwell. Practitioners may have tense muscles, or even worse, they may feel faint and oppressed; the side effects are very obvious. Unlike in the process of mind adjustment when a slight deviation from the principle of naturalness will not result in immediate physical discomfort, any forced attempt in the operation of breathing adjustment will result in instant side effects.

How can practitioners follow the natural way of breathing adjustment? By keeping the breathing easy and calm. Natural inhaling/exhaling are indeed the breathing of relaxation and calm. If practitioners persist in being relaxed and calm, they can be said to have maintained naturalness. Since the orientation of Rujing has been set up in the subconscious, the operation of breathing will gradually go deeper along the way, so practitioners need not force themselves to overreact.

Regarding adjustment of the body, relaxation is the aim. During this time calm and naturalness both serve relaxation, and they are the guarantees of relaxation. In order to relax, one should stop moving any of one's limbs. Only when practitioners calm down can their muscles relax well. Practitioners with waving arms certainly have difficulty in relaxing completely. During this time, calming down is the essential and only way to reach relaxation.

During the process of body adjustment the arms and legs should be in the right position; it is unnatural if practitioners have difficulty maintaining their posture, such as placing their heads on their feet, or their feet facing forward and their face facing backward. Practitioners cannot relax if they stay in wrong positions to practice Rujing, and they will not get good results. During the operation of body adjustment, all natural postures are easy; therefore, preserving ease preserves naturalness. One thing must be mentioned here. The easy and natural posture may not be the same for each person. As for sitting postures, some may feel at ease when sitting a little bit forward, while others may feel comfortable when sitting a little bit backward. The difference is due to the individual differences in physical conditions. How do we handle the distinction? The answer is for each person to follow their own way.

Here is a summary of the special emphasis on relaxation, quietness, and naturalness: a calm state of mind, relaxed arms and legs, and natural inhaling/exhaling. This emphasis is definitely relative. The fundamentals of relaxation, quietness, and naturalness go together during the practice. The emphasis here is to have common ground while maintaining the differences.

When practitioners understand relaxation, quietness, and naturalness, they will not go to extremes but just keep to the point. We must be aware that relaxation is not slackness in practice; quietness is not dead stillness; and naturalness is not indulgent and willful. Things that oppose each other also complement each other; if they go to extremes and have nothing of the opposite, then they themselves are without value. Therefore, during Rujing we must grasp the ties between relaxation and tension, between active and inactive, and between naturalness and intention.

Relaxation is not something absolute during the process of Rujing. During the operation of body adjustment, no matter what posture practitioners keep, some muscles always remain relatively tense. If practitioners are completely relaxed, they may simply collapse. Therefore, only when practitioners themselves maintain the correct posture in the practice of Qigong can their arms and legs be relaxed to their maximum limits. If they go past the limit and affect the practicing posture, they become slack and sluggish. The requirement for the relaxation of consciousness is the same. As we know, practitioners should also be alert when they at the high level of Rujing. Here practitioners need to be mentally a little bit tense, otherwise they will not only relax too much but also risk malfunctions. This also reveals the relative aspect of quietness in Rujing. Thinking activities are still existent. As for naturalness, it is restrained by the intention of Rujing. If a spontaneous tendency deviating from the intention arises, we, of course, must correct it. Can we let negative illusions go their own way when they occur in our minds? It is impossible. Even though they are only distracting thoughts, we still cannot let them go their own way, let alone negative hallucinations. We need to adjust our thinking and moods so as to gradually overcome them.

The principle of relaxation, quietness, and naturalness is an old story in Qigong practice. Yet this principle indeed reveals the core of Qigong operation. To grasp the key point, the core, is to have proper limits for relaxation, quietness, and naturalness. People often say that truth taking one more step becomes nonsense. If relaxation, quietness, and naturalness go a little bit beyond their limits, they will become their opposites. Of course, practitioners' attempts will be in vain if their practices do not meet the necessary requirements.

The second principle is to proceed in an orderly way, step by step. This is an expression of "following nature" in the process of practicing Rujing. To proceed in an orderly way and step by step means to progress steadily by following the procedure of increasing Qigong power. Do not take shortcuts in practicing Rujing, or cut out necessary steps to get ahead faster. Beginners are likely to be impatient in practicing Rujing. They hope to master the skill in just a few days and reach the high level of Rujing quickly. So they often ask their teachers if there is any shortcut they can take. Actually, the only shortcut in practicing Rujing is to proceed in an orderly way and step by step, because only by doing so can we take fewer detours, or avoid detours. Avoiding detours means taking the straight road. The straight road is a shortcut, isn't it? Certainly, due to different talents, some people may walk quickly and some may walk slowly, though they take the same road. No matter how quickly or slowly they walk, they need to complete their walking so as to reach the destination, and it is not acceptable to leave any part of the route unwalked.

During the operation of Rujing, generally speaking, practitioners should learn and keep the correct posture and the proper way of breathing, and then coordinate with concentrating thought. It is pretty good for practitioners to follow this principle. Cautious practitioners do not hurry to start mind adjustment before they have set themselves up in the correct posture and way of breathing. Otherwise, they will not get good results. In addition, the benefits of Rujing will come gradually once practitioners have mastered the methods of operation. Since everyone is different in many respects, there is a big difference in the time when each person starts to see results. Some can make big progress within ten days or a fortnight; others will probably get some results after several months' practice.

It is the same as learning any operational method. Achievements in Rujing also depend on following an orderly sequence, step by step. We must banish the distracting thoughts of impatience in order to succeed. We should march forward steadily, in line with our own conditions.

Just as the principle of relaxation, quietness, and naturalness should not be taken to the extreme, the idea of practicing in an orderly way and step by step should not be regarded as an absolute solution either. It can be different under certain circumstances. For example, if someone does Rujing practice with the purpose of prolonging his life and preserving good health, he should learn and practice systematically and appropriately, from the easy to the most difficult, and make progress steadily. Those who practice Qigong to cure their diseases, especially patients who are seriously ill, may choose to practice a section of a particular Qigong that will have a curative effect on the illness. They can have systematic practice later, when their illness has gone. That is what is said in TCM: bring about a temporary solution to disease when it becomes serious, and apply a permanent cure when the disease becomes less serious. In their ordinary lives, practitioners may possibly encounter unexpected events, so sometimes they have to make temporary changes in their routine practice. For example, if people are on a business trip, it may upset their systematic arrangements for practice. If this is the case, practitioners should not attempt to make progress in their practice. They can just maintain what they have achieved and continue to practice. When they are once again settled after returning from the business trip, they can move ahead.

The third principle is perseverance. We can say that the operation of Rujing is not complicated. Yet it will take time for practitioners to become skillful and reach perfection. In Chinese the notion of Qigong practice contains the meaning of "martial art," which means real skill, and which can only be achieved through efforts and exercise, day after day. One should not have the idea of making small efforts to get good results. People often say that martial art needs big efforts. It means that practitioners can gradually reach the peak only after they have made great efforts and laid solid foundations. So we say that, no matter what type of Qigong practitioners practice, they must make great efforts to lay a solid foundation. The main content of the fundamentals is to entirely and correctly master the skills of breath, mind, and body adjustment.

If we say practitioners need quite a long period of training to become skilled in the operation of Rujing, it will take even more time for them to cultivate and temper themselves and develop the spirit of unselfishness. This spirit and ethics are the necessary conditions for practitioners aspiring to an advanced study of Qigong. Practicing Rujing is like a furnace tempering one's character. Only through a long period of tempering can the character be purified and become crystal clean. In ancient times, when people wanted to learn martial arts, their masters would test their characters for a few, ten, or even dozens of years, before they really started to teach them the genuine martial art. They might have been too conservative, but long-term tempering of their apprentices' character, and cultivating their nobility, was one of the important reasons for this.

It is actually quite difficult for beginners to persist in their practice, especially for those who do not even know the ABC of the operation of Rujing and have not yet gained any benefit from their practice. Once they have experienced the benefits of practice and have reached the realm of Rujing, it is not difficult for practitioners to keep practicing every day. I mentioned earlier that people can become addicted to Qigong. Thinking of how difficult it is to have the diehard smoker quit smoking, you will understand that it is also not easy to get Qigong addicts to quit their practice. However, persisting in long-term practice is not all that perseverance entails. There is still more to it. That is to practice Rujing at any time and anywhere, and to integrate the practice into your life. It is more difficult for practitioners to reach this goal than to keep practicing several hours every day.

What is it to practice Rujing at any time and anywhere? How can people practice Rujing all the time? They have to eat, sleep, work, and study. Here we do not mean that people have nothing to do but to sit cross-legged all day long with their eyes closed for practice. We ask that practitioners, at all times and in all places, put their mental and physical experience gained in the practice of Qigong into their daily work and living. It is not at all that people should stop working and living, but rather to make their lives and work more comfortable, pleasant, and much easier. Does this mean that they are people with two minds, or working absent-mindedly? No, on the contrary, they should be wholly absorbed in their work and life. To concentrate their ideas is to focus their attention on what they want to do. It does not mean that people focus their attention mechanically; they should concentrate on the work with ease. Meanwhile, they should relax their arms and hands and breathe naturally. This not only relieves fatigue at work but also improves their work efficiency. The method of practicing while working introduced earlier is similar to this one. When you start to learn how to blend your practice of Rujing with your work and life, you can adjust your breath, mind, and body according to the demands of practice and take a few minutes, or even seconds, to enter the realm of Rujing; and then you can start to work. Keep on doing this, and you may gradually get into the habit. Later on you will gradually realize that you are in the state of Qigong at all times and in all places. Thus, you can improve your power of Qigong much more quickly.

The three basic principles of how Rujing works have important guiding significance. The principles need to be carried out completely, from the beginning to the end. Practitioners who have followed these principles avoid deviation and make great progress. The principles are a powerful guarantee of success in the operation of Rujing.

Mind Adjustment

Mind adjustment in Rujing has two elements: thinking adjustment and mood adjustment. We'll focus initially on the practice, processing, and content of thinking, and what is involved in adjusting moods will be discussed later in this section.

The Operation of Thinking

The thinking operation of Rujing is to change the activities of daily abstract and imagery thinking into the activities of sensory thinking (part of perceptual thinking, the advanced thinking required by Rujing). It includes three steps. These are the luring of the senses, sensory practice, and sensory judgment and distinction. Here are the details of the three steps.

THE LURING OF THE SENSES

In the operation of Rujing thinking the first thing to do is to adjust the concentration of thought. There are many ways to adjust consciousness in Rujing practice. These methods belong to two categories: Yi Shou (thought concentration) and Zuo Nian (creating an imagery focus). Yi Shou consists of interior visualizing and hearing, Shou Qiao (focusing attention on a selective point), etc. Zuo Nian consists of focused thinking, reciting from memory, etc. No matter which method it is, three stages are needed in the concrete operating procedures of all methods.

Setting Up the Aim of Concentration

During this stage, the operating methods for concentration (Yi Shou) and creating an imagery focus (Zuo Nian) are different. The distinction between them is the way of setting up the aim of concentration, and the exact process of operation.

In *thought* concentration, practitioners choose a concrete event as the object of thinking activity in order to establish the aim of concentration. The concrete object may be a part of their body, some physiological activity, or the outside scene. The chosen body parts are often acupuncture points, such as the Dantian, Yongquan, Baihui, and Shanzhong. The physiological activity that people most often choose is breathing. As for the outside scene, pines, distant mountains, the morning sun, and the full moon are mostly chosen.

In Zuo Nian, things are different. Setting up the aim of concentration does not rely on the choice of something that actually exists, but rather on the creation of an image as an object of thinking. These "fictitious" objects can be divided into two types, abstract and imagery, on the basis of their different characteristics. Abstract objects are formed by words, such as "relax," "quiet," etc. Silently repeating phrases such as "early recovery" and "conquering diseases," or mentally counting numerals, can also be regarded as belonging to this type. Imagery objects are constructed from images such as recollections of the sea, fresh flowers, and trees. Practitioners can also imagine that they are floating in water or in the air, etc. The "Zuo Nian" meaning is "to construct one's own concentration." Constructing means "imaging."

We can see that during the period of setting up the aim of concentration, thinking activities are still forms of reflection of daily abstract, imagery, and perceptual thinking. Setting up the aim in thought concentration is mainly based on the operation of thinking with concrete images. If creating an imagery focus, its successful completion results in abstract or imagery thinking.

The aim of concentrating thoughts is the initial step of this first stage. After this, practitioners should continue to focus on the aim, letting their thinking orient towards it, and banishing other thoughts. People often say that "one thought replaces all kinds of distracting thoughts." It means keeping to the aim we have already set up for concentrating thoughts.

However, on the issue of maintaining concentration, and in the operation of "one thought replacing all kinds of distracting thoughts," practitioners must be aware that while the words "maintaining concentration" are to some extent linked with the notion of maintaining attention in psychology, they are in fact greatly different. If practitioners confuse them, it will affect their operation of concentration.

The common element in "concentration" in Rujing and "attention" in psychology is that both are exclusive and mono-selective. The function of concentration is "one thought replacing all kinds of distracting thoughts": it requires concentration on one thing only. "Attention" is a human psychological activity geared and focused towards a particular object. It also requires concentration on one event.

Apart from this, the two differ in the following way: the word "attention" requires human psychological activities to have a certain direction and concentration; "direction" and "concentration" are the two characteristics of the word "attention." The direction of attention makes human psychological activities reflect selectively on certain objects at every moment. It indicates the object reflected on and its scope.

Concentrated attention means that the human brain has a clear, complete, and sound awareness of the selected object. At the same time, when human psychological activities are directed towards some object they also concentrate on this object. There is no concentration without direction, and direction also results in concentration. Thus "attention" makes human psychological activity focus on one point. If we use the same terminology to express the concept of thought concentration, we would rather say that concentration means the direction and focusing of human psychological activity on a particular object. Concentration and attention have only their directed nature in common; they are different in that they reflect the selected objects to different extents. Concentration does not require clear, complete, and profound representation on the selected object itself. It needs only a rough impression of the selected object. The main purpose of concentration is not to know and understand the object itself. We have already mentioned that concentrating on the Dantian does not mean studying what the Dantian is; it means inducing certain feelings and moods by focusing on the Dantian. After that, we should let the feelings and moods spread through the whole body or to an even larger field.

Metaphorically speaking, *attention* is like the saying "drink today while drink you may, you may never ever drink another day," and requires the wine itself. The word *concentration* is like the old tippler's delight not residing in the wine, so much as having other things in mind. If we compare the two, we can say that concentration is a kind of attention that guides towards certain feelings and moods.

Attention is the act of fixing the mind on something in itself. In addition, attention places emphasis on rational things; it usually leads to the deep understanding of objects. As for concentration, it places emphasis on perception of objects. Thus attention tends towards the opposition of subjective and objective, whereas concentration tends towards a mixture of the two. That is the key distinction. It demonstrates the different modes of handling things in the everyday state of the human body and in the state of Qigong. That is one reason why the states of Rujing and other types of Qigong are often different from the common sensations and understanding of ordinary people.

Now we know that concentration and attention are similar in form, but that the two are different in quality and purpose. The results are certainly different. We have analyzed above the difference between concentration and attention in the psychological state. Attention causes psychological activity to be very active, in both thinking and mood. It makes the cerebral cortex very excited. This is the procedure of *positive inducement*. As for concentration, it induces slow reflection and quiet feelings about things, eventually to the point where even concentration itself does not exist. It gradually strengthens the control of the cerebral cortex. This is the procedure of *negative inducement*.

Once we know the difference between concentration and attention, we are much clearer about how to establish the purpose of concentration. First of all, we choose or set up a concentrating thought, through concentration or Zuo Nian. We then lead the thinking activities to the concentrating thought. We will get the result of "one thought replacing all kinds of distracting thoughts." Once we have done this, we have completed the task of setting up the aim of concentration.

Inducing Sensory Experience

We mentioned above that one thought replacing all kinds of distracting thoughts is not the main purpose of setting up the aim of concentration. Its most important function is to induce the relevant sensory experience (including mood experience).

What about the concrete procedure? First we will talk about the processing of sense experience in Zuo Nian, because this is very typical. Then we will introduce the processing in concentration.

As an example, let's say we build up a concentrating thought of the sea through imagination. The picture of the sea appears in our minds. Meanwhile, we banish other distracting thoughts that have nothing to do with the sea. Now we have completed the task of setting up the aim of concentration. What is the next step? Does it require you to enjoy the beautiful scenery, turbulent waves, and flying seabirds? No. The next step is to mentally be there and indeed experience your feelings and mood as if you are standing on the beach. You don't need to have a very clear picture of the sea in your mind, but you should really feel open-hearted, and feel the soft, cool sea breeze, and even smell a salty, fishy smell. Thus, you will feel relaxed, content, and at ease. After that, you will be indulging in this sense and mood experience as if it were real. This is the sensation of vital energy, and a kind of sensation of floating in the universe and merging with it. In brief, from this point your sensory experience should be induced by setting up a concentrating thought that matches your sense experience. There should definitely be a premise—that is, you should have had the concrete experience, or at least have gotten the knowledge by reading some books. In other words, the superficial image that practitioners set up must be linked with their own sensory experience. If they cannot follow the principle, they had better not set up the aim. In that case they should build up a superficial image that they are familiar with and have experienced as their aim of concentration, so as to keep the inducement of their sensory experience running smoothly.

The sensory experience in concentration is not as straightforward as that in Zuo Nian, but the basic principle is the same. Let us talk about focusing concentrating thought on the Dantian, starting from the operation and the comparison with Zuo Nian. Focusing concentrating thought on the Dantian means that practitioners guide their thinking to the Dantian—and where is the Dantian? Have you ever seen it or touched it? The answer is clear. The

Dantian is known to lie in the abdomen but it can be neither seen nor touched. At the beginning, when they focus their concentrating thought on the Dantian, practitioners can only imagine that the Dantian is in their abdomen and focus their thinking towards it. From this point of view there is an essential difference from Zuo Nian. The only difference is that in Zuo Nian practitioners imagine the shape of a certain object in the outside world; and with regard to concentration, they only imagine some part of their bodies. One of the concentration exercises requires one to focus on a point three inches down from the Shenzhong acupuncture point on the chest. It is all very well that the activities of thinking point to that spot, but how does concentration induce the sensations?

Each kind of concentration is slightly different. When practitioners focus their thinking on the Dantian, their thoughts are directed to the area of the Dantian in their imagination. Based on this, practitioners may have one thought replacing all kinds of distracting thoughts, and they can evoke the sensation of vital energy from their Dantian. As described earlier, the actual process of evoking vital energy feelings from the Dantian is directly related to the internal movement of vital energy. Actually, in actively focusing thoughts on the Dantian, you are also conducting the operation of vital energy. As we know, the activities of concentrating thought are closely linked with the internal running of vital energy. That is what people often say: "Where the concentrating thought is, there is the vital energy." Your concentrating thought is directed to the Dantian, your internal vital energy turns to the Dantian, and the concentration of internal vital energy can then be felt. The vital energy sensation is induced by focusing the thoughts on the Dantian. In other words, practitioners can feel the concentration of vital energy in the Dantian. (In fact, only practitioners have this kind of Qi sensation. They know exactly the position of the Dantian—their guided thinking really has an aim.) Therefore, concentrating thought and vital energy support each other and are mutually interdependent. If you keep focusing and you have no sensation in the Dantian, this proves that you have not been successful. Because your concentrating thought in the Dantian is not coming together with vital energy, your concentrating thought is not attached to anything, and it is difficult to focus your concentrating thought on the Dantian. So it can be seen that, in concentration, sensory guidance to the aim of concentrating thought is a kind of vital energy sensation that is produced when the operation of vital energy is directly affected by the activity of concentrating thought. Compared with concentration, the vital energy sensation produced by Zuo Nian is indirect. But the vital energy sensation produced by Zuo Nian is complete from the beginning, while the vital energy sensation produced by concentration is only partial at the very beginning.

During the stage of inducing sensation, operating thinking activity is a process of transition from thinking activities that involve abstraction and images, to thinking activities based on sensation evoked by the thinking of concrete subject matter. Now we have the *sensation* of Rujing activities in sensory thinking, but the *activity* of sensory thinking is not yet in full swing.

The sensation needed in Rujing is not something arbitrary. It has special requirements. It is the strong sensation of vital energy and its movements, and the sensation of vital energy mingling with universal Qi—and it is also the sensation of comfort and relaxation. Due to the movements of vital energy in the body, practitioners may have all kinds of sensations, such as the "16 touches," but most of them are the by-products of the sensation of vital energy; they are not the sensation of vital energy itself. Another task for practitioners at this stage is to have correct judgment of what the sensation of vital energy feels like.

Abandoning the Aim of Concentrating Thought
This is the last stage of the luring of the senses, and also a very important one. During this stage practitioners will complete the transition from other modes of thinking to sensory thinking. Following this, practitioners have just stepped through the gateway to sensory thinking, and they are also on the elementary level of Rujing. In the process of practicing Rujing, this is a turning point for practitioners, from the ordinary state to the Qigong state.

In the operation of the two previous stages, we first set up the aim of the concentrating thought and banishing all kinds of distracting thoughts. Finally, we induced the relevant sensation. Thus, the task of concentrating thought has been completed. Now, we need to give up the aim of concentrating thought, and instead direct our thinking to inducing sensation. For example, if our focus of concentrating thought is the sea, then when we have all kinds of sensations of being beside the sea, we can give up the image of the sea in our minds, and make our thinking engage with the sensations we have just had. If the aim of concentrating thought is the Dantian, when you have the sensation of vital energy from the Dantian, you need only let your thinking be directed to the sensation of vital energy; you need not care about where the Dantian is. If the aim of concentrating thought is the words "relaxation" and "quietness," then, when you have had the sensation of relaxation and quietness, you should forget the words, and instead let your thinking grasp the sensation of relaxation and quietness. In sum, practitioners should give up all abstract image and concrete image-related thought content, which induced the sensations in the mind, that will enable them to enter into sensory thinking.

Please note that there is both a difference and a connection between abandoning the aim of concentrating thought and banishing distracting thoughts. "Distracting thoughts" here means all kinds of thoughts which have nothing to do with the practice of Rujing; and the aim of concentrating thought is related to the practice of Rujing. For beginners, this operational activity of concentrating thought is an important part of the thinking operation of Rujing. However, once it has completed its task, if thinking still relies on it, then it has become a distracting thought. Because at this stage the activity of thinking should stop, as the aim of concentrating thought has become redundant and has nothing more to do with the practice of Rujing. If practitioners do not make their thinking stop in time, it may go astray. Therefore, practitioners must give it up whenever it should be given up. Do not indulge it.

This process of abandonment is very natural. The main task of setting up the aim of concentrating thought is to induce sensation. When practitioners have had their sensations, and things are in full swing, the aim of concentrating thought can itself be eliminated, since it is no longer effective, and will gradually fade away. So in order to progress, practitioners naturally allow the thought to follow its own way and disappear by itself; otherwise, it cannot die away quickly. If practitioners try to do it purposely, the concentrating thought will reappear.

The three stages of sensory guidance seem like the process of learning to swim. In this analogy the human body is like the main part of our thinking; a rubber ring would be the aim of concentrating thought, and water represents sensation. At the beginning the novice wears a rubber ring and learns how to swim in water. In the end, he knows how to swim, and then he takes off the rubber ring, goes into the water, and swims freely.

After these three stages of sensory guidance, practitioners can feel relaxed and comfortable because they have got rid of everyday abstract and imaginative thinking and seem to have entered into a new world.

For beginners, the luring of the senses needs to be repeated many times, because it is hard for them to hold the induced sensation. They may lose the sensation due to distracting thoughts and unstable moods. For the masters it is not necessary to purposely induce the sensation. Once they have prepared for Rujing, the sensation will appear naturally.

THE OPERATION OF SENSATION

Sensory guidance towards sensory thinking is the first step in the whole process of Rujing. After that, practitioners should let their thinking directly operate their sensory experience and gradually approach the level of emptiness and the state of forgetting both the material world and self. The operation of sensation is the whole process of sensory experience in the operation of thinking. This is the main part of sensory thinking. The operation of sensation has three elements.

Expansion and Contraction of Sensation

At the beginning of Rujing, sensations of vital energy usually occur on one or several sensitive points. For example, someone may have Qi sensations in the Dantian or at Huiyin, and some may first experience the sensation in their hands and feet. As the level of Rujing deepens, practitioners need to expand Qi sensation from these sensitive points—for example, from the Dantian to the whole abdomen and to the whole body, or from the hands to the arms, from the arms to the shoulders and back, and from the upper body to the whole body. When practitioners reach the higher levels of Rujing, the Qi sensation of the whole body needs to be extended beyond the body, so as to let the individual's Qi merge with universal Qi and reach the realm of man and nature becoming one. At that point Qi sensation will have expanded without limits. In some specific forms of Qigong the operation of sensory expansion is the most important element.

For instance, "Brightness Section of ShiBien" (a Buddhist Qigong) requires practitioners to induce the sensation of brightness, and then expand it, in order to stimulate certain extraordinary powers, such as the power of clairvoyance.

Sensory contraction is totally different from sensory expansion. It requires the transferring of Qi sensation from the external world to the internal world, and from the whole world to one particular part. For instance, while practicing collecting Qi you need to collect Qi from the outside world, whether it is the essence from the sun or the moon, or from the Earth and the trees, and send it to your Dantian. If practicing Qigong to cure yourself of a disease, you sometimes need to get Qi to attack the afflicted part. Practitioners should also lead Qi from their bodies to focus on that particular part. In the process of recovery, any negative sensation will shrink. If the patient has something wrong with their abdomen, the uncomfortable sensation in their belly will contract to a small spot on the belly, and finally vanish.

Sensory extension and contraction are operations of sensory experience.

Strengthening and Weakening of Sensation

The strengthening and weakening of sensation is directly related to sensory expansion and contraction. If we try to expand a sensation, we must, first of all, strengthen it. The sensory strengthening is the premise of sensory expansion. If we want to extend Qi sensation from our Dantian, we must make the Qi in the Dantian full, and to some extent the Qi in our Dantian will expand naturally. Then we can guide the action adroitly according to circumstance, and successfully finish the task of sensory extension. If we want to extend the Qi sensation from any sensitive point, we first need to strengthen it and make it full of Qi. If we are reluctant to do this, but eager for quick success, we will spoil it and be unable to achieve what we anticipated.

Sensory extension usually relies on the strengthening of sensation. We may perhaps feel the Qi sensation strengthened, yet the sensory extension may not follow at the same time. They are interlinked, yet different aspects of the same matter. For example, extension is not a requirement if one wants to strengthen the sensation of weightlessness from being as light as a swallow to as light as smoke; or if one wants to strengthen the Qi sensation at the acupuncture point of TianMu in order to explore one's potential clairvoyance. Generally speaking, at the lower level of Rujing, practitioners often need the operation of sensory reinforcement.

At the advanced level of Rujing the operation of weakening sensation is used quite often. In the realm of emptiness, all sensations are gradually weakened. And in the state of forgetting the material world and self, all sensations seem either to vanish or to appear interchangeably.

The weakening of sensation has some links with sensory contraction. Sensory contraction often occurs after the weakening of sensation. When we need to diminish the range of some sensation, we'll first weaken it, and then it will dwindle naturally. Of course, like the relationship between sensory reinforcement and expansion, they are either correlated or not correlated.

The strengthening and weakening of sensation is the operation of sensory intensity.

The operation of sensation in its range and intensity is closely related to the operation of breathing. We know that many sensations are caused by the supplementing and spreading of internal vital energy in the body. Therefore, their range and intensity are directly affected by the movement of inner Qi. If one is full of inner Qi in the body, one has strong feelings in many parts. Otherwise, one has weak feelings. We also know that the movement of inner Qi is often based on breathing as its source and power. Thus sensory range and the change of its intensity are linked with breathing. Adjustments of mind and breath are linked. So the operation of sensory range and its intensity can change in line with the operation of breathing to some extent, and the two operations become integrated. Practitioners should fully observe and understand this.

Stability and Change of Sensation

Sensation in the process of Rujing develops step by step from a low level to a high level. Each level one experiences contains a period of transforming and stabilizing the sensations. When practitioners reach a new level, the fresh sensation is very weak and unstable, and needs to be stabilized. Sensory stability is related to the reinforcement and extension of sensation. The sensation within a certain range can be stable only when its intensity reaches a certain level. The stabilized sensation still needs to be gradually strengthened to a critical point in order to enter the next level. The critical point is a turning point. When a new sensation reaches that point, practitioners should seize the opportunity and transfer the sensation to the next level, where the process of stabilization and transformation is repeated, and so on, until the realm of Ultimate Emptiness is reached.

At the beginning of Rujing practitioners often have sensations of relaxation and quietness. When the sensations appear, they need to be stabilized, expanded, and strengthened. It may involve the process of expanding from a part of the body to the entire body, from being weak to being strong, and from being unstable to being stable. When the relaxed and quiet sensations are stable, practitioners will naturally have a Qi sensation coming from their Dantian. At that moment the sensation will change. The Qi sensation in the Dantian will gradually replace the sensation of relaxation and quietness to become the center of Rujing sensation, and will bring one to a new level. Practitioners still need to expand and strengthen the Qi sensation in the Dantian and make it stronger and more stable. When the Qi sensation in the Dantian develops to a new stage, it can appear and move up along the Du meridian, or rush to the part affected by disease, and proceed to a new level. After that, the center of sensation may transfer to operate and guide the movements of inner Qi. The process of Rujing continues step by step in this way.

Sensory stability and alteration create the *nature* of sensations. The operation of the nature of sensations is the key link in the activities of sensory practice. Whether or not practitioners can deepen their practice of Rujing depends mainly on this operation. People often say that practicing Qigong needs mastery of the "cooking temperature." What is the "cooking temperature"? It refers to the right time and opportunity for a change in sensation. When is the right time or opportunity? It is the time for the promotion of sensory transformation. If you start the transformation a little too early, you will fail; a little too late, and you will also fail. Taoists pay great attention to the opportunity and take it as the key point in success in the practice of "Dan" (internal essence). Because of its significance, and because mastery of it relies mainly on the comprehension of each individual, the knowledge of how to master this opportunity has been kept secret by Taoists. There is a saying, "The wise man teaches how to use the medicine and not how to make it. It is always just a few people who have the know-how."

The contents and operation of the key points in Rujing are different from the practice of Dan, but the basic principle is the same. They both require one to grasp the critical points; in other words, practitioners need to grasp the point which transforms quantitative change to qualitative change. The operation of forging the internal essence has a significant relationship with breathing. The transformation between different levels in Rujing is closely related to breathing—but more important still is the operation of thinking.

During the operation of sensory extension and contraction, of strengthening and weakening, it is quite easy to master the essential principle of following nature. As to sensory stability and transformation, this is not easy to do well. Human subjective reinforcement is easily added. Therefore, it is very important to stress comfort in the process of transformation. If you are eager to have quick success and speed up the process of transformation subjectively, the result is that the transformation will be an awkward one and will make you feel uncomfortable, because the existing sensory range and intensity have not met the requirement for producing a new sensation. If, on the other hand, you delay the transfer and maintain or strengthen the sensation which should be transformed, and are unable to bring the sensation to a higher level, then you may also feel upset and uncomfortable. But if you do it to just the right point and at the right time, it will bring to you the sensation of your heart's opening, and it will open a new world for you. You will certainly feel comfortable.

Comfort is significant, both in sensation and mood. To promote sensory transfer, a comfortable mood is far more important than the sensation of comfort. As mentioned earlier, patients who practice Qigong to cure their diseases really suffer pain when the diseases are almost cured, but they are in a pleasant mood. When they are suffering pain, the disease is disappearing; therefore, the pain is emotionally bearable. The patients may even request it. If this is the case, practitioners should follow their senses and make a quick decision to assist the occurrence of this pain and suffering in order to cure the disease instantly. That is an act of following nature. If we hesitate and miss the chance of facilitating this pain and suffering, we will have to wait days for another opportunity. Therefore, there is an important link between the grasp of sensory transformation and correct judgment of the sensations and moods.

Sensory Judgment and Distinction

Judgment and distinction of sensations is a very precise and complicated operation. In Chapter 2 we saw that there are all sorts of sensations with different levels in the process of Rujing. These different kinds and levels of sensations often have only subtle differences. Furthermore, when a new sensation appears, it is usually unstable. Most appear and disappear by turns or flash by, so it is even more difficult to distinguish them. Therefore, practitioners should improve their sensitivity all the time during Rujing. The state of Rujing itself has already provided the conditions for improving sensitivity. Generally speaking, practitioners will be more and more sensitive at the successive levels of Rujing they reach. All will be well so long as practitioners understand the importance of the matter and keep an eye on it in practicing Rujing. They don't need to (and should not) intentionally seek it.

If we say sensory guidance comes first and sensory practice second, sensory judgment and distinction must be carried through the entire process of operating sensory thinking in Rujing. It is not *beyond* sensory guidance and its practice, but it exists in each part of the operating process.

We need to judge and distinguish the sensation in its initial stage, as well as its developing and transforming stages. Besides, sensory judgment and distinction have a role to play when a new sensation appears. It needs to determine the destiny of the new sensation, and whether the sensation should be developed or given up. After a new sensation becomes strong, sensory judgment and distinction must often gauge its range, intensity, stability, and so on. Therefore, sensory judgment and distinction play the role of pioneer and guide in the operation of sensory thinking. We may say that the activities of sensory thinking cannot proceed smoothly without sensory judgment and distinction.

For judgment and distinction, we need a criterion. Our aim is to practice Rujing, so our criterion is the level of emptiness and the realm of forgetting the material world and self. All the sensations and moods that meet the needs of this aspect should be kept and expanded; otherwise, they should be given up and banished. As explained in Chapter 3, the term "Qi sensation" means the way practitioners feel vital energy gathering and expanding. In the process of Rujing, in a broad sense, it can be the sensations that meet the demands of reaching a high level in Rujing: whether or not practitioners are obtaining Qi in Rujing is essentially whether or not they really have this kind of sensation. During the operation of Rujing one thing should be paid attention to. The criterion in our minds should be mainly in our subconscious; it should have been established there during the preparation of Rujing. When Rujing begins, practitioners need not consider it deliberately, though it may escape from the subconscious and appear in consciousness.

Sensory judgment and distinction usually entail judgment in the following three aspects: the existence of sensation, the nature of sensation, and the scale of the sensation.

Judgment of the Existence of Sensation
During the operation of sensory thinking in Rujing "judgment" relates specifically to the initial occurrence of the sensation. Only when practitioners have the Qi sensation can sensory thinking be carried on. Judgment and distinction function at the second stage of sensory guidance, the stage of inducing sensory experience. During the guiding process, practitioners should continuously judge whether there is inner Qi moving, or a sensation that could lead to the realm of emptiness. If there is, we should keep it. If there isn't, we should continue to induce it. If something is wrong we should banish it. The sensory judgment and distinction at this time are a reference point for the later expansion of sensory thinking. Besides, later on, when practitioners enter a new stage of Rujing, the sensory judgment and distinction relating to a new sensation is of the same nature. But unlike the judgment of sensation at the beginning, judgment at this

time, precisely speaking, is judgment of the *nature* of the sensation rather than judgment of the *existence* of the sensation (since the new sensation is mostly transferred from the old sensation).

Judgment of the Nature of Sensation

This has two parts. One is to judge the type of nature of the sensation; the other is to judge whether its nature is stable or not. These two are linked together. When the nature of the sensation is unstable, its type is difficult to decide.

During the operation of sensory thinking in Rujing, practitioners need this judgment for any new sensation. New sensation may be a change in quality, or may be a change in quantity. Furthermore, sometimes the boundary between quality and quantity is not very clear. For example, in the "16 touches," there are two sensations of warmth and heat. Are they, in the final analysis, a change of quality or quantity? It seems reasonable to say they are changes of quantity, because too warm becomes hot, and slightly hot is just warm. It is also reasonable to say they are changes of quality, because warm makes people comfortable, but heat can make people uncomfortable and depressed. Feeling warm is the normal sensation, but feeling hot may be abnormal. In the process of Rujing there are many sensory changes; for example, cool and cold, heavy and very heavy, etc.

The reason for these sensory changes is that sensory changes mainly follow an evolutionary mode, and seldom the mode of revolution. In the process of evolution, the sensory changes are very slight. Although there is a big difference between the beginning and the end, it is very difficult to detect the slight changes throughout the process. Yes, there is the sensation of great change, such as getting through the Du meridian in a split second, and in a moment opening TianMu. A new horizon opens up before practitioners. It is easy to judge such a big change, but it is not easy to judge subtle changes in sensation. This must be related to the judgment of sensory scale.

Judgment and Distinction of Sensory Scale

This has three parts. These are the judgments of the position, scope, and intensity of sensations.

In the operation of sensory thinking, thought needs to know where the existing sensation is, where it is extending to, and how powerful it is. As the process of sensation develops, it also needs to be aware of sensory changes in these aspects. In fact, only when people grasp the changing sensory scale can they decide how to operate the sensation in the next step and guide it correctly.

It is easy to operate sensations on a small scale, but it is not easy to define its nature. It is easy to judge and differentiate sensation and its nature on a large scale, but not easy to operate it. If something is wrong, we can only slow down its speed and cannot give it up at once. Just as when we are taking strong medicine, we cannot suddenly reduce a large quantity without consequences.

As we pointed out in Chapter 3, in sensory thinking "sensory judgment and distinction" means changes of human sensations, not changes of abstract knowledge in sensation. Here we stress again that, in the actual operation of sensory thinking, sensory judgment and distinction are easily influenced by abstract thought. Practitioners should pay special attention to this. Sensory judgment and distinction are first and foremost the change of sensory experience, not the change of its knowledge; otherwise, it would be abstract thought, not sensory thinking. The condition of Rujing would be ruined. Of course, abstract thought, image thought, and concrete imagery thought cannot be taken separately. The factor of abstract thinking cannot and should not completely be beyond sensory judgment and distinction, but it can never, ever affect and replace sensory thinking in the prime position.

In the same way as the three modes of thinking are linked together, so sensory guidance, sensory practice, and sensory judgment and distinction are also related to each other. They are different stages and aspects of the operation of sensory thinking in Rujing. So, in the operation, practitioners cannot attend to one thing and neglect the others. They need to take care of everything.

The Operation of Mood

Earlier, we talked about the operation of moods in the operation of thinking. Here, I'd like to restate only one point: that when the operation of sensory thinking proceeds smoothly, the mood follows the sensation, and it too develops successfully. Now mood and sensation can unite as one and go forward together. When the operation of sensory thinking is not done smoothly—such as when practitioners have bad sensations—sensation and mood may occur separately. In this case practitioners should focus on the control of moods, reversing the priority of sensory thinking over mood thinking, and take mood thinking as the leading operation, to guide sensory thinking. If the sensation is already not good, we should not let the mood become a bad mood. If we cannot stay in a good mood, we should at least try to keep it in an ordinary state and avoid it following the trend of sensation. After that, we can let mood influence sensation and return sensation to normal.

For example, if a vicious hallucination appears in the mind and "demons and ghosts" are making an entrance, what practitioners do now is to operate mood. Facing demons and ghosts, it is impossible for practitioners to be happy. They must, first of all, calm down and not be frightened. When the mood comes back to a normal state, practitioners can start to deal with the hallucination itself. By this time the hallucination has appeared and been strengthened, so it is difficult for practitioners to get rid of it right away. A good method of handling this is to ignore it and let it disappear by itself, or to have another good concentration thought to replace it. No matter which method we choose, it is always necessary to maintain a stable mood. If practitioners are nervous and flustered at this time, they will be letting the sensation be buffered about.

Now we know that, in common cases, we cannot take special care of mood thinking, but if sensory thinking is not going smoothly, then mood thinking has to come along immediately and rescue sensory thinking from danger. It is like a first-aid kit. A first-aid kit is not used in the normal run of events, but in an emergency, we will have to use it.

Some kinds of Qigong always place the operation of mood thinking in the lead position, and assign subordinate status to sensory thinking. Take Xian-Tian (Natural) Qigong, for example. The Rujing operation of this Qigong requires the practitioner to calm his mood and not to experience any sensations. An old saying states that "all roads lead to Rome." Taking mood operation as the dominant factor for promoting practice is also one of the ways to reach the realm of Rujing.

Breathing Adjustment

Breathing adjustment in Rujing mainly consists of two parts. One is the operation of inhaling/exhaling, that is, breathing in and out in very soft way. The other is the operation of the manner of breathing, that is, changing from ordinary breathing to navel breathing, according to the demands of Rujing.

The Operation of Inhaling/Exhaling

In ancient times people thought there were four types of breathing in Rujing. For instance, in *Da An Ban Shou Yi Jing* (Breathing and Concentrating Scripture)[41] it says: "Breathing has four forms: the first is called Feng (wind), the second is Chuan (gasp for breath), the third is Qi (air), the fourth is Xi (gentle breathing). Feng means to breathe noisily; Qi means to breathe silently; Xi means to breathe in and out; Chuan means to breathe with difficulty."

There are further explanations in the Sui dynasty book *Tong Meng Zhi Guan* (Primary Methods of Cultivating Vital Energy).[42]

What is the state of Feng (wind)? If a noise can be heard as the air goes in and out through the nostrils as one breathes, that is the state of Feng. What is the state of Chuan (gasp)? Although there is no sound when people sit there breathing, there is a blockage in their breathing in and out. That is the state of Chuan. What is the state of Qi (air)? Although there is no sound and no blockage when people sit there breathing, the breathing seems a little heavy. That is the state of Qi. What is the state of Xi (gentle breathing)? Breathing silently, smoothly, and gently; breathing in and out softly and consistently. The breathing is sometimes noticeable and sometimes imperceptible. One is peaceful, calm, and in a pleasant mood. That is the state of Xi.

Rujing requires the last breathing form, namely the state of Xi. The three previous breathing forms should be avoided. The state of Feng makes vital energy scattered. The state of Chuan blocks the movement of vital energy. The state of Qi makes you feel tired. The state of Xi brings you stability. Only the state of Xi is beneficial in Rujing. The other three breathing forms may be used in some other types of Qigong. For example, in New Qigong Treatment the state of Feng is adopted. In some martial arts Qigong, the state of Qi is adopted. As for Rujing, none is effective except the state of Xi.

Xi, as described in modern language, is a deep, long, soft, tiny, and very weak breath. It is just like what Mr. Su Dongpo, a very famous Chinese ancient poet, used to say: "Xi is just like steam coming from boiling water in a kettle, or the steam from boiling soup in a pot; it comes in and out freely." Under these circumstances, when a feather is placed under the nostrils, the feather does not even move. We know that ordinary people breathe 16–20 times per minute. During Rujing, practitioners may reduce their breathing to 1–2 times per minute, or even once every few minutes. But the reduction in breathing frequency does not mean one has ceased breathing; that is to say, there is no pause between inhaling/exhaling. Practitioners extend the length of their inhaling/exhaling. Now we can imagine how deep, long, soft, and tiny their breaths are during this time.

People's regular breathing is between the states of Feng and Qi. It needs a lot of practice if practitioners are to change their regular breathing form to the Xi form. Take "Do Not Forget and Do Not Assist" as a principle; during the operating process practitioners should actively adjust their breathing and have it shift to a deep, long, soft, and tiny mode. They should not intentionally hold their breath and force themselves into that state, but get into it in a natural way. During the process of Rujing, practitioners may feel as if the chest is depressed, they may feel faint and tired, etc. All this is related to incorrect operation of their breathing. When we say "Do Not Forget and Do Not Assist" we mean to just have the idea of operating breathing in mind, but not to apply any force to implement the idea—using concentrating thought, not force. As the three adjustments affect each other in the process of Rujing, the breathing may naturally become deep, long, soft, and tiny. If practitioners try to influence it, they may go too far.

Once practitioners know how to adjust their breathing, the whole procedure of controlling breathing can change from conscious to subconscious. By now the consciousness will not pay any special attention to breathing, because the way of breathing now is deep, long, soft, and tiny.

In adjusting the breathing in Rujing one should alternately work and rest. In this way practitioners not only avoid tiredness but also develop gradually the ability to adjust breathing subconsciously. When the adjustment is active, you operate your breathing consciously; when it is at rest, you can completely ignore your breathing. As this is done alternately, the difference between the states of work and rest becomes smaller and smaller, until there is no difference. Then practitioners enter the stage of subconsciously adjusting their breath. We call this "Xi adjustment."

The operation of breathing in the adjustment is very closely linked with the operation of mood. The combined process of adjustment of breathing and adjustment of mind is based on the link between mood and breathing. A placid mood leads to stable breathing. Conversely, stable breathing leads to placid mood. They influence each other. Native Americans believe that when two people are talking to each other, if they keep the same rhythm and speed of their inhalation and exhalation, their hearts will beat in harmony and it will be easy for them to agree with each other. This is reasonable, because breathing and mood influence each other, and mood is closely linked with thinking activities. Therefore, when the rhythm and pace of human inhaling/exhaling are synchronous, the higher psychological activities, including thinking and mood, can be synchronous as well.

So, in the operation of adjusting breathing, if practitioners have fast breathing or very slow breathing, apart from the aspect of operating breathing, we should consider the operation of mood. This may be related to the moods of being eager for quick success, or being lazy. After adjusting the mood properly, the problems in the operation of breathing may be solved. If we combine the adjustment of breathing with mood adjustment, we can speed up the process of Rujing. This is a good experience that has been confirmed by repeated testing.

The Operation of Various Breathing Forms

The advanced form of breathing in Rujing is "TaiXi" (breathing like a fetus). There are two explanations of breathing like a fetus. One is to inhale/exhale from the navel. As an ancient belief states, "People beginning to learn the adjustment of their breathing must imagine that the air comes in and out through their navels, as if they were breathing in the womb as fetuses. Hence the name 'Fetus Breathing'." Ancient people practiced this breathing form in order to recover their youthful vigor. They believed that a baby in the mother's womb breathed through the navel. In the book *She Sheng San Yao* (Three Important Ways of Keeping Fit)[43] it says: "The fetus does not breathe through his nostrils and mouth. His navel connects with his mother's Ren meridian, which associates with her lungs, and the lungs link to her nose. So when the mother exhales, the baby exhales; when the mother inhales, so does the baby. The baby's breathing comes from the navel."

The second explanation of breathing like a fetus is body breathing; that is to say, the whole body breathes. Every pore of the body can breathe. Now, lung breathing may have already stopped. As it says in a book entitled *Su Shen Liang Fang* (Good Prescriptions of Doctor Su and Shen):[44] "Breathing goes by itself, it does not come in and out.

You can feel this kind of breathing. It spreads out from the thousands of pores on the body. It occurs without you noticing its beginning."

The two descriptions of breathing like a fetus may be taken as two stages or two forms of the breath. The former is the essential one, and the latter is developed from it. The breathing like a fetus that is required by the advanced level of Rujing is the latter; we call it "body breathing."

The natural breathing of people in everyday life is not breathing like a fetus. It needs training for someone to transfer from natural breathing to breathing like a fetus. The entire process involves three stages: chest breathing, abdominal breathing, and breathing like a fetus.

CHEST BREATHING

Chest breathing is the natural breathing of people when they are standing. Due to lengthy training, singers and sportsmen may have developed natural abdominal breathing, or a combination of chest and abdominal breathing. When people are chest breathing, you can see their chests rise and fall. The first step of breathing operation in Rujing is to guide natural chest breathing to deep, long, soft, and tiny breathing. As described above, the principle of operation is to practice with concentrating thought, not with force. But at the beginning, it is very difficult to operate the breathing without any effort. Practitioners mainly rely on their concentrating thought, and also make some effort. How do practitioners practice with just the right amount of force? As the ancients said, neither let breathing be blocked, nor breathe in and out quickly; keep breathing easy and smooth, and keep it within limits.

After breathing in and out has been adjusted properly, practitioners can lead the breath lower down and shift chest breathing to abdominal breathing. This change cannot be done suddenly. We should do it step by step. It should be achieved gradually. Usually we can adopt the method of guiding the Qi down in different sections. For instance, we can first let Qi down to Shenzhong (the acupoint in the pit of the heart). When this part is full of Qi and breathing in and out is stable, we can let it down to the navel area, and finally to the Dantian. During the process, chest breathing may switch to a mixture of chest and abdominal breathing. We can observe the rise and fall of both chest and abdomen.

During the period of chest breathing and transition from chest breathing to abdominal breathing, owing to short-term practice in breathing, it can be quite difficult for practitioners to have deep, long, soft, and tiny breathing. We cannot demand too much of them. We can have a long breath only when we take a deep breath, and only a long breath can become soft and tiny. In the operation of breathing it will be all right if practitioners can keep their breathing stable and at the right speed, and also gradually lead their breath down into the lower part of their bodies.

ABDOMINAL BREATHING

When practitioners are breathing with the abdomen, we can see their belly rise and fall. Abdominal breathing can be divided into two kinds: the "up" type and the "down" type. In operating the "up" type, your abdomen should swell up when you inhale. You belly should contract down when you exhale. The "down" type operates in just the opposite way. When you gradually switch from chest breathing to abdominal breathing, you will naturally switch to the "up" type of abdominal breathing. The "down" type of abdominal breathing requires special training and is a bit more difficult to adopt. For the purpose of Rujing, practitioners do not need to bother about which type to select. Any type will do, so long as it is formed with a gradual, natural development.

Some types of Qigong emphasize the training of the "down" type of abdominal breathing. They think it is much more helpful to push the inner Qi around. For example, when people move Qi along the Ren and Du meridians, they often adopt the "down" type of abdominal breathing. Inner Qi moves up to the acupoint Baihui when you inhale, and down to the Dantian when you exhale. In training the "down" type, practitioners should focus on exhalation and ignore inhalation from the very beginning. Concentrating thought will guide the inner Qi down to gather in the Dantian when practitioners exhale. If practitioners keep practicing for a long time, their belly will be full of air and bulge when they exhale, and be relaxed and shrink when they inhale.

Whichever type practitioners pick, they should avoid throwing out their abdomen intentionally. Bulging and shrinking of the abdomen are the natural consequences of inhaling/exhaling. Practitioners should not force it. When practicing, they need only to focus on inhaling/exhaling. Their abdomens should only coordinate and assist. Deep, long inhalation usually makes the abdomen bulge, and when practitioners contract their abdomen, the pressure naturally releases the air.

At the beginning, with abdominal breathing, practitioners feel as if they are breathing with their whole abdomen. It is the same as the lobes of the lungs bulging and shrinking with chest breathing. Gradually, a clear and specific breathing point will appear as breathing becomes deep, long, soft, and tiny. This is a central gathering point in the abdomen as it bulges and shrinks. Later on, the air will go to this point when practitioners inhale, and out from it when they exhale. The point is the Dantian. Breathing from the point is breathing with the Dantian. Now we know that breathing with the Dantian comes from abdominal breathing. People have different opinions about the location and scope of the Dantian. From our own practice of operating breathing, the location of the Dantian varies from person to person. It may be big or small, and located accordingly a little above or below the navel. Referring to the acupoint position, the Dantian is three *cun* down from the navel (one *cun* is equal to the widest part of the testee's thumb). This position is basically correct and applies to most people, but some people think the Dantian is the navel. The point three *cun* down from the navel is the position of the Dantian when people are lying down. According to this viewpoint, breathing with the Dantian is also breathing with the navel, and that is the initial stage of breathing like a fetus.

Strictly speaking, once abdominal breathing has developed and has a clear point from which to operate (that is, today, breathing with the Dantian has developed), this is just the beginning of adjusting breathing in Rujing. The purpose of chest breathing is to switch to abdominal breathing, and operating abdominal breathing is to develop the operation of breathing with the Dantian. As we know, a type of breathing required by Rujing is breathing like a fetus. Breathing with the Dantian is only the beginning of breathing like a fetus.

Long training is required when we try to turn breathing with the Dantian into deep, long, soft, and tiny breathing. The first step is to keep the Dantian breathing point stable and let breathing take root at the Dantian, and then make the Dantian more substantial and gradually fill it with Qi. It takes a long time to learn and we cannot accomplish it in one day. As the Dantian gradually fills with inner Qi, its volume may increase. At the beginning its breathing point may be the size of a bean; later on it may become as big as a date, or even an egg. It is related to personal martial art, and also related to individual living conditions. We cannot require all practitioners to be the same.

How can we judge when breathing with the Dantian has been established? That is when the Dantian is full of Qi and it transforms from a negative to a positive position. Now practitioners need not take air in and out of the Dantian by concentrating their thoughts. The Dantian alone can control breathing. The Dantian opening means inhaling, and its closing means exhaling. It does not need practitioners to operate it deliberately.

Once we understand the opening and closing of the Dantian, the abdomen's bulging and shrinking gradually becomes even, and its movement gets smaller and smaller. Finally, practitioners do not even feel the rising and falling of their bellies. Now deep, long, soft, and tiny breathing has been formed and it has reached the stage of being extremely soft. Inhaling/exhaling are very natural, without any sign of a pause or shift. It is called "potential breathing" in some books. When practitioners have this kind of breathing, they can start the transition from abdominal breathing to breathing like a fetus.

BREATHING LIKE A FETUS

Breathing like a fetus here means body breathing, and does not mean breathing with the navel. Breathing with the navel at the primary stage is the same as breathing with the Dantian, so when we introduced breathing with the Dantian (above), the primary stage of breathing with the navel already played a role. Here we recommend the advanced stage of navel breathing.

The main difference between body breathing and breathing with the chest and abdomen is that, subjectively, your breathing channel is no longer your mouth and nose. Chest and abdominal breathing, including breathing with the Dantian, all come through the mouth and nose, although the breathing point changes. They involve either inhaling/exhaling through the nose; inhaling through the nose and exhaling through the mouth; breathing both in and out through the mouth; or breathing in and out through both the mouth and the nose. Some types of Qigong require practitioners to inhale/exhale through alternate nostrils. Thus, in the practice of Qigong, there is quite a refined use of the breathing channels in the adjustment of breathing. Regarding the breathing operation of Rujing, it requires practitioners to inhale/exhale through the nose as much as they can. Under some special circumstances, practitioners may breathe with the mouth as a support.

Body breathing is different. It requires air to go in and out through the pores of the whole body, and avoids using the mouth and nose. At the beginning of body breathing, the breathing point may remain in the Dantian, but air goes directly in and out of the Dantian through all the pores of the body, and no longer through the mouth and nose. In a subjective sense, practitioners only feel all the pores of their body opening and closing, and air going in and out through them. Meanwhile, there is no air being breathed in and out of the mouth and nose.

How do practitioners complete the transition from mouth and nose breathing to pore breathing? As we know, on the basis of potential breathing, the air from the mouth and nose becomes weaker and weaker; gradually it seems sometimes to exist and sometimes not to exist, and tends to stop. On the other hand, as Qi fills up the Dantian, it spreads out through the whole of the body. The sensation of Qi has been formed throughout the whole, and it continues to spread out of the body to merge with Qi from the outside world, and eventually become one with it. Gradually (and finally), air from the mouth and nose stops altogether. It is natural for air to be exchanged through the pores with the air on the outside. The operation of body breathing has formed. During the operation, as soon as we continuously strengthen our sense of Qi in the Dantian, it will naturally spread out through the whole body, and then outside the body, and the flow of air through the mouth and nose gradually weakens. We simply follow the trends of the Qi sensation strengthening in the Dantian and the air weakening through the mouth and nose. The aim of body breathing is reached naturally.

I mentioned above that when body breathing is just forming, we can take the Dantian as a breathing point. Now it seems that other parts of the body no longer exist, and the boundary between the body and the outside world becomes blurred. It seems that the Dantian is the only point existing in this world, and that it is slowly opening and closing. Except for this, everything around becomes vague. As body breathing further develops, the sole point, the Dantian, will also gradually vanish. Practitioners can feel the internal and external worlds become one integrated mass, a galaxy of air. Right now there is no opening and closing of body pores, nor opening and closing of the Dantian. The whole body seems to have completely dematerialized. It makes no difference whether we are breathing or not. Air is everywhere, inside and outside, in one integrated mass; what is there to be exchanged? This is chaos; this is man and nature becoming one.

We know from all that has been explained above that the adjustment of breathing at the advanced level, and the activities of concentrating thought, are both closely linked with the adjustment of mind at the advanced level. Concentration and Qi (vital energy) now become one at this high level of Rujing. During the Rujing process, the operations of adjusting breathing and mind both develop together.

The adjustment of breathing and adjustment of mind are normally both on the same level, so we need to pay attention to the balance between them. When practitioners have their minds full of distracting thoughts, their inhalation and exhalation cannot easily become deep, long, soft, and tiny, not to mention breathing like a fetus; and if people are gasping for breath, they cannot expect to know the state of emptiness, either.

Body Adjustment

Compared with breathing and mind adjustments, body adjustment is much more flexible and does not have many requirements. This does not mean that body adjustment is not important. The reason is that posture change itself is quite simple because the practice of Rujing is different from martial arts. Furthermore, the operation of posture has been done at the stage when practitioners start doing Rujing. People need not change their postures continuously along with the deepening of their practice. This is unlike the operations of adjusting breathing and mind, which have to be carried out through the entire procedure of Rujing.

Body adjustment consists of the following two elements. One is the arrangement of posture; the other is the tenor of the operation.

The Arrangement of Posture

The first step of body adjustment is to select a posture. This part of the work should be finished before the process of Rujing. It is preparation for Rujing. Due to the posture arrangement of body adjustment we should not only consider the subjective and objective conditions as a whole, but also as these directly relate to the concrete contents of adjusting mind and breathing and the need to cooperate with them. Therefore, it is different from ordinary preparatory work, which is why body adjustment is discussed in this section.

As we discussed in Chapter 3, the sitting posture, especially cross-legged sitting, is the best posture for the practice of Rujing. Every practitioner is different, but he or she should consider the aspects described below with regard to selecting a Rujing posture.

HEALTH CONDITIONS

There are two aspects to this: general health conditions, and health conditions in the practice of Rujing.

Here we are talking about health conditions and physical constitutions. A sick practitioner may consider his disease when he selects his posture. For example, conditions such as high blood pressure or glaucoma make people weak in the lower body. Sick practitioners may select a standing posture for training in order to mitigate this. They relax from the upper part to the lower part of the body in Rujing. Lying on the left or right side is good for practitioners who have gastric ulcer or hepatitis, as it can reduce pressure on the sick part, which can then relax well. A half-prone posture is good for people with heart problems or asthma. This posture uses very little strength, and they can breathe smoothly. Practitioners can choose standing, sitting, or prone postures according to their own health conditions. You can stand if you are in good health, or select a prone posture if your health is not good.

Health conditions mainly determine whether people feel tired or are all right when they practice. If they feel very tired, they can select an upright sitting posture or prone posture. If they are full of energy, they can choose a standing posture or cross-legged sitting posture.

THE TRENDS OF CONCENTRATING THOUGHT AND QI

A proper posture is helpful in setting up the aim of concentrating thoughts and forming the breathing point. Hence it is also good for adjustments of mind and breathing. For example, when people are maintaining concentration on the acupoint Yongquan, or leading Qi down to the heels, a standing posture is good. Feet are the lowest part of the whole body, and a standing posture can help in concentrating thought and leading Qi down smoothly. It is easy to operate.

Lying on one's back is also good. The whole body is even and straight, and it makes the aims of concentrating thought and inner Qi straightforward to achieve. Compared with the first two postures, the sitting posture is not advantageous.

However, if practitioners are concentrating on the Dantian and have Dantian breathing, then the sitting posture is the best. Cross-legged sitting is, in fact, superb.

If practitioners have crossed the boundary into chaos, man and nature become one and form body breathing. Then, although the sitting posture is good, the standing posture is even better. The standing posture has the semblance of a gigantic stature. It can assist practitioners to experience man and nature becoming one, making this posture better than others.

In sum, practitioners should choose their posture according to which parts they are concentrating thought on, and the pathways of inner Qi moving around. The basic principle is to follow the way of nature.

THE LEVEL OF RUJING

Beginning Rujing on a basic level, beginners may select a standing posture; sitting or prone postures are also all right. They can make a free choice. If practitioners have reached the advanced level of Rujing, the sitting posture is good, and the cross-legged posture is even better. The sitting posture is always the best until such time as one reaches the level of man and nature becoming one. Practitioners can choose a standing posture when they have reached this level. Of course, it is all right to continue using the sitting posture. If practitioners reach the highest level of "discovering the power of understanding" (as it is called by Buddhists), they can bring their practice of Rujing into their everyday life. Then, no matter which posture they use—walking, standing, sitting, or prone posture—they can practice all the time and anywhere. It makes no difference what posture they use.

LIVING HABITS

If a person practices twice a day, it is good to select a standing posture in the morning and a sitting posture in the evening. This also follows the way of nature: in the morning people want to get up, so practitioners are following the inclination to stand up; in the evening people need to go to bed, so practitioners are following the inclination to sit cross-legged for a while on the bed. If practitioners can practice one more time, at noon, it would be better to choose the prone posture. Lying on their back, they can have a nap if they fall asleep; they can enter the state of Rujing for a while if they cannot fall asleep—and it is also good to have a rest at noon.

Although the choice of posture is comparatively free, people should keep a correct and fixed posture. Once they set a posture, it is not good to change it frequently. For instance, if one assumes a standing posture in the morning, a prone posture at noon, and a sitting posture in the evening, one should fix this set of postures. People should not change them at will. According to the postures selected for concentrating thought or breathing, practitioners can change posture when the requirements of concentrating thought or breathing change. Considering postures selected on account of disease, sick practitioners can decide whether to make a proper adjustment of their posture once their conditions begin to improve. Free selection and "chopping and changing" are two different things. Practitioners should not change their posture for no good reason if the postures are fixed.

The Tenor of the Operation

The main points in posture operation that we shall endeavor to discuss in this section concern some general problems that may arise in the operation of all postures. This is to provide a common guide, but we shall not discuss specific problems in this section.

Here are some words that the ancients used to talk about the operation of body posture: standing like a pine; sitting like a clock; and lying prone like a bow. Standing like a pine means that the standing posture makes people stand straight. Sitting like a clock means that the sitting posture makes people sit stably. Lying like a bow means that the prone posture makes people curve freely when they lie on their side. These words are suitable for the posture operation of Rujing. In particular, they illustrate the different characteristics of standing, sitting, and prone postures, which correspond with the demands of posture in practice. However, what the ancients were talking about is still a matter of posture operation in general. As far as the posture operation of Rujing is concerned there are detailed requirements for each part of the body, to which we have to pay attention. Now we'll discuss these details, from head to foot.

HEAD AND NECK

The head must be straight. In some Qigong we are told that the head is "suspended." It means that the top of your head is lifted up by a piece of string. If you think of it this way, your head will be naturally straight. That is not the full meaning of the head being suspended. It is also a means to let your neck relax, because if your head is lifted up by a piece of string it reduces pressure on your neck and the cervical vertebrae can relax, which is helpful for clearing the Du meridian. A straight head is not absolute. In fact, the head tilts forward a little bit. When you practice, you should only retract the lower jaw slightly. Why? Because when the head is completely straight, the cervical vertebrae are compressed and the neck cannot extend. Only when the head tilts forward can the cervical vertebrae extend fully. Look at Buddhas in temples: their heads are all tilted slightly forward. In addition, the lower jaw is slightly retracted. The head tilting forward is closely related to the operation of toning up one's back. We will mention this topic again later.

The gaze should be straight ahead or slightly downwards—for example, fixed on the tip of your nose. In some types of Qigong vision is required to focus on your navel. The requirement for vision has nothing to do with opening or closing the eyes. No matter whether your eyes are open or closed, your vision is actually fixed on what you really are visualising. Your vision is closely related to your concentrating thought. Concentration on the Dantian and inner vision of the Dantian is the same thing. Now we can see the importance of operating vision. Do not suppose that when you close your eyes there is blackness in front of you. You can see nothing. Generally speaking, looking straight ahead is mostly required when people are in the standing posture. In some forms of Qigong, the eyes are required to look up a little bit. They should look down slightly when people select the sitting posture, of course. (They can also look straight ahead.) Practitioners are required to close their eyes slightly in the practice of Rujing. It is easy for beginners to feel sleepy, or their concentrating thoughts are not focused, so they may slightly open their eyes. When practitioners reach a certain level they may continue Rujing to another level even when they are opening their eyes. If they are trying to reach the high level of Rujing, it is better to have the eyes closed.

Practitioners should gently keep their mouths closed and their tongues in a natural position. For many kinds of Qigong, practitioners are asked to place their tongue against the upper tooth ridge in order to keep the Ren meridian open. If practitioners do this, the vital energy may stop in the upper gums. So it is essential for practitioners to rest the tongue against the upper tooth ridge if they are practicing Circulation of Qi. It is not the purpose for the practitioners of Rujing to open up their Ren and Du meridians. Therefore, they are not supposed to rest the tongue against the upper tooth ridge. There is no harm in doing this if they find it comfortable, and they are not obliged to do it. The position for the tongue is the point where the roof of the mouth meets the central upper teeth. Slight contact is all that is needed.

One more thing should be paid attention to with regard to the posture of the head. That is to smooth the brow and relax the cheek muscles. This is related not only to posture, but also to mood. People often say that practitioners are required to smile in Rujing. The word "smile" here indicates a relaxed and pleasant mood. The mood is revealed in a smooth brow and relaxed cheek muscles during the posture. A smile is not a laugh showing amusement. As practitioners are in a pleasant mood, their mouths turn up at the corners. We usually think of expression as showing people's mood and sensations by changing their gestures. During practice, the expression not only shows the importance of the posture of the head, but also the need to pay attention to the posture of the arms and legs.

UPPER LIMBS (SHOULDERS AND ARMS)

Relaxed shoulders and dropped elbows are the basic and main points. First of all, let the shoulders relax and drop down naturally. Practitioners never hunch their shoulders. Hunched shoulders make muscles tighten, obstruct the flow of vital energy down to the lower part of the body, and also make abdominal breathing difficult. It is easy to have hunched shoulders when practitioners raise their arms in the standing posture, especially if they raise their arms too high. Therefore, no matter whether practitioners are making the gesture of holding a ball in their hands while standing up straight, their arms should be in the position between the Shanzhong and the Dantian. Practitioners often make the mistake of hunching their shoulders when they are practicing in the standing posture. The same mistake is also made in the sitting posture. They hunch their shoulders slightly, and this too requires attention.

Dropped elbows are the continuation of relaxed shoulders. Loose shoulders not only let the shoulders relax, but let the elbows relax, too. When both the shoulders and the arms stay relaxed, we get dropped elbows as a result. No matter whether practitioners are in the standing or sitting posture to practice Rujing, the elbow position is usually a center of resistance and a turning point of the shoulders and arms' falling force. In attending to our elbows, our purpose is not to let the center of resistance move up.

In addition, practitioners are also required to pretend to "carry their armpits under their arms"—in other words, not to keep their arms close to the sides of their chest, but to have space between them. This also helps to make the arms and legs spread and feel more comfortable. If the arms are clamped to the sides of the chest, the circulation of vital energy and blood is certain to be blocked.

CHEST AND BACK

Slightly dropping the chest and toning up the back are the basic and main points. As we know, dropping the chest is helpful in letting vital energy move down to the lower parts and facilitates abdominal breathing. Tightening one's back is good for extending the spine and allowing free Circulation of Qi along the Du meridian. This operation is so important in Rujing.

A common mistake is to overdo it. Actually, withdrawing one's chest simply means not straightening the chest (and in so doing slightly tightening the lower jaw). Practitioners need not press their chest down. There is a close relationship between withdrawing one's chest and slightly tightening the lower jaw. When people lower their head in everyday life, their chest usually goes backwards. If a person only lowers his head without withdrawing his chest, his neck will stiffen. Withdrawing one's chest as required in Rujing means slightly sinking the chest. So it is all right, as long as practitioners do not deliberately straighten their chest and consequently slightly tighten up their lower jaw. Withdrawing one's chest and toning up one's back must be done at the same time. If, in sinking the chest, practitioners go past the limit, they will not so much tone up the back as become round-shouldered. Toned up means straight, not crooked. Therefore, when one tones up one's back correctly, the spine is basically straight. Spines have physiological curves in the lumbar and thoracic regions. The consequence of tightening up one's back partially offsets the physiological curves, so that the spine is now straighter than in everyday life. Since the lower jaw is slightly tightened, it too partially offsets the cervical curve of the spine. Therefore, the whole spine can fully extend along its whole length if we know the principle. We can see that it is totally wrong if we become round-shouldered instead of tightening up one's back.

LOWER BACK AND HIPS

A straight back and relaxed hips are the main points. No matter whether practitioners select the standing or sitting posture, the training of straightening their back and relaxing their hips is very important throughout the entire operation of the postures. A key item is straightening one's back and relaxing one's hips, which makes sitting and standing postures in Rujing different from those in everyday life. When people stand up and sit down in everyday life, their back and waist are not straight, and their hips are not relaxed either. Only when they "stand to attention" or "sit up straight" might they straighten their back and relax their hips. In this respect, postures required in Rujing are similar to the postures of standing to attention and sitting up straight.

Straightening one's back means that the waist should be extended and straight, and should not be bent or curved. The function is mainly to let the lumber spine straighten. Note that straightening your back does not mean throwing out your abdomen. The belly should go slightly back. Relaxed hips means that the hips should drop down. Practitioners should keep their hips a little bit backwards when they are in the sitting posture. The purpose is to relax the hips. When practitioners are in the standing posture, they should keep their hips on an imaginary high stool, for the same reason. Furthermore, a straight back and relaxed hips are helpful for extending the spine. They can also bring the body's center of gravity down to the lower abdomen, even if practitioners are in the standing posture. Lowering the body's center of gravity helps to focus vital energy on the Dantian. When we relax our hips, we have to pay special attention to ease and naturalness. Especially when the hips go backwards, we should not exceed the limit. Otherwise, it can stiffen the muscles of the lower back and abdomen. This is the opposite of what we want.

LOWER LIMBS (LEGS AND FEET)

In the lower limb posture there is a big difference between the standing and sitting postures. When practitioners are in the standing posture, keeping straight, their legs should be as relaxed as possible, and both knees should be slightly bent. The bend should not go past the tips of the toes. The feet should be shoulder-width apart. The toes should slightly clutch the ground. There are three types of foot position. One is like the Chinese character "eight" (an upside-down V shape). Another is like a reversed Chinese character "eight" (inverted V shape). The third is parallel, shoulder-width apart. The upside-down V shape is standing with the toes of both feet touching. This posture makes practitioners stand stably, and also makes it easy for them to bend their knees in order to protect themselves. This kind of posture is closely related to the standing stake step in the art of attack and defense in martial arts. The V shape is standing with the toes pointing outwards. Compared with the first, this posture lacks flexibility and stability. It does little to help practitioners in Rujing to have a quiet standing posture without stepping forwards and backwards. Standing in parallel style is also called "Horse Stance." It is quite stable and flexible, and also accords with the natural human standing position. It is not invented; therefore, this posture is ideal for the practice of Rujing. Since each practitioner has individual conditions and different habits, he may select any of these three postures, including a V or an inverted V, so long as it is comfortable and natural.

Further, the body is not totally straight and still when practitioners practice in the standing posture. Normally practitioners sway a little bit. This is not to stand unsteadily, but to stand more steadily. Besides, compared with standing totally still, standing with a slight sway can save practitioners' energy, and also help them relax. In the standing posture, standing with a slight sway relies mainly on the lower limbs. When practitioners do it they must keep the practice to the point and never, ever sway too much. Generally speaking, it is fine for practitioners to sway just a little bit, going with the relaxing and tensing of the muscles.

Compared with the standing posture, the lower limbs can be more relaxed when using the sitting posture to practice Rujing. But when practitioners are in the regular sitting posture, some tensions in the lower limbs are still needed because they have a lot of weight on them. When they sit regularly, the position of practitioners' feet is the same as in the standing posture. When people are in the cross-legged or kneeling posture, their lower limbs are compressed. After practice, they should tap and massage them in order to stimulate the circulation of vital energy and blood. In the management of posture from head to feet, practitioners should pay attention to relaxation and tension everywhere and all the time—relaxed, but not slack; and firm, but not still; that is, we may say, an absolute law of posture operation. For those practitioners doing it well, it is natural and comfortable. Furthermore, it is also very important to proceed in an orderly way and step by step with posture operation.

We should say that it takes time for practitioners to master the correct posture in the practice of Rujing. They cannot do it well after just a bit of training. Correct and graceful posture always keeps in step with the continuously improving level of Rujing. At the beginning practitioners need not mind too much about postures if they cannot exactly copy the correct ones. It is all right for them to follow the correct postures in principle. It is not necessary to be upset about incorrect postures being an obstacle to Rujing. That is to "give up eating for fear of choking." When practitioners have laid some foundations, they are naturally able to correct their faulty postures, because they tend to feel uncomfortable if they keep doing them wrong. In addition, someone may not learn a correct posture quickly because he has some discomfort, such as a stomach ache. When sick practitioners practice, they cannot easily straighten their back. They will gradually straighten their back as they get good results by practicing Rujing. Once they straighten their back and can do the correct postures, they have already recovered.

There is one more thing we should say to beginners. That is, no matter which posture they choose for the practice of Rujing, they will feel tired after practicing for a while. In this situation, practitioners should keep on practicing properly. They should not keep it up for too long at a time, but just continue for a while, so that they can gradually improve, and also follow the postures they have selected. If they go past the limit, they will be going against the principle of comfort and naturalness, and unable to do Rujing well. Practicing Rujing is not like physical training, which can make practitioners sweat all over, gasp for breath, and then need a rest. Rujing practice tells practitioners that they should stop when they feel tired, and stay interested in it. No matter which form of Qigong practitioners choose, it is always a question of training that takes a lot of time and practice. Practitioners never, ever lack perseverance.

Coordination and Unity of the Three Adjustments

We are familiar with the principle of three adjustments becoming one. We need not discuss this topic here, but it is not easily done during practice. When beginners start to learn Rujing, they have too many things to take care of, all at the same time. They take care of breathing and cannot take care of their postures; when they take care of their breathing and postures, they leave concentration behind. In order to avoid this situation at the beginning, practitioners should put postures first, and then focus on the adjustments of breathing and mind. Practitioners can also choose an operating method as an ABC of breathing and mind adjustment. They can choose, for example, from breathing by counting numbers, or breathing by listening. This way, they can adjust their breathing at the same time as concentrating, and success will come easily.

When practitioners practice to a high level, their bodies, minds, and vital energy are linked together, and there is no distinction among them. We say that a slight movement in one part can affect the whole situation.

Chapter 7

Malfunctions in Qigong

Malfunctions that occur during the practice of Qigong are a matter of great controversy. Some people deny the existence of this malfunction. They believe that the phenomena of the so-called malfunctions are actually temporary reactions in the process of Qigong, and that these reactions may even be associated with the cultivation of human latent powers. Others are of the opinion that malfunction in the process of Qigong does exist (even though it may be just a temporary reaction), and that it should be regarded as such when it occurs. This viewpoint, taken to the extreme, believes that malfunction frequently occurs in the process of Qigong. I believe that malfunction does exist, but does not occur as frequently as some people think.

Malfunction may also occur in the process of Rujing, which is, after all, a type of Qigong exercise. Yet it is relatively "safer" than other types of Qigong. The occurrence of malfunction is, indeed, rare.

Identifying Malfunction and Its Causes

We should first define the notion of malfunction before we start to discuss it. It is not easy to define. The argument about malfunction amongst practitioners of Qigong is more or less linked with the ambiguity of its definition. I am not going to redefine the notion, but just to provide you with an overview of the notion.

It is known that once you enter the state of Rujing, your body and mind are certain to show some sort of response. Responses can be classified into two groups in terms of the positive or negative impact they have on your body and mind. Those that are good for your health are positive reactions, and those that will do harm to your body and mind are negative reactions. This division may sound a bit too assertive, because the negative consequence of some of the reactions cannot be seen clearly. We cannot mechanically put them into either of the two groups. For instance, when you have a feeling like ants crawling on your body in the process of Rujing, can you tell whether the feeling is positive or negative? It is hard to tell. But in order to have a better understanding of malfunction in Qigong, this simple division may enable us to distinguish the most significant positive and negative reactions. Since we are discussing the *malfunction* of Rujing, naturally we'll study mainly the negative reactions.

Can we say that all the negative reactions that occur during the process of Rujing are malfunctions? My answer to this question is both yes and no. As far as the nature of the reaction is concerned, if the reaction occurring in the process of Rujing jeopardizes the practitioner's health, it is a malfunction. There is no doubt about it. Considering the degree of the reactions, some may affect the process of Rujing, but with so little negative impact that they can be corrected immediately. If we treat these as serious malfunctions, it seems we are making a mountain out of a molehill. We should not regard these reactions as malfunctions.

If we judge negative reactions by both quality and quantity, we can define malfunction and negative reaction respectively as follows. The notion of malfunction consists of two meanings: in a broader sense, it refers to all negative reactions during the process of Rujing; in a narrow sense, malfunction refers to the negative reaction that causes serious harm to the body and mind. Therefore, malfunction is divided into two types: *serious* malfunction, which causes greater harm to the health of your body and mind; and *slight* malfunction, which causes less harm to the health of your body and mind.

What kind of negative reaction can be regarded as serious and more harmful to the health of your body and mind? We may define it as follows.

When you have stopped practicing, and have tuned your body with the correct operation of the three adjustments, the symptom of discomfort still exists and the negative reaction continues to disturb your everyday life and work. This reaction will be regarded as the more serious kind. This is serious malfunction. The negative reaction that ceases as soon as you stop practicing, or is corrected with little effort, will be regarded as a minor malfunction.

Now let's discuss the causes of malfunction.

There are more or less two factors that may cause malfunction in the process of Rujing. One is incorrect operation during the process. The other is the condition of one's physical constitution. Operational failure in any of the three adjustments will cause malfunction. For instance, incorrect operation in the adjustment of mind will make you feel dizzy; incorrect operation in the adjustment of breath may make you have a headache and have difficulty breathing; and flaws in the adjustment of the body may cause you to feel weary and exhausted. Since the operations of the three adjustments in the process of Rujing are usually mild and gentle, once they are operated incorrectly, you will feel mentally and physically uncomfortable. They are easy to identify and correct. Thus those malfunctions caused by faulty operation are minor and not serious. They often occur among beginners, since beginners are still unfamiliar with the operation. Also, since they are eager to be successful, they are quite likely to neglect training in the basic skill. The result is that minor malfunction occurs now and then. Beginners' hope for quick success will actually be delayed, since they are over-eager to achieve their goal.

The serious malfunctions are mostly caused by both faulty operation and the hidden problems of physical constitution. The latter are actually the main reason, and faulty operation is the triggering factor. This malfunction is difficult to correct, yet it is also rare to see practitioners in such cases not recover. It is estimated that these occurrences make up only 0.01 to 0.1 percent of total numbers.

The most serious and typical consequence of this malfunction in Rujing is that the practitioner becomes mentally ill. Generally speaking, those who are mentally ill due to malfunction in the process of Rujing are also those who have a family history of mental illness, and themselves usually have a personality disorder. Without those problems with your physical constitution, even if the malfunction leads to the symptoms of mental illness, you will recover soon after you stop practicing and have had a good rest. It will not develop into a typical sort of mental illness. Those practitioners who are diagnosed with schizophrenia or mental illness are mostly already potential patients before they turn to Rujing.

Therefore, it is unfair to blame serious malfunction on the practice of Rujing. Those who have potential problems with their physical constitution may become ill even without practicing Qigong or Rujing. This is why some people insist that practicing Qigong will not cause any malfunction at all. This raises the question of what kinds of people are not suited to practice Qigong or Rujing. It seems that, apart from those who have a family history of mental illness, people with a family history of some other genetic condition are also not suited to practice Qigong. "Not suitable" does not mean absolutely forbidden. If they want to practice, they can do so under the guidance of Qigong masters and choose the right type of Qigong.

Types of Minor Malfunction and How to Correct Them
Let's discuss the minor malfunctions first.

SWIRLING SENSATION AND HEADACHE
This is the most common malfunction that occurs in the process of Rujing. It usually occurs at the beginning of practice, and does not diminish immediately you have stopped practice. It may even be worse after you have stopped practicing. It will not affect your normal work and daily life. In serious cases, it may be accompanied by nausea.

The occurrence of this malfunction is due to incorrect operation in the adjustment of mind and the adjustment of breathing. As for the adjustment of mind, it is usually due to the fact that one has spent too much energy on concentrating on the acupoints, especially those on the head. Therefore, if you concentrate on Baihui or Yintang, or other acupoints on the head, you should be aware of the intensity of your concentration. If you apply the same strength as you would do to concentration on the Dantian, you will certainly have a swirling feeling, as the acupoints on the head are more sensitive. As for the adjustment of breathing, if you are forced to reduce the rate of your breathing and stop breathing for too long, you will feel swirling and dizziness due to the lack of oxygen. In addition, the practitioner with high or low blood pressure and neuropathic headache may have these symptoms, as well as the reaction to incorrect operation. This will contribute to a very serious problem. The swirling feeling caused by overdoing concentration will disappear when you stop practicing or give up the concentration. Those caused by incorrect breathing or by the misguided Circulation of Qi may not be so easily got rid of. They may last for a couple of days. Recovery will come after a good rest. If the situation gets much worse, you should stop practicing Qigong and resume your practice only after all the symptoms of malfunction have disappeared.

BREATHING DIFFICULTY

Beginners may sometimes feel difficulty breathing, since they are not used to deep, slow breathing. They will come back to normal by giving up the breathing rate required by the adjustment of breathing, or after they have taken some deep breaths. In serious cases, one may feel suffocated, and this can even turn into a breathing disorder. The causes of this malfunction are the incorrect operation of the adjustments of body and breathing. The practitioner may not be widening his waist and chest enough, which results in inadequate expansion of the lobes of the lungs. The air has difficulty flowing in and out. The practitioner begins to feel suffocated and very uncomfortable. Faulty operation in the adjustment of breathing is usually the result of overdoing long, deep breaths. One may be using too much effort in breathing. The muscles of respiration and the diaphragm become overworked.

To correct this problem, one needs to readjust one's posture and breathing. This works almost immediately. One can also stop practicing for a little while, and then the symptoms will quickly disappear. It is quite rare for the problem to last for days.

POUNDING HEART AND PALPITATIONS

Some practitioners will have the problem of the heart pounding while practicing Rujing. One's heartbeat may be accelerated, or one may feel the heartbeat heavily. As a result, one may feel a bit scared. These symptoms usually occur soon after one starts practicing Rujing. How long it lasts varies from person to person. A serious case may affect continuity of practice. If not corrected in time, one may feel quite anxious. Gradually this may develop into a stimulus–response pattern and one's heart may pound whenever one starts to practice.

All these reactions are related to the practitioner's physical constitution and incorrect operation of the process of Rujing. One may not be relaxed enough. The posture becomes rigid, unnatural, and uncomfortable. Overdoing concentration and breathing are other factors that cause malfunction. An additional reason may be the psychological burden on practitioners who worry about their poor practice. As far as the physical constitution is concerned, many of those who have experienced malfunction in Rujing are people whose nervous system is unstable, who are sensitive and susceptible to auto-suggestion. Those who have heart disease or cardiovascular neurosis easily experience the heart pounding and palpitations.

This reaction may be repeated in the process of Rujing. It takes time to correct them completely. The first thing one needs to do is to be relaxed in the process of the three adjustments. One should do everything naturally and comfortably. You should feel relaxed and release all psychological burdens. If you chose the left-side lying posture for practice you should change it to the right-side lying posture, or face-up lying posture, as the left-side lying posture may cause a little pressure on your heart. If the reaction is too strong, you should change the type of Qigong to one that is more relaxed and requires less intense concentration. You should not practice the original type of Qigong until the reaction has disappeared. Those who have heart disease should consider appropriate medical treatment.

DRY MOUTH

Some practitioners may feel that their mouth and tongue are very dry during the practice of Rujing. Yet they may not necessarily want to drink, except for a little water to cool and clear their throats, because they are not really thirsty. It is just that the secretion of saliva has been temporarily inhibited.

The main cause is still incorrect operation of the adjustment of breathing. The practitioner may not be inhaling properly, or may be holding the breath in a faulty pattern. It is known that if a single inhalation is too long, or if one holds the breath too long after the inhalation, the sympathetic nervous function will be reinforced and this consequently restricts the secretion of saliva. Another factor that accounts for the dry mouth is that the practitioner is usually breathing through his mouth (inhaling in particular) during the process of Rujing. If the practitioner also has problems with his digestive system, this may also be reflected in reduced secretion of saliva.

To solve the problem, you should first change your breathing habit. Try to avoid breathing through the mouth. Follow the natural pace of breathing; don't try to interfere with it. You can also imagine yourself eating some sour food, so as to stimulate the secretion of saliva. Your body does not really need any water at this moment. So long as the secretion of saliva becomes normal again, the problem has been naturally solved.

DIZZINESS AND SLEEPINESS

This should not be regarded as a malfunction, since dizziness during the process of Rujing does not seem to be harmful to the body. Yet I still prefer to treat it as a malfunction, since it is very bad for the process of Rujing. We have learned that Rujing doesn't mean sleeping. If it is not corrected, we may get into the habit of going to sleep in the process of Rujing. Then we may always go to sleep while practicing Rujing, and never actually be able to enter the state of Rujing.

Both Rujing and sleep are the process of the pallium being constrained. There are some similarities, so it is easy to mix them up. It is quite likely that you will feel dizzy and sleepy as you approach the deep realm of Rujing. At this moment the practitioner should take care with the distinction between dizziness and chaos. Chaos is the ultimate stage of Rujing. It is vague, clear, and empty. Dizziness is related to the state of sleepiness; it is dark and unclear. If it is clear, then one is in the waking state. In the state of chaos, one is consciously awake, while in the state of dizziness one is consciously foggy. Maintaining a clear and alert consciousness is the key to overcoming dizziness. Whether or not you can handle this is most significant for success in Rujing.

To avoid dropping off to sleep, you should practice Rujing only when you feel very energetic and fresh. Don't try to practice when you feel tired and exhausted. Don't choose the lying posture—take the standing or sitting mode. Don't close your eyes completely; keep them open slightly to let some weak light in. When you feel dizzy in the process of Rujing, you should stop practicing and do some exercises to get rid of the fatigue—such as rubbing your face with your hands, or covering your ears with your hands and then taking them away again quickly. You can also take a short walk or do a little Taiji. When you feel fresh you can continue to practice Rujing. If you only feel a bit sleepy (not dizzy) in the process, you should also try to differentiate between it and the feeling of swirling, and see if there is any other flaw in your manner of practice.

Types of Major Malfunction and How to Correct Them

Let's talk about the serious malfunctions of disturbance of Rujing.

SUDDEN DISTURBANCE OF RUJING

This is a mood disorder caused by sudden, intense stimuli in the process of Rujing. The practitioner appears to be very upset, anxious, dizzy, and swirling. He may feel terrified by the practice, since the disturbance may disrupt the circulation of vital energy. One may feel the vital energy moving randomly. This symptom may last for several days, or even several weeks.

Stimuli that cause this reaction include sudden noise in the outside world, being shaken hard, or being touched suddenly—for example, the sound of an explosion from a construction site, the sudden swerve of a boat or a bus, being hit by a running child while practicing Rujing in a park, etc.

The occurrence of hallucination associated with horrible images in the process of Rujing can also lead to shock. During the process of Rujing, the pallium is in a state of protective suppression. Its response to regular stimuli is weakened. Once an intense stimulus imposes itself, the pallium is forced to awaken and this causes a temporary functional disorder, which results in the disturbance of Rujing. The degree of disturbance depends on whether or not one is prepared for it. If one is prepared, the effect of the disturbance will be minimal, even if a sudden, strong stimulus occurs. Readiness does not mean one is consciously reminding oneself of the possible occurrence of strong stimuli, but something that is stored in one's subconscious. Just like most people would feel scared on hearing thunder on a fine day, but no one would be bothered on hearing it on a stormy day.

Once the disturbance has occurred, one should stop practicing Qigong. One needs to be comforted psychologically and guided to do something happy, so as to shift the attention and focus of consciousness. The symptoms of disturbance will shift to the positive side, so long as one is no longer feeling mentally rigid. If the disturbance is serious and the person is really scared, I suggest that medical advice is sought.

Avoiding this kind of disturbance from happening is important. One should select a quiet place for the practice of Rujing; to avoid the occurrence of negative hallucinations, try to eliminate the possible strong stimulus. One should also be psychologically prepared for the occurrence. For instance, when practicing Rujing on a bus or a boat, or in a park, one should keep somewhat alert. If a powerful event occurs, one should still be able to maintain the state of Rujing as if one had not seen or heard anything happen. Just ignore what has happened. This will help you not to be disturbed by the incident. This is just like a case cited in Zhuang Zi's book *Da Sheng Pian*

(Understand Life): "A drunkard fell off a cart. He was injured, but got away with his life." This is because "he was in a drunken state and did not know he was on a cart, nor did he know that he fell off the cart. He did not care about anything such as life and death, upset and fright. That was why he fell but did not die."

DISORDER IN CIRCULATION OF QI

The disturbance of Rujing can lead to disorder in Circulation of Qi. When your consciousness guides Qi incorrectly, Circulation of Qi may also be in a state of confusion. Disorder of Qi circulation means that the Qi does not circulate along the route of the meridians. It moves randomly, without a clear orientation. Where it moves, the practitioner will feel pain or itching in that place, or feel very uncomfortable. If the Qi goes up to the head, one may experience headache and swirling. Other symptoms such as insomnia and anxiety will also occur. If the Qi goes everywhere in your body, it will cause you to feel your whole body itching and swelling. In serious cases the patient will suddenly wake up from sleep if the Qi is moving chaotically. Disorder in Circulation of Qi is not a regular occurrence. One feels upset and agitated when it occurs. This illness may last from a few days to several months or even years.

Disorder in Circulation of Qi mainly occurs among practitioners who are intentionally seeking the feeling of Qi circulation. They often have a strong will to make their consciousness guide the movement of Qi. Many of them are physically sensitive. Since the inner Qi in their body has not been stabilized and fully realized, and their ability in handling the inner Qi is also not adequately developed, the circulation of inner Qi easily gets out of control and runs aimlessly all over the place, resulting in various symptoms. In fact, the feeling of Circulation of Qi does not correlate with one's mastery of Qigong. It is taboo in Qigong to pursue the feeling of circulation.

Once the disorder occurs, one should stop practicing Rujing. Don't let your consciousness follow the sensation of the movement of Qi. Just ignore it. You can also do some physical exercises. Those who have the Qi rushing up to their heads can practice Qigong that is aimed at relaxing them from head to toe, and guide the Qi to the Yongquan acupoints on the soles of the feet. Those who are seriously affected by the disorder may ask an experienced masseur to give them a massage or other kind of therapeutic treatment. Patients should stop practicing Qigong for some time. They can resume practice when the symptoms have completely disappeared. Furthermore, all the patients should maintain a happy mood, avoiding all negative moods such as anxiety, agitation, etc. Tranquilizers do not work very well with this condition.

OBSESSIVENESS

This means that the content of your consciousness during the process of Rujing remains in your mind and you cannot get rid of it. The content could be the image you invest in the process, or the parts you try to concentrate on in the adjustment of breathing. For instance, you may always see flowers and trees in your mind and cannot get rid of those images; as you breathe, you can clearly feel the air flowing in and out; or you may clearly see the outline of the Dantian or Yongquan points, etc. When it is serious, you cannot get rid of those images, not only while practicing Rujing, but also after practicing.

This condition is similar to obsessive-compulsive disorder (OCD). It is one of involuntary thinking. What is different from OCD is that it derives from a different source. The practitioner cannot get away from it, as he is so eager to be successful, and, in wanting to have a strong idea of it, becomes obsessed. This intensity and eagerness in the mind cause anxiety and over-concentration. This is no longer the normal concentration required by Rujing, but an overdone version. Thus the obsession is caused by the overdone determination during the process of Rujing. It violates the maxims of adjustment of mind, and is a typical example of being too demanding to achieve anything.

Once the obsession develops, one should stop practicing Rujing. After a few minutes' rest, one should change the target one was concentrating on before. For instance, if one was concentrating one's consciousness on breathing, one could change it to concentrate on the Dantian. If one was concentrating on the Dantian, one could change to concentrate on some other mental images. Remember not to concentrate totally on the event, and just concentrate in a loose manner—neither reinforce it, nor be distant from it. Those with a strong obsession should stop practicing for several days. Meanwhile, they should try to release their mind and shift their focus and attention to other things. When the obsession is eradicated they can resume their practice of Rujing.

According to the book *Qigong Xue Gai Lun* (An Introduction to Chinese Qigong), one can use the following method with a patient who has an obsession with his breathing pattern. Let the patient lie down on his back and insert something under his back so as to maintain a sloping position. Tell the patient to relax his whole body and concentrate his consciousness slightly on his toes. With heels touching the ground, he should then swing his feet slightly from side to side and count from 1 to 100. Then re-count the numbers over and over again. At the beginning the patient can swing his feet rapidly, so as to avoid swinging in time with his breathing and achieve better concentration. Then he can gradually slow down the swing. This method can correct the breathing obsession and exclude distracting thoughts at the same time.

In addition, one should always try to prevent the occurrence of the obsession during the process of Rujing. One should realize that the ultimate realm of Rujing is something shapeless and invisible. Concentration only works as a means of transition from the visible to the invisible. Beginners need to exclude their distracting thoughts by concentrating on a particular event. This concentration should turn to something vague, along with the improvement of their skill in Qigong. Their thinking pattern should gradually transfer from abstract, imagery thinking to sensory thinking, and to a realm where even sensory thinking becomes vague and blurred. Only by doing so can they enter the realm of Ultimate Emptiness. Therefore, one should not always literally concentrate on one particular event during the process of Rujing, but use the visible object to help oneself reach the realm of emptiness. This is the basic solution for avoiding obsession, and is the correct mode of thinking operation in Rujing as well.

OVERREACTION AND ENCHANTMENT

These are two related yet different malfunctions. Overreaction relates to severe, uncontrollable movement of the body during the process of Rujing. Slight moving and shaking of your body are normal. Even in the practice of the autokinesis type of Qigong, the movement of the body and limbs cannot be regarded as a malfunction, although the movement tends to be more obvious and wider in range and scale. These actions are usually not very fierce and violent. Overreaction is, on the contrary, fierce and violent, and the movement of the body is also larger in range and scale. For instance, someone may jump, fight, roll, and twist on the ground. He is unable to control his action, but lets it go until he is exhausted or stopped by an external force. After the overreaction, he may need several days to fully recover, as the overreaction has taken most of his energy.

"Enchantment" refers to the mental disorder that occurs in the process of Rujing when the practitioner is infatuated by the illusion. These illusions may be positive or negative. If someone is taken in by a negative illusion, he may become very upset, frightened, and rigid, and even go crazy. If someone is taken in by a positive illusion, he may pursue it, and when his demands are not satisfied, he may become very indifferent and melancholy. Enchantment is a most serious malfunction in the process of Rujing. It will have a severe impact on the practitioner's mind and body. It may make the practitioner manic and restless.

These two malfunctions may be observed at the same time, and their manic nature is also one of the reasons why they occur together.

Overreaction is also closely related to the disorder in Qi circulation. This is due to confusion of the movement of Qi, and the Qi moves chaotically everywhere in the body. The chaotic movement of Qi will not only make one feel uncomfortable, but also cause the limbs to shake and swing endlessly. As a result, overreaction occurs. Overreaction is to some extent caused by incorrect operation of the adjustment of mind and breathing. Breathing too huskily or too heavily, and attaching too much importance to the results of guiding Qi with consciousness, are some of the main causes of overreaction.

Some occurrences of overreaction have something to do with one's physical constitution. For instance, if one of the practitioner's meridians is blocked, overreaction may occur as the inner Qi comes in a rush. There is only a fine line between overreaction and autokinesis. If it is controllable, it is spontaneous movement. If it is out of control, it becomes overreaction. Spontaneous movement is also driven by the inner Qi. It is related to illness in the practitioner. When the Qi reaches the afflicted part and tries to clear the blocked meridians, spontaneous movement may occur. Once it occurs, one should handle it with particular caution. Try to avoid violent and fierce movement, to prevent the overreaction from occurring. On the other hand, do not persue autokinesis. Asking for too much of it is one of the causes of overreaction. Some people erroneously believe that the occurrence of autokinesis will cure the illness one has. This has been proved not to be true. Many practitioners have their illness cured without experiencing autokinesis. The purpose of our practice is Rujing, not autokinesis. Movement or no movement—let nature decide.

The key issue that leads to infatuation is our belief in the illusion. Why we tend to believe the illusion is complicated. Upon the occurrence of an illusion, one person may ignore it, while another may believe it without a single doubt. Here one's understanding of the mechanism of Rujing and the instructions for practicing it plays a vital role. Those who are enchanted often have irrational ideas about the effects of Rujing. They may also be influenced by certain religious doctrines, and often have the ambition to become holy by practicing Qigong. Therefore, they easily fall into the trap when illusion and hallucination occur. Those who possess a scientific understanding of Rujing will not be so easily affected. They are immune to infatuation. Apart from mental factors, the factor of physical constitution should also not be ignored. Seriously enchanted practitioners often have a family history of neurosis or personality disorder. They are susceptible to suggestion and have introverted personalities. Once they become enchanted, it is not easy to cure them.

Why do practitioners encounter illusion and hallucination in the process of practicing Rujing? We have discussed this in Chapter 2, "The Realm of Rujing." The ancient Chinese believed this was due to impurity in the process of Rujing, that it happened when one forced oneself to enter the state of Rujing before all distracting thoughts had been excluded. That is to say, it was due to failure in the adjustment of mind. Of course, this is only one of the reasons. It is much more complicated in reality. Even if one has not made any mistakes in the process of Rujing, an illusion may still occur once one enters a certain level of Rujing. It is the result of the operation of the subconscious, just like dreaming when one falls asleep. We all understand that the occurrence of dreams has nothing to do with correctness in the process of falling asleep. Thus, the occurrence of illusion is natural.

Now let's discuss the prevention of overreaction and enchantment.

To correct overreaction, the practitioner should first try to control his movement. He may be able to stop practicing Rujing and readjust his body into a very relaxed mood. If he still can't control his movement, you can ask him to stand with his feet shoulder-width apart and drop both arms down by his sides. Have the palms facing down towards the Earth, as if pressing on the ground. The fingers point forwards and stretch open. Let all his tension and strain go into his fingertips. Then ask him to shake his wrists and fingers to resolve the uncontrolled movement. If the practitioner cannot control his motion at all, invite a Qigong master to help by tapping and pressing his acupuncture points to stop him overreacting. For instance, pressing the Hegu and Quchi acupoints may work for the arms; as well as Zusanli and Sanyinjiao for the legs. Once the movement has stopped, the practitioner should stop practicing Rujing for several days, so as to regain his energy.

Tranquilizers may be prescribed for those who still feel rigid and upset after the treatment described above. Acupuncture and massage can also be used to remove the muscle strain and clear the meridians.

Chinese herbal medicine for soothing the nerves and removing inner tension can also be considered.

To prevent the occurrence of enchantment, it is necessary to have a correct understanding of Rujing first. Don't be obsessive. The benefit of practicing Rujing is to cure illness, improve health, cultivate latent potential, and acquire a better insight into the world. This has nothing to do with becoming holy or a saint. The connection between Qigong and religion, and the non-scientific character it has been given throughout history, make it difficult to expect all practitioners to have a correct opinion on the practice of Rujing. Practitioners are more or less superstitious, and dream of the miracles. This is often the cause of enchantment. Therefore it is necessary, indeed vital, to learn and master some fundamental knowledge of Qigong—which is often ignored by beginners. Besides, as we have already mentioned earlier, the occurrence of illusion is natural in the process of Rujing. If it does occur, no matter whether it is good or bad, the sole correct attitude is to forget about it. This principle is applicable both to illusions and to other external stimuli. That is, to see but not to be seen, and to hear but not to be heard.

The Chinese proverb says: "The bewildering will no longer be bewildering if you don't take it as something bewildering when you see it." This is the best way to deal with illusion. If a negative illusion occurs during the process of Rujing, remember: first, don't be taken in; second, keep calm. If you believe it, you may lapse into enchantment; if you become upset, the disturbance may overcome you. Try to do some easy exercises to activate your body, then slightly open your eyes to make the illusion disappear. And then stop practicing, and shift your thinking by doing some pleasant activity such as listening to music, playing ping-pong, etc. You should stop practicing Rujing for several days and resume practice only when you have really recovered emotionally.

Correcting enchantment is much more difficult. For someone who is still rational and able to obtain a correct understanding of himself, we can try to comfort and counsel him. Explain clearly the scientific principles of Rujing and enchantment to him, and release his mental burden. Those who can be diagnosed with neurosis, we can refer to the doctors. We should also be aware that these patients (if they do not have a family history of neurosis or personality disorder) may have minor symptoms and the illness may be brief, so they may have a better prognosis. However, this is quite different from typical neurosis.

Besides western medications for neurosis, Chinese herbal remedies such as Kuang Dian Meng Xing Tang (Chinese herbal medication for insanity), Huang Qi Jiang Zhong Tang (Chinese medicine with Astragalus membranaceus root as the main ingredient), Tian Wang Bu Xing Dan (Chinese medicine for heart disease), etc., may also be a medical practitioner's choice for these patients. Other applications such as acupuncture and therapeutic massage can also assist treatment.

AGGRAVATION OF ILLNESS

Another malfunction in the process of Rujing can be that, instead of being cured by practicing Rujing, your illness becomes aggravated. We need to be clear about two points. First, we need to be sure if the illness is really aggravated. Sometimes the symptoms of the illness may seem temporarily aggravated when the inner Qi attacks the illness. For instance, one may start to feel more pain or numbness than before, but the illness is actually developing towards a recovery. The phenomenon and essence are temporarily separate. To diagnose the situation, one should find out whether the patient is comfortable and relaxed, or worse after the pain. If the former, it is a good sign. Second, we need to find out if the aggravation of the illness is the result of practicing Qigong, or just a natural development of its own. Sometimes the illness gets worse after Rujing. This is because of the illness itself. For instance, terminal cancer tends to worsen anyway, regardless of the practice of Rujing. One should note if the practice quickens or slows down the aggravation of the illness. If the latter, it is a good thing.

The aggravation that is indeed caused by the practice of Rujing is often due to mistakes the practitioner makes during the process of Rujing. For instance, a practitioner who has high blood pressure should usually concentrate his consciousness on acupoint Yongquan, or other acupoints below his navel, so as to correct his condition of being solid in his upper body and void in his lower body. If he mistakenly concentrates his consciousness on Baihui or Yingtang, or other acupoints, that will be like pouring oil onto a fire. His blood pressure will become even higher. Patients with asthma or tracheitis should use normal breathing in their practice of Rujing. If they try deep inhaling/exhaling they will feel suffocated and out of breath. The cough and asthma will get worse. Patients with heart disease should be aware of the amount of practice they do. If they practice far too long in a standing posture, something unexpected may happen. Patients with epilepsy or mental disorders should be particularly cautious about their practice. Without guidance from experienced masters, they should not practice Rujing.

If the illness gets worse after two or three weeks of Rujing practice, one should stop and check out the causes. Correct them if they are operational faults; change to another type of Qigong if your physical constitution and illness do not allow you to practice Rujing.

Chapter 8

Piao Hua Gong

A Type of Rujing

Piao Hua Gong was created especially for the further study of Rujing. Its creation is not only an adoption of Rujing operating techniques in many kinds of Qigong, but also the sum and enhancement of Rujing experiences from Qigong masters.

Piao Hua Gong features a very scientific operating process. Each of its operating steps was designed after scientific studies of the mechanism of Rujing. Each step is concise and reasonable, and it is not easy to run into malfunctions. It is also easy for self-learning. Moreover, Piao Hua Gong is not merely a simple design without advanced features. It can be used not only as an ABC for beginners, but also as a foundation for further development in order to reach the higher levels of Qigong. Therefore it is suitable for practitioners at all levels, for men and women, young and old, and healthy people as well as sick people.

Regarding its operating principles and benefits, readers may refer to Chapters 3 and 4. I will not repeat them, but mainly introduce its design idea and operating procedure.

Design Idea

Piao Hua Gong is a kind of Qigong meditation aimed at achieving the state of Rujing by inducing and experiencing a "body floating and diffusing" process. The term "Piao Hua" ("floating and diffusing") is the aim of consciousness in the process of concentration, as well as being the realm one ought to achieve during practice.

The realm of Piao Hua actually refers to the Ultimate Emptiness and the state of oblivion of the outside world and self. These two ideas seem rather abstract and archaic. The term Piao Hua is more popular and gives people a feeling of something living and concrete. Therefore, selecting floating, and diffusing as the aim of concentrating thought has the effect of inducing practitioners into the sensation of the high level of Rujing. It will also be easily accepted by most people. Taking Piao Hua as the aim of concentrating thought has another advantage; that is, it has several inducing functions. As a term, it is abstract; as a description, it is imagery; and as a type of feeling, it is also concrete. In other words, it has the aspects of concept, superficial image, and objective form. So it is ideal as the aim of thought concentration. Compared with focusing on the Dantian or on the seaside as the aim of thought concentration, it is direct and precise. When the term Piao Hua is taken as the aim of thought concentration to induce sensation, we may say it is easy to operate, simple to understand, and highly efficient and effective.

"Floating" and "Diffusing" are the two stages of this Qigong exercise. Each stage can be classified into several subdivisions.

Floating is the primary stage. This is the stage when body and heart become one. In this primary stage one may experience all kinds of sensations that may possibly occur during the three stages that we discussed in Chapter 2.

As for the relations between body and mind, all kinds of feelings one experiences during Rujing, whether pleasant or unpleasant, are evidence of the fact that one's body and mind have not yet integrated into one. Because during the process of Rujing when one is looking forward to the state of Ultimate Emptiness and oblivion of the outside world and self, one does not need to feel all the sensations. Only when all the kinds of experiences utterly disappear can the Ultimate Emptiness that the mind is looking forward to come out through the body's actual experiences, and what the mind expects to be realized. So up to this point, the integrity of body and mind will be realized.

During the Floating period the mind is looking forward to floating. The aim of concentrating is to float. When the whole body starts to feel floating, the body and mind merge together and become unified. At that moment, practitioners will just feel their bodies become weightless and as light as a wisp of smoke or fluffy white cloud. The body and mind are free and happy. The soft pores of the whole body open and close naturally. The shape of the body is only vaguely known, and the air going in and out of the mouth and nostrils almost stops. During this time the practitioner may feel that his body is weightless, but may still feel the form of his body.

Diffusing belongs to the higher stage. The stage of Diffusing is the stage when man and nature become one. This stage is equivalent to the emptiness stage introduced in Chapter 2, which is the stage of man and nature becoming one and forgetting the material world and self.

Entering the stage of Floating, the body–mind is healthy and purified, and becomes weightless and misty. Gradually practitioners may feel as if the universe has a special magnetic force and is trying to magnetize the purified body–mind back to nature. Now we come to see the trend of man and nature becoming one. The practitioner's body–mind is experiencing the transition from the period of Floating to that of Diffusing. Since man and nature become one, the form of his body has to disappear. What is "heaven," then? Heaven is the natural formless gas of the universe. The body can merge with heaven only when it is dematerialized. Therefore, what the practitioner is doing at this moment is to accumulate his vital energy continuously and make the body become like air. So the body becomes lighter and lighter, and its form gets more and more vague. Finally, one's vital energy and the formless gas of the universe mingle together and become one. The main difference between the stages of Floating and Diffusing in terms of sensory experience is that Floating makes the body weightless but still retain its form, while Diffusing makes the body lose both weight and form.

The state of Diffusing may continue to deepen. The body has turned into formless gas; it seems to exist and also not to exist. So does the breathing. As the internal vital energy and external gas in the universe have merged, do we still need to breathe? In this realm where the body and mind and the concentration and Qi have magnificently become one, the adjustments of body and breathing are suspended. This means that the adjustment of mind will also cease. Now we have reached the highest level of Piao Hua Gong. The operations of all three adjustments of body, breathing, and mind are virtually suspended. No concentration, no breathing, and no body—that is the state of triple non-existence. It is also the level of forgetting the material world and self. In this realm it seems that everything has ceased to operate, and yet everything is still operating. Everything seems not to be in existence, and yet everything is clearly seen to be there. These words sound very contradictory, but that is what the realm is. Here, we are perhaps at the limit of language.

When practitioners have completed the studies and exercises of all levels of these two stages, it does not mean that they have already reached the highest level of Rujing.

After the highest level of the Diffusing stage there is a vast range of prospects, such as the exploration of man's latent energy, the occurrence of all kinds of extraordinary power. They all may emerge after practitioners reach the level of Piao Hua, but that is beyond the Piao Hua Gong.

Thus, Piao Hua Gong is a kind of Qigong practice which will lead practitioners to the advanced level of Qigong.

Operating Procedure
Mind Adjustment
First of all we should follow the order of the three stages of sensation inducement. We start from producing a concentrating thought of floating. Practitioners can repeat the word "floating" silently in order to banish distracting thoughts and induce the body to experience the sense of floating at the same time. If practitioners feel awkward repeating one word, they may add more words or phrases, such as *floating up*, *my body floating up*, etc. They may imagine their bodies

floating in air, or like floating white clouds or balloons, etc., so as to produce an image for concentration. In sum, the key content in concentrating thought is floating. When practitioners start to construct the concentrating thought they may select different methods according to their own preference. So long as these help practitioners to banish distracting thoughts and induce the creation of a floating sensation, all different forms from which concentrating thoughts of floating can be constructed may be adopted. When practitioners have the sensation of floating, it does not matter whether it is partial or entire. (In general, it is the feeling from the entire body, but may not be well proportioned. One may have a stronger sensation in one part of the body than in another.) They should continue to guide and induce the sensation in order to strengthen and expand it. Once the sensation of floating is stable, practitioners may give up the aim of concentration in time. (No matter whether it is imagery or abstract.) They should let their thinking directly manipulate the sensation of floating, and enter the stage of sensation operation in floating.

At the beginning of the sensation operation stage, the main task is to make the sensation of floating be continuously expanded, strengthened, stabilized, and coordinated. The partial sensation of floating should gradually become the whole one. The blocked sensation of floating should gradually transform into the relaxed one. The sensation of floating may only be a short-term experience. After this, one should make it a long-term one. An unbalanced sensation of floating should gradually change to a balanced sensation. Through this operation, the sensation of floating will on the whole become stronger and stronger. Practitioners may change to the operation of diffusing when they start to feel that their feet have left the ground (in the standing posture) or that their hips are suspended in the air (in the sitting posture); the body has become weightless, and the sensation of body form gradually becomes vague.

The change from the state of floating to diffusing is a gradual transformation. In operation, practitioners need to continue to strengthen the sensation of floating so as to make their bodies lighter and lighter. On the other hand, they need to continue to fade the vague shape of the body from their memories and gradually make it vanish.

Now they need to adjust both their breathing and their minds. The purpose of adjusting breathing is to make vital energy fill and extend, so as to spread it out. The purpose of adjusting mind is to wipe out the boundary of the shape of the body, so as to make the vital energy merge with the ether in the universe. During this time we may use the words "floating," "diffusing," and "melting," or imagine that the body is merging with the ether in the universe to induce the sensation of diffusing. Once there is no outline of the shape of the body, body and mind will gain an incomparable sensation of freedom. Practitioners have never experienced this sensation before. They will feel extremely relaxed, comfortable, and content. This is a delicate and remote sensation of happiness. This happiness is way beyond any entertainment in the world.

Although the forms of their bodies have already disappeared and the internal and external Qi have been blended together as practitioners entered the realm, Qi which belongs to the body can still be very "strong" and is out of balance with the gas in the universe in the mixture. In addition, practitioners may have very strong concentrating thoughts. They have not fully experienced the pleasant mood and their body's breathing seems to be felt. During this time, practitioners should continue to practice the sensation operation, so as to let the vital energy from the body and gas in the universe gradually come into balance and combine evenly. In this way practitioners improve on the level of man and nature becoming one. This operation is mainly to extinguish the sensation of Qi in the body in order to bring it into balance with the Qi outside the body. So practitioners should now strengthen the operation of Qi spreading out to let Qi fully extend and go far, far away, until finally it blends evenly with the Qi of the whole universe. Since concentration and Qi have already become one, the Qi operation of spreading out and the operation of floating and diffusing are unified. When concentrating thought goes far, far away, it is the same as the Qi spreading out.

When the level of man and nature becoming one has been reached, the body and mind have already purely and evenly melted into the universe. I am the universe; the universe is me. I am the same as the universe, which is infinite and eternal. Now practitioners should continue to work to reach the level of emptiness and forgetting the material world and self. The aim of this operation is to extinguish all sensations. Whether it is the sensation of happiness, the sensation of melting, or the sensation of infinity, everything should vanish. Gradually, nothing is different. Happiness, melting, space, and time—they are all the same thing. They have mixed together, vanished, and melted. So the actual state of emptiness is really arriving. Actually, even the word "quietness" seems unnecessary. Quietness is the sensation of happiness. It has already vanished. Only one thing is left, and that is emptiness. It is very clear and purified emptiness—that is, empty purity. It is also a purified heart; it is a spotlessly clean heart.

Is there any activity of concentrating thought? The answer is that it seems there is none, and it also seems that there is some, but mostly none. Sometimes it has and sometimes it has none. It is mostly none. We say none is still none.

Breathing Adjustment

The key point is to follow the way of nature. It is not necessary for practitioners to force themselves to do it. As long as practitioners' breathing is smooth and stable under the control of the concentration aim of floating and diffusing, they can gradually have deep, long, soft, and tiny breathing. Meanwhile, they can change everyday normal breathing to body breathing.

During the Floating period, the type of breathing will gradually change from normal breathing to navel breathing, or breathing from the Dantian. At the same time the deep, long, soft, and tiny breathing is improving at the same speed. The operation of breathing is directly related to the production and movement of Qi. Along with the increased need of the inner Qi, the inhaled air gradually sinks down to the Dantian and roots there, and finally it will lead to breathing from the Dantian. Breathing from the Dantian will continue for quite a long time. The sensory operation of floating is based on breathing from the Dantian. Qi from the Dantian will rise and grow stronger with the inducement and promotion of breathing. Later on, it will spread to the outside and cause the floating sensation. When Qi has spread out evenly through the whole body, it seems that the whole body is the Dantian. When the whole body breathes in and out is the time when breathing from the Dantian changes to body breathing. At this point the Floating stage is close to ending, and the Diffusing stage has started.

At the beginning of the Diffusing stage, breathing from the Dantian is changing to body breathing. Practitioners need not force themselves to do it. Let it happen spontaneously. When breathing from the Dantian initially switches to body breathing, the Dantian breathing point still exists. The breathing channel is not via the mouth and nose. The breath directly gathers and spreads out through the pores of the whole body to the Dantian. Breathing through both the mouth and nostrils and the pores of the whole body may also occur during this period. Some time later, the Dantian breathing point will gradually diminish and finally vanish. Breathing in and out of the pores of the whole body will no longer focus on and spread out from the Dantian, but will be soft and continuous and spread evenly through the whole body. The rhythm of breathing will also cease. The reason why it vanishes is that the rhythmic periodicity of breathing becomes longer and longer. When periodic length becomes unlimited, the rhythm will no longer exist. With no breathing point and no breathing rhythm, breathing that relies on the mouth and nostrils as a channel can simply stop, but body breathing continues, and it will keep on for a long time. During the entire process of the Qi from the body and the ether in the universe mixing, body breathing will exist from beginning to end, but it will gradually weaken until the merging process is complete. Body breathing cannot vanish until we have no sensation of body shape.

Are there ultimately any breathing movements at all? Please see the last paragraph of "Mind Adjustment" earlier in this chapter.

Body Adjustment

Practitioners may select any postures at will, standing, sitting, or prone postures, according to their own conditions. For beginners, it's better to choose standing or sitting postures, as the prone posture easily makes practitioners fall asleep.

The key points of whole body posture operations were described in Chapter 6, "Rujing and Its Components." We won't repeat the contents here.

If practitioners select the standing posture to practice Rujing, they should also be aware that they need to be standing steadily on their feet, in addition to the main operating points we mentioned before, such as head up, relax the shoulders and drop the elbows, tone up one's back, drop the hips, and have the feet parallel. Before practitioners get into the standing posture, they should know whether the ground is even or not. They must not stand with one foot lower than the other. If there are obstacles where they are trying to stand, they should move them away. This is because practitioners' bodies may shake slightly during the primary stage of Floating and Diffusing Gong. If they are standing unsteadily, they may easily shake past the limit and even fall down.

During the stage of Floating, when practitioners are in a standing or sitting posture, they can keep their arms in position by holding a ball or touching a desk, or they can hold out their arms to both sides in the "outspread wings" position. Practitioners have a free choice in this, according to their own habits and what is comfortable for them. Staying in the correct position, they may also shake slightly in order to let their bodies increase the sensation of floating. If they keep the posture of holding a ball, their arms may act as if playing an accordion. If they are in the posture of touching a desk, their arms may move up and down. If they are in the posture of "outspread wings," their arms may rise up and fall down. In addition, during the operation, they can deliberately change postures, so long as they do it naturally. For example, they may keep the outspread wings posture and later on change to the position of holding a ball or touching a desk. The reason is that the outspread wings posture has the strongest influence on practitioners in terms of the sensation of floating. The postures of holding a ball or touching a desk give practitioners a sense of ease. As the arms move up and down, the body may also shake slightly or move forwards and backwards, to left and right, or turn round freely. The body's center of gravity may shift, along with the movement of the body.

But here we must be aware that waving arms or a shaking body do not indicate stimulation of the circulation of the blood, or cause muscles and joints to relax, and it is also not the same as the body moving spontaneously. The only purpose is to change the body's center of gravity, and the point of muscle activity is to achieve the sensation of floating easily, and to strengthen it. Therefore, the operation of body adjustment must match the operation of mind and breathing adjustments. We cannot deviate far from the principle of floating. As long as we keep the principle in mind all the time, the arms waving and the body shaking must be slow and slight, not quick and active.

When we have the sensation of floating and continuously strengthen it, the limbs' light movements gradually weaken until they vanish. (Although there is no movement, practitioners may not keep absolutely straight in standing or sitting postures, as they may move slightly—subconsciously and passively.)

It is best for beginners to select the standing posture because it makes the active body more flexible. It may also help practitioners to have the sensation of floating through body movement. Compared with the standing posture, the sitting posture cannot guide practitioners to Rujing by changing their postures. During the Diffusing period, body activities have stilled because practitioners have no necessity (and no way) to use body activities to induce the diffusing sensation. In this period, what practitioners need to operate is to make the sensation of body shape gradually vanish, and the first thing is to make the body inactive, because it is difficult for practitioners to have the sensation of their body shape vanish if their body is in activity. Therefore, as for the operation of body adjustment, the change is from slight movement to stillness and from the state of Floating to the state of Diffusing. After that, the sensation of body shape will gradually diminish.

All the sensations from the body will gradually be replaced by the sensation of Qi following the operation of breathing and mind adjustments, and the whole body will be completely dematerialized. As the transparent body merges together with Qi in the universe, the sensation of body shape vanishes. As I have already said, when the body shape just vanishes, Qi from the old body may be strong; therefore, practitioners may have a vague sensation of body shape. As their Qigong improves, Qi from the body will eventually become even with the Qi in the universe. The universe is boundless, the body is also boundless, and a boundless body means no body shape.

During the Diffusing period the body shape gradually vanishes and the postures are of no use, but we should take care not to select postures that impose a burden on the sensation of body shape. Sitting and standing or even prone postures are OK. Further, practitioners may select postures according to their own needs in practicing Rujing. For example, if they are trying to stay in good health, practitioners can choose the standing posture; if trying to discover their latent powers, select the sitting posture, etc. We cannot list them all here individually.

Do practitioners have operation of body shape if they are in the highest level of the Diffusing stage? Please read the last paragraph of the section on "Mind Adjustment" earlier in this chapter.

A Few More Points
Summary of the Main Points in Piao Hua Gong
Do not seek concentration on the Dantian. Do not seek abdominal breathing. Do not seek specific postures. Keep the sensation and experience of floating and diffusing as the key points, so as to operate the three adjustments.

Finishing Practice
Piao Hua Gong has no special mode of finishing practice. If practitioners want to end their exercises, what they can do is to slowly

bring their concentration back to their everyday state (thinking, mood, breathing, etc.), as well as slowly rub their hands and faces and slightly move their bodies. Practitioners may engage in other activities once their minds and bodies have returned to the everyday state, but they should not busy themselves with anything as soon as they finish their exercises. There needs to be a transition between the practice of Rujing and other activities.

Other Points of Attention

Practitioners should enter the stage of Diffusing when they have completed the Floating stage. Do not mourn the loss of the old stage and hesitate. Practitioners missing the old stage may not make any improvement. During the period of Diffusing, practitioners should always maintain concentration on diffusing, and do not lose their way because everything has vanished.

Practicing Time

As for practicing time, practitioners may practice once or twice a day. It requires 30–60 minutes each time. It is suitable for practitioners to practice in the morning or in the evening, because it is very quiet at those times. Otherwise, practitioners can practice at any time and anywhere if they are free—at noon or in the afternoon or early evening.

Advice for Sick Practitioners

Piao Hua Gong is efficacious against many diseases, not against one or two specific diseases. Some sick practitioners can take this Qigong as the main mode of treatment. Whether practitioners take Piao Hua Gong as the main or supplementary mode of treatment depends on their conditions, and also their reactions while practicing Piao Hua Gong. Therefore it is difficult to give each practitioner the same set of recommendations. Generally speaking, when practicing this Qigong, sick practitioners who feel changes in sensation in their affected parts should continue their practice and may find it effective.

The effects of illness may mean that, when sick practitioners begin to practice, they will not be able to meet the standards for the operation of the three adjustments. They may not even be able to finish their practice. During this time, sick practitioners should not lose confidence and let this be a burden to them. What they should do is to keep the main principles of Piao Hua Gong in mind and manage their practice flexibly. Later on, they will gradually find themselves on the right track.

We already know that floating means body and mind becoming one, and diffusing means man and nature becoming one. By the time sick practitioners achieve the state of body and mind becoming one, they will have fully recovered. In other words, here we say that the state of Floating achieved is a high standard. Practitioners are required to blend their feelings and experience of floating into their everyday life—to maintain a relaxed and pleasant state all the time and everywhere, and let nothing be a burden to them. By then they will have fully recovered from their illness.

Endnotes

1. Qigong: Traditional Chinese psychosomatic operational skill aimed at cultivating human potential through the unified three adjustments of mind, breath, and body.

2. Lu Xun (1881–1936): A great Chinese writer and thinker, well known for his critical essays on the characteristics of Chinese.

3. Meridian: The main and collateral channels through which vital energy circulates and along which the acupuncture points are distributed.

4. *Compendium of Materia Medica*: A very famous ancient Chinese medical text written by Shi-Zhen Li (1518–1593), a well-known ancient Chinese physician during the Ming dynasty.

5. Yin and Yang theory: In Chinese thought there are two basic opposing principles in nature. Yin represents the feminine/receptive/negative; Yang represents the masculine/active/positive, etc.

6. A type of Qigong meditation state, characteristic of which is attaining a mental stillness where the consciousness ceases working and itself becomes nothing but pure, ultimate existence. In general, this meditative state is achieved by operating particular thinking processes.

7. He Ming (1983) *Exploring Qigong*. Shi Jia Zhuang: Qigong Coaching Station. p.3.

8. Tian Hong Ji (1987) *Xu Ming Gong* (Void and Bright Qigong). Hei Bei province: Science & Technology Press. p.3.

9. Preliminary Committee of the Association of the Science of Qigong, Qihua University (1988) *Zhong Guo Shen Gong* (Magic Qigong in China). Beijing: Qinghua University Publishers.

10. Ma Ji Ren (1983) *Zhong Guo Qigong Xue* (The Study of Chinese Qigong). Xian, ShanXi province: Science & Technology Press. p.240.

11. Zhao Bo Feng (1987) *Qigong Xue Gai Lun* (An Introduction to Chinese Qigong). Beijing: People's Health Publisher. p.368.

12. Dantian: The point about an inch below the navel, in which the vital energy is collected and concentrated.

13. Baihui 百会 DU20.

14. Yongquan 涌泉 KI1.

15. Shanzhong 膻中 RN17.

16. Huiyin 会阴 RN1.

17. Chengjiang 承浆 RN24

18. Changqiang 长强 DU1.

19. A concept from Taoism, relating to something produced by collecting and concentrating vital energy through Qigong or other self-cultivation skills.

20. *Jin Dan 400 Zi* (Four Hundred Words on Golden Dan): A classic source on the cultivation of Dan.

21. Part of the human body, located in the skull.

22. Part of the human body, the area between the brows.

23. Part of the human body, the abdominal area.

24. Part of the human body, the area to either side of the spine.

25. *Liu Miao Fa Men* (Six Magic Skills): A reference book of self-cultivation in Buddhism.

26. *Tong Meng Zhi Guan*: An elementary book on the concept and process of self-cultivation in Buddhism.

27. By Zhuang Zi (369 BC–286 BC): Named Zhou; representative of the Taoists in the Warring States period in ancient China. He and his successors wrote a book entitled *Zhuang Zi*, which was a typical Taoist work.

28. Also called "Geju" (Heritage of the Secret) school: A Tibetan school of lamas, founded by Marlba in the eleventh century. The monks always wear white skirts and shirts; therefore it is also called "the White School."

29. *Xin Ming Gui Zhi* (Precious Instructions on Cultivating Mind and Body): A Ming dynasty book on Taoist Qigong.

30. *Chan MiGong* (Zen and Mystic Qigong): A pamphlet on Zen and Mystic Qigong.

31. The term "visual thinking" does not entirely cover my concept of this particular form of thinking. I use this term to emphasize the realistic aspect of the constituents and process with which this thinking process operates, which should go beyond visual experience to include all sensory modalities (hearing, smell, touch, etc.). What one experiences in visual thinking is as realistic as a dream, but one is completely conscious and in total control of the experience.

32. Used to distinguish between elements in one's visual thinking and objects in the physical world (outside the mind). In the visual thinking process one works virtually, with the objective form, through which one experiences the real feeling just as it would be derived from the corresponding experience with a concrete object in the physical world.

33. *Yi Wen Ji* (The Diary of Anecdotes): An ancient book of bizarre and incredible anecdotes from China.

34. Qian Cheng, Zhou Xin (1988) *Gui Bao Zhi Guang* (The Light of Treasure). Beijing: Workers' Press.

35. Kang: In northern China people use bricks to construct a large bed. They may put a big mat on top of it. In the middle of the bed there is a cooking stove connected to the chimney outside. People can make a fire and warm themselves by it.

36. *The Medical Canon of the Yellow Emperor*: The best-known ancient Chinese medical text.

37. The "third eye" is concealed in the forehead, behind and between the brows. It is said that its sensory function is developed through practicing Qigong.

38. Daisaku Suzuki (1870–1966): A well-known Japanese Zen monk.

39. Twenty-four solar terms or periods: 24 periods of approximately 15 days each, into which the lunar year is divided, corresponding to the days on which the sun enters the 1st or 15th degree of one of the 12 zodiacal signs. Each period is given an appropriate name indicating obvious changes in nature at the time of its occurrence. The names are as follows: Beginning of Spring, Rain Water, Waking of Insects, Spring Equinox, Pure Brightness, Grain Rain, Beginning of Summer, Lesser Fullness of Grain, Grain in Beard, Summer Solstice, Lesser Heat, Greater Heat, Beginning of Autumn, End of Heat, White Dew, Autumn Equinox, Cold Dew, Frost's Descent, Beginning of Winter, Lesser Snow, Greater Snow, Winter Solstice, Lesser Cold, and Greater Cold.

40. *He Tu* and *Luo Shu*: Two legendary ancient Chinese texts. In Chinese mythology it is said that in the time of Fu Xi (an ancient Chinese emperor) a dragon horse appeared on the Yellow River with a square of numbers on its back, and hence was named He Tu; a heaven turtle appeared on the Luo Shu River, with a particular texture on its back, hence the name Luo Shu.

41. *Da An Ban Shou Yi Jing* (Breathing and Concentrating Scripture): A Buddhist classic on breathing and concentration skill.

42. *Tong Meng Zhi Guan* (Primary Methods of Cultivating Vital Energy): A Buddhist classic that introduces some primary methods about how to adjust mind, breath, and body to cultivate vital energy.

43. *She Sheng San Yao* (Three Important Ways of Keeping Fit): An ancient Chinese text on health preservation.

44. *Su Shen Liang Fang* (Good Prescriptions of Doctor Su and Shen): An ancient Chinese collection of traditional prescriptions.

Tianjun Liu, O.M.D., is Director of the Qigong research laboratory at Beijing University of Chinese Medicine, where he has taught Qigong for more than twenty years. He is also First Vice Chairman and Secretary General of the China Academic Society of Medical Qigong, Secretary General of the National Qigong Education and Study Association, and the first government approved academic mentor for Ph.D. candidates in the field of medical Qigong in China. For the past decade, Dr Liu has been Editor in Chief of Chinese Medical Qigong, the only official Qigong textbook used in universities and colleges of traditional Chinese medicine in China.